THE FUTURE OF SOCIALISM

THE FUTURE OF SOCIALISM: PERSPECTIVES FROM THE LEFT

Edited by William K. Tabb

Monthly Review Press
New York

"Prometheus Rebound?" by Daniel Singer, "The Future of Socialism" by Samir Amin, and "Is Socialism an Alternative for the Third World?" by Carlos M. Vilas all appeared in *Monthly Review*, July-August 1990.

"Has Socialism Failed" by Joe Slovo is a condensed version of a pamphlet by the same title published in 1990.

"Revolution in Eastern Europe" by Andre Gunder Frank first appeared in *Third World Quarterly* 12, no. 2 (April 1990), and is reprinted with permission.

"Perestroika and the Future of Socialism" by Harry Magdoff and Paul M. Sweezy is the second part of a two-part article that appeared in *Monthly Review*, March and April 1990.

"Why Not the Capitalist Road?" by William Hinton is a condensation and combination of "Tiananmen Massacre: June 1989" and "Why Not the Capitalist Road?" which appeared in *The Great Reversal: The Privatization of China, 1978–1989* (New York: Monthly Review Press, 1990).

"Marxism Is Dead, Long Live Marxism!" by Michael Burawoy was first published in *Socialist Review*, April-June 1990, and is reprinted with permission.

"Why Is There No Socialism in the United States?" by Eric Foner was first published in the *History Workshop Journal*, Spring 1984, and is reprinted with permission.

"Self-Governing Socialism" by Pat Devine is an updated summary of his book *Democracy and Economic Planning* (Boulder, CO: Westview Press, 1988).

"Postscript on Post-Revolutionary Society" by Paul M. Sweezy was written as the preface for a new Japanese edition of *Post-Revolutionary Society* to be published in 1990 by Shakaihyoron-sha.

Copyright © 1990 by William K. Tabb
All rights reserved

Library of Congress Cataloging in Publication Data

The Future of Socialism : perspectives from the left / edited by William K. Tabb.
    p.   cm.
    ISBN 0-85345-820-0 : $32.00 — ISBN 0-85345-821-9 (pbk.) : $15.00
    1. Socialism   2. World politics—1985-1995.   I. Tabb, William K.
  HX73.F88   1990
335'.009'048—dc20   90-13451
                                            CIP

Monthly Review Press
122 West 27th Street
New York, NY 10001

Manufactured in the United States of America

10 9 8 7 6 5 4 3 2 1

CONTENTS

v

THE FUTURE OF SOCIALISM

WILLIAM K. TABB

WHERE WE ARE IN HISTORY: INTRODUCTORY THEMES TO WORLD-TRANSFORMING EVENTS

The end of the postwar era is marked by the demise of the Soviet system and a trumpeting of the victory of capitalism. With so many people either gloating or shaking their heads in disbelief, it is hardly sufficient to respond that the failures of the Soviet model are historically specific and therefore cannot be considered evidence of the unworkability of socialism—which, after all, is not about centralized control from above but economic democracy from below. The Soviets did not develop very far in this direction in significant measure because of the hostility and unremitting destabilizing efforts of the Western capitalist states. Indeed, all of the early attempts to build socialism occured in relatively backward nations and produced centralized, nondemocratic regimes that bore the deep scars of their Czarist or Mandarin pasts, the burdens of backwardness, and the costs of defending themselves against a hostile capitalist system.

At the same time, we must interpret the world as it is, including the fallout from the announced victory of capitalism, the prospective incorporation of its Eastern European periphery, and the imposition of privatization on third world debtor nations, all of which appear to be creating a more uncontested capitalist world economy. These developments have suggested to some that we have reached the end of history. If so, it is one of those improbable Hollywood endings where complex problems have suddenly been happily resolved, an end moviegoers hardly expect to be sustained in real time. The Eastern European workers who innocently endorse market freedoms will learn soon enough about unemployment and life without the

1

collective provision of basic needs. The Stalinist economic model is being dismantled and national economies privatized by local elites, in cooperation with international capital. The cost of this restructuring will inevitably be borne by the workers, who face inflation, unemployment, and the loss of state subsidies and other protections. Meanwhile, austerity programs in the third world debtor nations will resolve nothing in the long run. The solidifying of class positions cannot but be the final result, for working people will not benefit from unleashing the magic of the market; nor will they starve quietly. Revolutionary struggles will continue. The questions are how, in what manner, and with what intensity.

The United States and the Critique of Capitalism

Even in the United States, such prosperity as there is—which is to say, as there is not for the majority of working Americans—is a false prosperity, not only because it is narrowly shared but because it is based on the temporizing expedient of a debt incurred by corporations, consumers, the government, and the nation itself (as an international debtor). The United States is left with an increasingly noncompetitive and noninclusive economy dominated by financial speculation. The mainstream financial press joins radical economists in wondering how long the excesses can go on without triggering financial collapse. Politicians scurry to denounce the very excesses without which there would have been precious little growth over the past decade.

The question of where we are in history, from the point of view of those who manage the system, is that "we" are not doing badly. Yes, there is instability and the threat of a serious downturn, but there always is, and "we" know this as well as any Marxist. The task is to postpone the reckoning and when it comes to have others pay—the third world debtors, small businesses, the working class, and the poor at home. "Our" profits and share of the market are holding up, even as the majority of "our" citizens experience declining or stagnant living standards.

Three ideological props have dominated postwar American consciousness: the Cold War, the Stalinist Soviet system, and U.S. hegemony. The passing of these, along with the arrival of a new fourth factor—the looming environmental crisis—will shape U.S. politics in the coming decades. Without attempting to spell out in detail the political implications of these epoch-defining changes, I will sketch how the loss of these props signals the start of an era in which the abuses of the capitalist system will be more difficult to mask and those criticizing its irrationalities harder to silence.

In the postwar period, the Cold War was used extremely effectively to demobilize the left. Not only Communists, but all kinds of class-conscious militants were thrown out of the labor movement by an employer-state alliance that used anti-Communism as a powerful weapon to assert class power. At the same time, the growing military budget claimed funds that could have gone to the social provision of goods and services for use outside the market-exchange structure. This thinned the ranks of the helping professions and disorganized and isolated those service recipients most in need of allies. By building up the military sector and shifting state expenditures to the Florida-Texas-Washington "missile crescent," the industrial Northeast was deprived of revenues. At the same time, a population shift produced congressional seat gains for the nonunionized Sunbelt states and created millionaires more than willing to recycle some of their largesse to right-wing politicians, who in turn engineered tax and spending priorities that continued to enrich the beneficiaries of militarism.

It is worth noting that while the arms race stimulated the U.S. economy—or at least certain parts of it—the much smaller Soviet economy strained at the seams, taking resources from badly needed consumer goods and light industry to build weapons it could ill afford. This forced march strengthened the Soviet government's command structures and repressive apparatuses, and gave authority to hardliners in all areas of Soviet life. Thus elites in both East and West benefited from a powerful external enemy that could be used as a rationale for silencing dissent.

In the United States, support for the military comes from a belief that such expenditures are good for the economy, but once the Soviet Union gave up control of its empire, the continued production of unneeded weapons is not as easily accepted by the American people. Nor will U.S. invasions of other nations be so palatable. It is becoming clear to more and more Americans—and will become clearer still as social suffering becomes more generalized in the next economic downturn—that meeting public needs must come first. Even within the ruling class, there are those who have come to believe that a bloated military is not in their best interests either, that it is detrimental to the overall health of the economy.

The questions of what should be produced and how the pieces of the economy should fit together are also informed by the demise of the Stalinist system. For the Soviet Union, this has meant a closer consideration of the costs of giantism in planning.[1]

The extent to which the drive to industrialize in the Soviet Union and Eastern Europe has extracted a horrendous price in environmental destruction is now becoming clear. The productionist bias of Soviet planning has been both ecologically destructive and wasteful in conventional economic terms. We now know from Soviet figures how much food rots before getting to market and how much production is of such low quality that it cannot be sold, even to goods-starved citizens. We also know something of the corrupting influences of inefficient incentive systems and the lack of worker control over the *nomenklatura*. These problems do not condemn socialism as such, however, but speak to the shortcomings of a historically specific social formation that was shaped in no small measure by the unrelenting pressures of the far stronger, hostile capitalist world.

Such revelations can lead to a "their system is worse than ours" mentality, which distracts from the ecological crises and increasing poverty in the United States and the third world, often the responsibility of U.S.-based transnational corporations pursuing devastating development policies in search of profits. In this regard, the two systems have much in common: a mania for growth at the expense of the environment and the human community is integral to the logic of development in the United States as well. The critique of Stalinism points to the waste and social inefficiency inherent in our own system, the result of substantial and ill-considered subsidies and a disregard for social costs. To choose one example: huge subsidies to California agribusinesses for water, beneficial land taxation policies, transportation subsidies to interstate trucking, a flagrant disregard for the ecological costs of gasoline consumption, pesticide use, and other false economies of U.S. agriculture have all led to the destruction of regional farming and the creation of a costly, unhealthy, and environmentally destructive agribusiness. The commonalities between the U.S. and Soviet systems can now be addressed more easily and the solution examined, both here and over there.

Indeed, the unthinking rush to the market is a good occasion to rehearse the waste inherent in planned obsolescence and endless style changes, and the ability of advertising to create a shop-until-you-drop response on the part of the consumer, playing on socially constructed personal insecurities that are created to sell products. It is widely accepted that capitalism's greatest strength compared to the Stalinist regimes has been its ability to "deliver the goods"—to make desirable consumer products widely available. But much of this is mythical, a media fantasy that jams the transmission of reality. U.S. television viewers watch *Miami Vice,* tantalized by the clothing, music, and feel of a glamorous reality more exciting than the unsafe streets outside their own windows, where real police are scarce and ineffective. The same viewers watch dedicated and handsome young doctors who appear to have only one case a week, while in the real world patients sleep in the hallways or are refused admission to hospitals because they do not have health insurance. The power of this constructed reality extends to the way events in the Soviet Union, Eastern Europe, and China are presented—as the failure of socialism and the triumph of capitalism. But this is a mythic capitalism.

The loss of the "enemy" will be both painful for the powerbrokers and profiteers and can be potentially energizing for the left. The end of the Cold War will disarm the red-baiters and make a shift in resources toward the progressive agenda more plausible. The corruptions of the Drexel-Burnham—Savings-and-Loan—HUD scandals, taking place at the same time as rising income inequalities and widespread homelessness, argue for a pendulum swing to the left in the 1990s. It is of course quite possible that drug wars and antiterrorist rapid deployment forces—to say nothing of bank bailouts—will eat up the "peace dividend," but such an outcome is subject to a popular contestation that is more likely as the perception that U.S. capitalism is performing poorly permeates popular consciousness.

The struggle will take place in a United States that no longer has the relative dominance it once had. The end of the postwar period is marked by the emergence of Germany as the unofficial capital of a Europe that will stretch from the Atlantic to the Urals and have a population of over 700 million, and by Japan's successful effort to establish an updated version of its Asian co-prosperity sphere, eclipsing U.S. dominance in the region to a remarkable degree. At the same time, the United States, despite its efforts to extend its economic hegemony over Mexico and Canada (through free trade agreements) and to maintain its dominance in the Caribbean and Central America, is becoming the weakest of the three power centers. These developments herald the next step of the journey to a single world economy. Today more than ever, the nation state must be seen as part of a world system. Just as, in the nineteenth century, regions of the United States became integrated into a vast national economy with the building of the transcontinental railways, so innovations in transportation and communication are today bringing a single world market more fully into being. The relationship between the three trading blocs—Europe, Japan, and the United States—is still to be defined, but what is clear is that the United States is no longer the hegemonic leader of the triad. The "allies" are increasingly unwilling to make the adjustments necessary to finance U.S. interests, while foreigners are increasingly able to do serious damage to the U.S. economy.

These developments do not necessarily mean that individual nation states have lost all room for maneuver. Those European countries that have most forcefully protected their domestic economies from free market forces—Austria, Switzerland, and Sweden—have done far better than those of their neighbors that acquiesced more fully to the demands of foreign capital.[2] The experiences of the state-led regimes in East Asia adds further support for the view that it is possible to influence the terms of insertion into the global economy. Other states may be in a weaker position because a weak local bourgeoisie or poor resource base give them less bargaining power, but the ideological steamroller that insists that "we" in the United States have no choice but to accede to the demands of transnational capital can be rejected. There is room for effective politics by progressive movements within individual states.

Furthermore, the left in the United States has relatively more opportunities for autonomy than does the left in many other countries. "Bourgeois democracy" is not that common among the world's 170 nations. Ironically, this autonomy is also almost completely unused: the United States remains among the most politically underdeveloped nations, the range of political discourse, that between Republicans and Democrats, the narrowest political spectrum, although the dramatic success of the presidential candidacy of Jesse Jackson shows an impressive potential. As the objective situation becomes worse, the educational impact of these changes may lead toward an understanding that capitalism cannot be tinkered with but must be replaced, lock, stock, and barrel. Those who are already convinced of this will undoubtedly be disappointed by the speed of such developments. For one thing, the effects of the demise of the Soviet system in Eastern Europe will mean a period in which all suffering will be blamed on the old "Communist" regimes.

In the meantime, the task is to prevent the uncontested acceptance of the idea that all markets must be deregulated, and to attempt to limit the damage that the rush to the market causes. In Europe, working-class movements will struggle to retain welfare state protections and extend social control over capital mobility in the post-1992 economy. These and other struggles will reverberate in the United States. At the same time, the decline of U.S. hegemony will encourage the working class in the United States to think about capitalism differently. The belief that the labor movement gains from imperialism, held by the leaders of the AFL-CIO and not a few union members, will be hard to maintain as relative privilege erodes. The cost of third world interventions will come to be seen in a different light as exports from third world police states, protected by the CIA, produce profits that are unavailable to U.S. workers, further lowering their living standards and threatening their jobs. Again, it would serve no purpose to exaggerate how fast such a learning process will go forward, but there is no doubt that American exceptionalism is on the decline.

For centuries humanity has acted as if the earth's resources were essentially unlimited and used the carrying capacity of the ecosphere as if there were no limits to its recuperative powers. From Bhopal to Chernobyl, from holes in the ozone layer to acid rain, the cost of greed is increasingly evident, as is the neccesity of a collective effort to reverse the destruction. These changes have created an opportunity to redefine such basic constructs as security, which until now has been seen purely in military terms. Martin McGuire, for example, asks:

> Is preservation of our standard of living a security problem? Does dependence on foreign savings present a security problem? Is economic volatility, high unemployment, and profoundly unequal and unfair income distribution a security problem?. . . Ruinous inflation? AIDS?[3]

And David Boren, chair of the Senate Intelligence Committee and a conservative on military matters, has warned that "the United States risks losing its preeminence if it fails to adjust to a new world order based on economic, rather than military, might."[4] This type of questioning is indicative of changes in mainstream thinking.

The end of the Cold War, the loss of U.S. hegemony, the demise of the system Stalin created, and the ecological limits to current patterns of growth all open up political space for progressive movments in the 1990s.

The next wave of socialist struggle will be internationalist in ways that transcend the more limited consciousness of earlier movements. This is because the development of the world system is both a constraint on, and a generator of, socialist movements. While individuals act locally, to be politically effective, a movement must also learn not only to think globally but to act globally. In Daniel Singer's phrase, internationalism has been forced upon us.

The Writing of the Present as History

Each generation, facing a unique set of circumstances, interprets its past as that which produced what it believes to be its present reality. Succeeding generations see that reality in the light of "new" hindsight. Earlier events are rewritten. There is no history, only histories. At any point in time actors occupy different realities. The one that becomes what happened is the hegemonic grand narrative of official history. The "reality" which has become "what happened" is written by the powerful and their representatives.

In this reconsideration much of the last seventy years of world history will be rewritten. The experience of Soviet statist regimes, after what *may* prove to be the watershed year 1989, will doubtless be reinterpreted. (While 1789 has remained a milestone, and the French Revolution a turning point, we must wait before we claim too much for 1989. Nevertheless, our working assumption is that 1989 is also such a year.) Although the immediate comments of some academics that our understanding of Communism must now be discarded seems excessive, reassessing the "end of Communism" will be a growth industry in the social sciences for years to come. In this reconsideration there will also be time to reflect on Eduardo Galeano's comment that in the rush to the funeral, they are burying the wrong corpse. The Promethean project that is socialism, as Daniel Singer tells us in his essay in this volume, has been declared dead many times before. At the same time there can be no doubt, as Luciana Castellina writes from a lifetime commitment to a Communist Party that has ceased to exist in name or politics, that the world of the left has indeed changed forever.

This is neither a collection of homogeneous essays by unreconstructed defenders of the faith nor a celebration of the triumph of capitalism, but a response from the left to the celebrants of a moment that in fact has great historical ambiguity. The essays included here are by journalists, academics, and intellectuals. Some are the testimonials of participants; others are the reflections of historians, economists, and sociologists. Some have the immediacy of reports from the saddle; others have been included to give necessary perspective. Most were written out of the passion of a life commitment to socialism. It is not that the crimes of Stalin, and the inanities of bureaucratic stupidity, are not deeply felt and condemned, but that there is at the same time a belief in Marx's vision of the self-emancipation of the working people, of a society directed by the ordinary folks—one that goes far beyond (although it certainly includes) elections and formal freedoms of the press and speech to meaningful direct participation in making and carrying out the decisions that affect people's core being as members of a caring, shared society. This vision of a participatory economic democracy is as far beyond voting every four years for the lesser of two evils as our limited democracy is beyond feudalism. It is a powerful vision that has motivated, and continues to motivate, millions.

The debate over the prospects for socialism takes place in the context of an understanding of a world capitalist system that has been briefly described above. Yet this is a system that is understood differently by analysts, and that range is reflected in this volume. Andre Gunder Frank offers a pessimistic account, one that seems to preclude the possibility that individual nation states can separate from the hegemonic, all-encompassing world system, and also denies the possibility that the system can be transformed. To both Samir Amin and Christopher Chase-Dunn, on the other hand, the contradictions of the system are so great that both see dynamism and the inevitability of change—Amin from the perspective of the periphery and Chase-Dunn from that of the core.

While the emphasis here is on events in the (formerly?) Communist states, the full impact of the vision would be better served by the inclusion of essays from South Africa, Korea, the Phillipines, and other places around the world where struggles to transform an unjust capitalist order are in motion. One such country, Brazil, is represented by an essay by Maria Helena Alves, who conveys the power of the Workers' Party. Her discussion of how its socialism addresses the issues of participation and social justice is important for us because Brazil is not a well-known case in the United States, despite the popularity of "Lula," the metal worker and trade unionist who came within a hair's breadth of winning the presidency of a country that is larger and more populous than all of Eastern Europe. In such countries, as Alves shows, the promise of socialism is far from dead, but it will take a different form because of different local conditions and because of Brazil's particular place in the world.

The failures of the first attempts to build socialism were not only due to external factors, but, as Harry Magdoff and Paul Sweezy argue in their contribution, to a lack of internal democracy. Sweezy and Magdoff deconstruct the essentially technocratic discourse of *perestroika*, as articulated by Gorbachev and his advisors, grounding their analysis in terms of the historical evolution of class and strata relations in the postrevolutionary Soviet Union. William Hinton's discussion of the history of the Tiananmen Square massacre points in a similar direction: new elites usurp power and come to rule in the name of the party and the people.

In the coming debate, non-Leninist models of democratic party building, in which social movements, the gender issue, ecological concerns, and complex localism will play a prominent part, will lead to an expanded understanding of labor and class. Phil Hill shows how these concerns demand a "greening" of left politics. While these "new" issues will become more prominent in future discussions and organizing efforts, traditionally important questions will also have to be reassessed. One of these is Leninism itself, and not surprisingly it is seen quite differently by different contributors. Most divergent perhaps are Joe Slovo's defense of Leninism from the perspective of the South African Communist Party and Michael Burawoy's dismissal of it based on his recent experiences in Hungary. There are also different degrees of optimism and pessimism regarding the reforms now under way, including whether the introduction of markets and private forms of property are consistent with (a perhaps broader) concept of socialism. Indeed, the very term reform is a semantic Rorschach test and contested ground among competing discourses. One of these involves the issue of market socialism, which Pat Devine argues is at best an inadequately theorized construct.

The third world (itself an increasingly problematic term) has generally been ignored in discussions of the "end" of the Cold War. Capitalism means Western Europe, Japan, and the United States—not Asia (outside of the Newly Industrializing Countries, or NICs), Africa, or Latin America. But, as Carlos Vilas explains in his essay, the prospects for socialism in these parts of the world have grown dimmer as a result of events in the Soviet Union, in part because the United States has more room to intervene without fear of superpower confrontation. These sentiments are echoed by Pablo Gonzalez Casanova in his discussion of antisystemic movements in the third world and the impact of the loss of Soviet support. For the third world, the Cold War has always been about imperialism's attack on their right to pursue a noncapitalist road to development. The end of the big power confrontation does not change this; it only means the loss of an important ally in the struggle.

What of the United States itself? Why is there no significant socialist movement here, no workers' party? These questions are addresssed by Eric Foner, while Paul Buhle, in a prophetic essay, suggests how a socialist movement in the United States will be different because of our particular national experience and diverse cultures.

The final words go to the dean of U.S. Marxists, Paul M. Sweezy, who takes the long view, confident in final victory but taking into account the complex interactions of consciousness and material developments that will proceed the birth of a successful internationalist social movement.

Most of the essays were written expressly for this volume. Three—those by Daniel Singer, Carlos Vilas, and Samir Amin—appeared in the Summer 1990 issue of *Monthly Review*, while Michael Burawoy's contribution is taken, with permission and thanks, from the April-June 1990 issue of *Socialist Review*. Many of the contributors attended the 1990 Socialist Scholars' Conference, held in New York City in April 1990, which I co-chaired with Bogdan Denitch. It was at the conference that, with the help of Susan Lowes, Director of Monthly Review Press and editor of this volume, the project was conceptualized. The book is thus in many ways a collaboration between myself and the press's talented and politically astute editor. While it will take decades to put the events of 1989 into perspective, we felt a pressing need at this particular moment, close upon the abrogation of power of the entrenched Communist parties, to ask what they may mean to us.

In the wake of events in Eastern Europe and the Soviet Union, the cheering section for international capitalism has grown bolder. Pundits like Flora Lewis write: "It is strange now to recall what panic, what lack of confidence drove the democracies to feel they were in danger of being overwhelmed by Communist ideas, not by Red armies."[5] It is only now that they feel safe at last that such thinking surfaces. Yet any security for the regime of capital must always be temporary, and at its center false.

The Cuban writer Pablo Armando Fernandez, when asked about how the world-transforming events of 1989 are being interpreted by the Colossus of the North, wrote:

They are happy now. They are celebrating. For them the world has ended. History has ended. Ideology has ended. How very silly to think that! Communism has not disappeared. The utopias of socialism and communism are not going to disappear as long as there are exploiters and exploited. You have to be very happy having one piece of bread to eat while others throw meat to their dogs. I didn't have to read Marx to know the difference.[6]

Marxism and the socialist vision have always begun with capitalism and its inadequacies as a social system. The promise is that once the forces of production are developed—at great cost to the vast majority—the system will be replaced through the self-conscious revolutionary activities of these same people. The experiments, the first strivings, to create a socialist system have not succeeded for reasons and in ways that are discussed at some length in what follows, but history does not march backward and it would seem the safest of predictions to say that socialism—by whatever name—cannot be dead as long as capitalism lives.

Notes

1. Paul Kennedy, *The Rise and Fall of the Great Powers: Economic Change and Military Conflict from 1500 to 2000* (New York: Random House, 1988), p.493.
2. Goren Therborn, *Why Some People Are More Unemployed Than Others* (London: Verso, 1986).
3. Martin McGuire, "The Revolution in International Security," *Challenge* (March-April 1990):5.
4. Quoted in Michael Wines, "U.S. Urged to Emphasize Economic Strength," *New York Times*, 4 April 1990, p. A5.
5. Flora Lewis, "A Necessary Cold War?" *New York Times*, 3 February 1990, p. 25.
6. "All We Have Are Mosquitoes, Cubans, and the Revolution," interview with Pablo Armando Fernandez conducted by Marc Cooper, *Village Voice*, 1 May 1990, p. 24.

RESPONSES TO THE EVENTS OF 1989

DANIEL SINGER

PROMETHEUS REBOUND?

To suffer woes which Hope thinks infinite;
To forgive wrongs darker than death or night;
To defy Power which seems omnipotent;
To love, and bear; to hope till Hope creates
From its own wreck the thing it contemplates. . . .

—Shelley, *Prometheus Unbound*

"In Russia the problem could only be posed," wrote Rosa Luxemburg, referring to the realization of socialism, "it could not be solved in Russia." I am not quoting Luxemburg because she was the only person treating the Bolshevik revolution as potentially an episode; when she wrote those lines in the summer of 1918, its hold on power was very uncertain. I mention her because she seemed more than anybody else to view revolution as a worldwide phenomenon spread over a historical period, thus involving advances and retreats, victories and defeats. This vision of seizure of power as provisional added even more importance to her emphasis on the need to stick to socialist principles in order to show an example, to prepare the ground for future fighters and coming generations. It took clever servants of our establishment a great deal of chutzpah subsequently to present that great woman revolutionary as the scourge of the Bolsheviks. In fact, even in her most critical pamphlet from which these quotations are taken, she hailed them for doing everything that could be done "within the limits of historical possibilities," thus

17

saving "the honor of international socialism."[1] But she also warned Lenin and Trotsky not to make of necessity a virtue, and of the limitations dictated by circumstances an example for the movement at large. What in their case was still a minor blemish was turned into a calamity, as Stalin forged his system and imposed it on an obedient international movement as the undisputed model of socialism. An exorbitant price is still being paid for this confusion of the Stalinist nightmare with the socialist dream.

Such thoughts came to mind watching the dramatic unfolding of events in 1989. The year of the bicentennial of the French Revolution was to be celebrated as marking the burial of all radical breaks. History, as if offended, then quickened pace. Prompted by Gorbachev's *perestroika* and fed by domestic discontent, a tidal wave swept across Eastern Europe, toppling a series of regimes that were Communist in name only, in Warsaw and Budapest, in Berlin and Prague. Before the year was out even Ceaucescu, the Roumanian Caligula, had left the stage with bullets in his head. We were clearly watching the twilight of a reign, the end of an era, the collapse of regimes that were the result of revolutions not only carried out from above but imported from abroad. We were also attending the final funeral of Stalinism as a system. In February 1956, in his famous "secret" indictment of Stalin, Nikita Khrushchev stunned the faithful by revealing that the corpse of their demigod was stinking. The shock was terrible. Yet it took a third of a century for the system based on this cult to be dismantled throughout the empire.

Behind these certainties lurks a question mark. For the first time it is necessary to ask whether 1917 marks the beginning of an epoch, like 1789, or whether it inaugurates a heroic but tragic experiment, the abortive search for a shortcut, and is therefore in historical terms merely a parenthesis. The problem, whatever the answer, is crucial. When the balance sheet of this era is finally drawn up, it will not be as one-sided as the assessments improvised today on the spur of the moment. The impact of the Soviet experiment on the outside world illustrates this complexity. There is no doubt that the identification of Communism with the Russian concentration camp or with the Soviet tank contributed to the current discredit of the very idea of socialism both in the West and in Eastern Europe. But it is also true that the pioneering exploit of the Bolsheviks, the seizure of power by the workers, gave hope to millions of downtrodden throughout the world, encouraged them to resist and to rebel. Not all the subsequent revolutions were sponsored from above. Or, to take another instance, it is absurd to suggest that the foreign policy of Stalin and his epigones was driven by the desire to spread revolution and Communism throughout the world. On the contrary, the international revolutionary movement was strictly subordinated to the interests of Soviet foreign policy. Yet the very existence of that policy sometimes acted as a limit on the expansion of western imperialism. (Today the Brezhnev doctrine is fortunately vanishing, but the Monroe doctrine, in its Bush version, is alas stronger than ever.)

There are more immediate reasons why we must face up to this issue. The collapse of the East European regimes is trumpeted by the propaganda machine as final proof that socialism is unworkable. Capital hates frontiers that limit its field of action. It now eyes with growing appetite both Eastern Europe and the Soviet Union as territory to swallow in order to both expand its rule and extend its survival. This, however, is the potential prize for tomorrow. Meanwhile, there are ideological benefits to be gathered. Francis Fukuyama, the poor man's Hegel, describing capitalism as the culmination of history was only part of a vast chorus singing the vanity of any attempt to get rid of the prevailing system.

However noisy, this propaganda can actually be countered quite easily. To die you must have lived, and what we have known so far is really inexisting socialism. Besides, the prophets now announcing the final death of socialism are the very same who only yesterday, with equal conviction, spoke of the immutability of "totalitarian Communism," the hell from which there was and there could be no exit. The Fukuyamas can also be reminded that they are saying what the servants of the ruling system have always proclaimed, namely that history did exist but has come to an end with the victory of their masters. Yet before scoring debating points, itself quite a useful exercise, we must ourselves grasp what is really collapsing on the

Eastern front, ask why it is falling to pieces, and guess what is likely to be put in its place.

The "Original Sin" and Its Consequences

To seize the tragic dimension of the Soviet revolution it is indispensable to go back to the "original sin," if one may use such a religious term, of its inception, to the contrast between the Marxist design conceived for the advanced capitalist countries of Western Europe and its application to backward Mother Russia, to the "proletarian revolution" carried out in a land where the working class, shrunk by civil war, was surrounded by a huge peasant sea. Russia was supposed to be only the "weakest link" in the chain. The center of gravity was to shift to Germany and beyond as the revolution spread westward. But the revolution failed to spread. The Bolsheviks could either surrender, or they could cling to power hoping their isolation would prove temporary.[2] In that case, in the meantime they had to carry out by themselves their country's unaccomplished task, its industrial revolution. Isolated, surrounded by enemies, the Soviet Union had to achieve within a decade—because the danger was immediate—what in the West had taken over a century with the help of colonial plunder and a ruthless uprooting of the peasantry. The highly contradictory term, "primitive socialist accumulation," coined by Vladimir Smirnov and elaborated by Yevgenii Preobrazhensky, sums up the terrible, completely unexpected task thrust on the revolution's agenda.[3]

Barbarism, as Lenin put it even more bluntly, had to be uprooted in Russia by barbarian means. Does this mean that only a Georgian tyrant could fulfill this function? Personally, I am not convinced that Stalinism, with its concentration camps and its Byzantine cult of the leader, was inevitable in the circumstances. This, however, is not the place for a complex discussion of this subject. For the sake of our argument only two points have to be made. The first is that the system did fulfill its role for a time and in its own fashion. It turned peasants into workers, spread skills and education. The crude economic command from above did function as long as the "planning" was mainly concerned with the coordination of a limited number of huge plants. The industrialization at breakneck speed provided the Soviet Union with the guns, tanks, and planes thanks to which the Red army was able to resist the German invasion and then liberate Europe from the Nazis.

The counterpoint is that this process of development, hardly the most efficient, had very little to do with socialism. It was not a case of capitalism being superseded because it had reached its full potential. The Soviet peasants did not join collective farms because the private ones had got beyond the point of highest efficiency; they were driven into the *kolkhozy* by a bloody collectivization. The Bolsheviks did not inherit a complex industry which required planning for coherent growth; they had to build an industry almost from scratch using methods borrowed from F.W. Taylor. Altogether, either in economic or political terms, the ruthless mechanism of command *from above* had nothing in common with Marx's vision of freely associated producers gaining mastery over their labor and leisure, that is to say, over their lives. But this strange product of unexpected circumstances was painted as a workers' paradise and imposed as a model for the world at large. The more or less necessary evils were hailed as virtues. Worst of all, friends and foes alike seemed agreed that what was being forged in the Soviet Union was socialism.

However, Stalinism too contained the seeds of its own destruction. The political system designed for uprooted and half-illiterate *muzhiks* became increasingly obsolete as the population grew more urban and better educated. An economy more complex and more sophisticated rendered the crude dictation from the top and from the center counterproductive. By mid-century, the whole structure was held together only by the conditioned reflexes of an aging dictator, and in 1953 his successors were faced with the need for a complete overhaul. Though their problem was immense, the basic question could be worded rather simply: how do you make people work if you wish to get rid of a system of coercion based fundamentally on the fear of the concentration camp coupled with moral exhortations and do not wish to replace it by the capitalist system of coercion based on the fear of unemployment linked with the dazzling tyranny of the market?

A socialist answer to this question required in Russia nothing less than a democratic revolution. Democratic relations were needed on the shop floor, giving the working people a real say in the organization of their own work and the general division of labor, if the slogan about "our factories" was to cease to be a hypocritical metaphor. But this was not enough. Democracy had to be spread, or rather invented, at all levels of the country's life so that planning, the need for which would not vanish, could cease to be an alien dictation and become the self-management of a society seeking to master its own destiny. These major questions, which have not yet been tackled, let alone solved, by Gorbachev's *perestroika*, could not even be raised by Stalin's epigones.

Nikita Khrushchev, half-peasant, half-townsman, and as such a symbol of the Soviet Union in transition, did show a striking awareness of the need for radical change. However, he chose a constituency—the party apparatus—utterly unsuited to this task. The *apparatchiks* saw nothing wrong with the inherited system except Stalin's propensity to purge his own faithful servants (his bloody way to prevent the crystallization of a ruling class). What they wanted was Stalinism plus security of tenure. Even Khrushchev's haphazard half-measures were too much for them, and they toppled him when the reforms seemed to threaten their position. The man they picked to replace him, Leonid Brezhnev, made the unwritten pledge never to endanger the interests of the privileged. He kept his word and his job for eighteen years. The political price paid for this unexpected longevity was what is now known as the age of stagnation. All important reforms were shelved. After a time Brezhnev also reached a truce with the working class: you don't mix in politics and we shall not drive you too fast on the assembly lines. The inevitable happened. The Soviet economy slackened its pace. The returns on investment diminished. Housing and the welfare state were squeezed in the process. But if the economy came almost to a halt, society kept on changing, with peasants moving to town, with less frightened and much better educated generations entering the labor market. They had been promised "goulash socialism" and were getting neither. The potentially explosive mixture of economic stagnation and social discontent could not last. The *apparatchiks* showed their resistance to change by selecting the decrepit Konstantin Chernenko as a stopgap leader. By 1985 they had to resign themselves to Mikhail Gorbachev and radical reforms. But before we tackle *perestroika*, we must have a glance at the area where its results were to be most spectacular in 1989, at the empire Stalin acquired, not in any fit of absentmindedness, but in the struggle for survival against the Nazis.

"Socialism" in a Single Bloc

By one of those ironies of which history is apparently fond, Joseph Stalin, champion of "socialism in a single country," spread his version of socialism to the east bank of the Elbe. At first he saw the conquered land as merely a protective glacis. (Otherwise, punitive reparations against East Germany, a future partner, would not have made sense.) He then decided to reshape it in Russia's image. Thus Stalin's armies, like Napoleon's, altered the social order in the countries they crossed. Throughout Eastern and Central Europe, they eliminated factory owners and uprooted landlords. This was their revolutionary heritage and, whatever may be written today, their progressive function.

Unfortunately it was linked with less progressive features. The revolution was an imported product, and by this very nature had not been carried out by the people but imposed on them from above. Later the split of the world into two blocs, with the ensuing separation from the international division of labor, was a serious drawback, particularly for more industrialized countries like Czechoslovakia. This third handicap might have been more than compensated by the advantages of an alternative system, if the imposed model was not the Stalinist one which, in political terms, meant one-party dictatorship, police repression, and Moscow-like trials, and was economically obsolete from the very start.

Naturally, things did not look quite as bad at the time as they do now in the hour of bankruptcy proceedings. Though imported, the regime was not always unwelcome. Pro-Russian feelings were strong in, say, Bulgaria, and Czechoslovakia had deep left-wing traditions. Even in Hungary or Poland, where hostility was greater, the memories of the prewar regimes, of their failures and their injustices, were sufficiently fresh for quite a number of people, particularly young intellectuals, to greet a new regime promising a radical break with the past (some of these early enthusiasts are today lecturing on the evils of socialism in western, particularly American, universities). But all over Eastern Europe, the story of the last forty-five years has been one of missed opportunities and broken illusions.

The effects of the failure of Stalin's successors to reshape his heritage spread beyond Soviet frontiers. The year 1956 was probably the last moment of great expectations throughout the area. In Poland's "Spring in October," the hopes were provisionally confirmed as the (once imprisoned) Wladyslaw Gomulka returned to office. But the limits of change were at once written in blood by the Soviet troops crushing the Hungarian insurrection. Nevertheless, the "revisionists," those thinking that the regimes were fundamentally right though in need of radical reform, could still cling to their belief for a time, even if the redundant name given to their next project, the Czech "socialism with a human face," showed how much the very idea was now in need of qualification. And, in 1968, the Soviet tanks entering Prague put an end to a whole period. The Polish workers who climbed on the stage next were not talking of reforming the regime but of changing it.

Indeed, instead of widening, the social base of these regimes kept on shrinking. Stalin and the iron fist provided a myth, and for a time there were still many believers. Khrushchev replaced the ideology by the promise of a new deal for the consumer. Brezhnev had nothing to offer. The health and education services open to all, the prospect of social advancement for children of workers and peasants, all yesterday's attractions, were falling victims of stagnation. "Socialism" no longer meant only the Soviet tank and repression. For millions it also stood for economic backwardness. The prewar past was now sufficiently distant to be idealized for the new generations, and the West sufficiently dazzling to be perceived as a cornucopia. Propped up only by the fear of Soviet intervention, the ruling Communist parties were ready for history's broom.

The case of Poland, often a pioneer of change, shows how the movement first turned against the regime and then swung to the right, two trends that should not be confused. The illusion that Gomulka would radically reform the system did not last. By 1970, Poland's workers won from their "workers' state" in bloody battle the right to veto the government's policy on consumer prices. Six years later, as the party vainly tried to abolish that veto, a small band of intellectuals came to the rescue of the battered workers. This alliance was reenacted in that glorious summer of 1980, when the intellectuals offered to serve the workers who were asserting the then unprecedented right to form an independent union. The victorious workers were no lovers of "really existing socialism" but, in very Marxist fashion, they presented their own interests as "the superior interests of society as a whole." And the year after, Solidarity, their union, was talking in terms of self-management both in the factories and the country at large. Indeed, the vague project of a new parliament, with a lower house in which the Communist Party still had a guaranteed majority, and a senate representing workers' councils and other forms of *autogestion*, was probably the last chance of transition in a non-capitalist direction. The Communist Party chose otherwise. It was ready to make a deal with the Catholic church, but not with the workers. It opted for the military coup that crushed the labor movement—not badly enough to impose an economic reform, and this is why it had to resign itself to new talks within a decade, but sufficiently to alter the balance of forces within Solidarity. In 1989, when it came to the new historical compromise and the transfer of power, the intelligentsia was in charge and the proletariat was part of the electoral fodder. And the resulting government had dropped its vision of workers' democracy for the sake of the monetarist vision of Milton Friedman.

When one comes to study carefully the sweep and speed of this metamorphosis, all sorts of factors will have to be taken into account, and the circumstance that during its years underground Solidarity was helped by American money (channeled through the AFL-CIO) is not to be neglected. But the real reasons are much deeper. Actually, the strong Western emphasis on the immediate conversion to capitalism, as we shall see, came only later. To understand why a Tadeusz Mazowiecki, once a progressive Catholic trying to reconcile socialism with Christianity, becomes a prime minister who presides over Thatcherite privatization, or why a Vaclav Havel, who a few years ago described himself vaguely as a socialist, no longer does so today, one must keep in mind the extraordinary change in the ideological climate. The bankruptcy of the command economy has been interpreted as that of democratic planning, the fiasco of neo-Stalinism as the funeral of socialism, and the failure of a Mitterrand to build something different as the final proof of the absence of any radical alternative. To talk of "the end of ideology" is as absurd today as it ever was. What we have been witnessing for some years now is the ideological hegemony of the capitalist gospel. But I am running ahead of the story. Mazowiecki's premiership, Havel's presidency, or the crumbling of the Berlin wall for that matter, were inconceivable without the crucial shifts in Moscow.

The Center and the Periphery

Mikhail Gorbachev was accepted by his peers because the economic stagnation had reached the point of potential political explosion. Though himself a member of the ruling group, he belonged to the fraction pleading that a radical reform had become inevitable. He also understood, unlike the Chinese and unlike so many Western advisers now suffering from amnesia, that to reform the economy it is necessary to proceed with a deep political transformation. If he may not have known from the start how far this would take him, he has shown a great capacity to sail forward with each new tide. Thus in its first years *perestroika* offered the exhilarating experience of a country awakening from its slumber, recovering its memory and its voice, of a people learning to debate, to choose between various versions and different candidates. As books were published, plays staged, films shown that had no chance of being produced a few years earlier, as newspapers changed their nature and television its coverage, the Soviet Union became an altogether different country. All these freedoms of speech or assembly, it will be objected, are merely the bourgeois revolution come to Russia two centuries late. But freedoms are no less precious because they were originally bourgeois, and they change content, raising new issues, in a country where private ownership of the means of production was eliminated.

It is in economics that *perestroika* has so far failed to produce results. It was supposed to alter the system entirely, shifting it from a command mechanism to some form of market economy. According to its critics, up to now it has begotten the worst of both systems. The main reason for this failure is that the leadership does not really know where and how far it wants to go, and this brings us back to politics. In Stalin's time all social forces were reduced to obedient silence. Under Brezhnev the premise was that interests would neither be hurt nor expressed. It is only now that the interests of the various classes and social groups begin to crystallize and seek political expression. The most articulate grouping, and a pioneer of *perestroika*, is the potential *priviligentsia*—the managers, economists, and all sorts of other professionals whose numbers have grown and who want to have more say in running the factories and the rest of the country. They want the market, big income differentials, incentives involving different standards of housing, health, and education for the successful. Contrary to legend, they are not for introducing privileges into an allegedly egalitarian society. They are for shifting privileges and power from the obedient *apparatchiks* to the dynamic managers, from the *nomenklatura* to what they would describe as the meritocracy. Are they not perturbed by the prospect of where the logic of the market might lead? The lessons of Eastern Europe have induced them to urge that the process of reform be speeded up and not slowed down or altered.

These developments have also led to a divorce between Gorbachev and some of his original supporters, based on political rather than philosophical grounds. Mikhail Gorbachev has too sure a grasp of Soviet realities to believe that he can win backed simply by a section of the *intelligentsia*. He has always known that to break the resistance of the bureaucracy he needs the support of the workers, whose interests are threatened by the reform. The idea of having managers elected by the staff, which has not got very far, was conceived as a stratagem to gain their sympathy. Above all, he realizes that in a country affected by shortages, the prospect of unemployment, of ostentatious social differences, and the current resentment against private speculators (barely disguised under the cooperative label), may well allow the conservatives to mobilize, pretending not to defend their own interests but those of the country's downtrodden.

In the ambiguous controversy over economic reform one voice is still too faint, that of the socialist opposition—trying to reconcile the workers with a good part of the *intelligentsia*, admitting the need for incentives yet setting them in an egalitarian perspective, defending planning while attacking the bureaucracy—all this by a movement from below, by spreading democracy well beyond the bounds conceived by Gorbachev and his reformist critics, through self-management on the shop floor leading to self-government on the national scale. Only such an attempt to answer questions facing society since Stalin's death can, in my opinion, provide a solution to Russia's predicament, and, possibly, preserve the Soviet Union as an entity.

That the union should now be threatened is Gorbachev's heritage, not his accomplishment. *Perestroika* merely released the accumulated tensions and *glasnost* revealed them to the world. It does not betray one's belief in democracy to observe that when the lid was finally lifted all the smell that surfaced was not Chanel No. 5. There also came a stench of prejudice, jingoism, anti-Semitic hatred, an odor that spread well beyond the allegedly patriotic *Pamyat* society. Old ghosts are being joined by new monsters, and this is not surprising, the irrationality of the government having abetted the forces of unreason in the society at large. In particular, the Great Russian chauvinism, encouraged by the Georgian tyrant, stimulated nationalism in the republics and prevented it from finding a natural outlet. Now the regime is faced not only with the reasonable aspirations toward autonomy but also with atavistic hatreds and medieval passions. The union will not be kept together without a renewed community of interests cemented by some form of ideological cohesion.

In this short survey I have purposely excluded foreign policy—where Gorbachev has scored serious successes and altered the international equation—except as far as it affects the Soviet bloc in Europe, that is to say tremendously. For years all the protest movements in Eastern Europe knew that there was a Rubicon, crossing which would provoke a Soviet intervention, and all the achievements at the periphery were fragile as long as reform was not consolidated at the center. *Perestroika* changed all that. When Mikhail Gorbachev dropped the Brezhnev doctrine, or at least its provision that members of the Warsaw Pact could not alter the prevailing social order, he signed the death warrant for regimes which, by then, were only resting on the threat of Soviet intervention. He can thus be described as the stage manager of the revolutionary events of 1989. If he did not necessarily desire the outcome nor set the exact timetable, we now know that he did accept well in advance the Soviet retreat from Eastern Europe.[4]

Quite naturally, the countries of imported revolution have gone much further in their restoration than Russia. Here the ghosts from the past seem to have taken over the whole stage. Though the revival of capitalism is for tomorrow, all the prewar parties are being resurrected without paying much attention to the intervening social changes (such as the reduced role of the peasantry). Actually, the new governments in Budapest, Prague, and Warsaw, including Communists in senior or junior positions, act as if they wanted to wipe out half a century and recover their prewar position in Europe, forgetting that except for the Czechs they were then very poor relations. Contrary to some of their expectations, the East Europeans will not be offered the choice between social-democratic Sweden and Thatcherite Britain. Their comparative rank will be closer to that of Mexico or Bolivia. The new rulers are not deterred. Will they be followed? The people of Eastern Europe have shown with their feet and their ballots what they do not want. They still have to determine what they wish to put in its place.

Open Frontiers and Restoration

When regimes tumble every week, it is presumptuous or foolish to forecast the course of events in the months to come. But one can venture hypotheses about deeper trends. This is the sense in which I want to suggest that all the countries of Eastern Europe, including Russia, will first move in a capitalist direction. This concept, however, has to be defined. The existence of a market does not mean a return to capitalism. Any transition to a socialism worthy of the name will take time and involve a long period with a mixed economy. The search for a proper yardstick or incentives does not mean capitalism either. What is at stake is the general sense of direction. Is the economy moving toward a system in which production, consumption, and investment will be shaped by the conscious will of society, or toward one in which the main outlines of the economy will be determined by profit-oriented forces of the market? I suggest that Eastern Europe will be moving toward the latter if it proceeds with its intention to open up its frontiers, accept full convertibility of its currencies, and recover its place in the international division of labor.

When the Bolsheviks introduced their monopoly of foreign trade, they knew that their departure from the international division would be costly. But this was the price they had to pay, as Preobrazhensky put it, to dissociate their "private economy from the world private economy toward which it was tending." The hope was that as the revolution spread to more advanced capitalist countries, the damage would be limited. Then Stalin invented the theory of "socialism in one country" and coined the slogan: "To catch up with and overtake America." But though he spread his regime up to the Elbe, he did not produce an alternative society, and though Russia began by closing the gap, it still lies far behind. Indeed, the frontiers are being opened at the worst moment, after a period of stagnation. Knowing the tendency of the capitalist market to remove obstacles and the prevailing discrepancy in productivity or technological know-how, the outcome of an open contest is beyond doubt.

A bridgehead, however, should not be confused with a successful invasion, and here one must draw quantitative differences between the various countries of Eastern Europe and a qualitative one between them and the Soviet Union. All these postrevolutionary states, while nowhere forging a socialist society, had nationalized the means of production. They are now faced with the unprecedented task of privatizing not a plant or an industry but the bulk of the economy. The Poles have opted for a shortcut to capitalism, on which you can break your political neck. The Czechs, whose crisis is less acute, are proceeding more slowly; even their monetarism is supposed to have a human face. Yet in all these countries where socialism is now perceived as an alien imposition and the leaders of the conversion as yesterday's resisters, capitalism will have to show its seamy side— the unemployment, the yawning gap between rich and poor—for an entirely new left to emerge. In the Soviet Union the turning point may come at an earlier stage.

Whether the resistance will be successful is another matter. These regimes are more complicated than they are now being described. They preached one thing and practiced another. This gap between promise and fulfillment greatly contributed to the political apathy and cynicism. Yet the socialist ideal, in some curious fashion, also managed to sink in. Eastern technocrats, who (whether they still hold a party card or not) sound like Harvard Business School graduates, have joined the International Monetary Fund and bitterly complain about their worst handicap—the egalitarianism and thirst for social justice of their populations. It remains to be seen whether the quite understandable resentment against "really existing socialism" will prove stronger and more lasting than the socialist unconscious. All that can be said for the moment is that this is the beginning of a long conflict, that the main confrontation will take place in the Soviet center, not at the periphery, and that only early in the next millenium will it be possible to answer the crucial question at the heart of this essay: Was 1917 the beginning of a heroic yet tragic diversion ending in capitalism or was the revolution, though premature and then perverted, a positive step on humanity's road toward mastery over its own fate?

The Abuses and Uses of the Eastern Question

Even this bird's-eye view of the Eastern scene shows how its dramatic metamorphosis is vital for the Western world, both for our rulers and for parties and people who consider themselves progressive. For the capitalist establishment, Eastern Europe offers a tantalizing prize and its members have descended upon it like vultures. Special envoys of the IMF and the World Bank, of the European Commission and the OECD, prepare the ground. Bankers, industrialists, ministers, and presidents, the German chancellor and the Japanese prime minister follow with their checkbooks and the common query—"What's in it for me?" Liberty and democracy have been quickly translated into freedom to sell and then export profits. Incidentally, "socialist market" has proved a short-lived craze, both East and West now apparently only interested in the noun. To those who, in keeping with common East-West fashion, claim that there is no need to mention democracy in the same breath as the market because the former is by definition inseparable from the latter, one is tempted to reply they should preach their sermon in Johannesburg. Actually, because it will be difficult to push the "market economy" down the throat of a surprised population, voices are already raised suggesting "special powers" in Poland and "authoritarian rule" in Russia, on the ground that the market must come first and democracy will follow after. The invasion has begun. Whether the capitalist conquest will succeed is still uncertain.

The ideological dividends, on the other hand, are already being collected and have been for some time. In the mid-1970s, when a deep capitalist economic crisis followed student protests, the system felt threatened. The *gulag* campaign—the discovery by latter-day Christopher Columbuses, the *nouveaux philosophes,* of Soviet concentration camps—came to the rescue. Describing the search for any radical solution as leading inevitably to a totalitarian dead-end, it helped capitalism to survive, to break the resistance of the labor movement, and to reassert its ideological domination. The reactionary trends in the two halves of Europe fed one another. This helped the rightward swing in the East, and the tide has now gathered much momentum. The ambition today is to break the Promethean spirit altogether, to destroy the belief in a radical alternative. It is no longer "totalitarian communism," it is capitalism, whether you like it or not, which is being presented as a system from which there can be no exit, since it marks the end of history.

This line of the establishment, carried with Eastern help and mass mobilization of the media, dictates the strategy of the left. We no longer need to defend in Eastern Europe the right of expression of people with whom we disagree; many former victims are now in the corridors of power. We can pick and choose our allies, broadly where latter-day Black Hundreds or neo-Nazis are a serious threat, more selectively when we seek partners to struggle together for a socialist resurrection. It may be objected that at least to begin with there will not be many candidates for that struggle in Eastern Europe. Undoubtedly. But we can help to shorten that period in many ways by reminding, for instance, the East Europeans who look at their prewar past through rosy spectacles of its real color, recalling Admiral Horthy for the Hungarians, Marshal Pilsudski for the Poles, reacting against the new Russian myth that the left-wing critics of Stalin were as bad or worse than the dictator. Yet our main task is obvious. It is human and natural for East Europeans, who waste hours standing in line or otherwise chasing scarce goods to be dazzled by our glittering city lights and our tempting shopping centers; for people who had to deal with a stupid censorship to be thrilled by our freedom of expression at once real and apparent. But we must show them the seamy side of our societies.

This is our duty to our Eastern friends, but also to ourselves, because of the damage wrought here by the huge propaganda machine. We must restate some fundamental truths about our system. Our inability to organize society to the best advantage of its population is such that we turn even our technological genius into a handicap: higher productivity leads to more unemployment. Shocking discrepancies between the haves and the have-nots are not the only feature of this increasingly two-tier society. Its prosperity rests on the poverty and exploitation of the rest of the world. We are unable to insert our economy into its natural environment and can only deal with pollution *ex post facto* so as to provide room for profit once again. Our alienated and alienating society has made little progress toward equality of sexes, but has shown a peculiar talent for commercializing culture, for turning everything into merchandise. These are only some of the points which must be expanded to draw a genuine picture of really existing capitalism.

Only dinosaurs, the post-moderns on both sides of the Elbe will object, can use such antediluvian concepts as capitalism or socialism. If you wish to be up to date the operating terms are "rule-of-law," the "law-abiding state," the "Rights of Man," in short, the vocabulary of democracy. So let us take them at their word. Democracy is crucial for a socialist. Though Russia should never have been our model, nor any other place for that matter, it would be foolish to deny the heritage and refuse to learn from bitter experience. Rosa Luxemburg was prophetic when she pleaded for the "active, untrammelled, energetic political life of the broadest masses of the people" and warned that "without general elections, without unrestricted freedom of press and assembly, without a free struggle of opinion, life dies out in every public institution, becomes a mere semblance of life, in which only the bureaucracy remains as the active element."[5] The most important lesson from the Soviet past is that when people are deprived of say over their lives, however temporarily and for however justifiable reasons, they will find it extremely difficult to recover their rights, and the price paid for this allegedly temporary exception proves prohibitive and long lasting. This is an additional reason why democracy must figure at the very heart of any revived socialist project.

But it must be real democracy and not the empty phraseology of our trend-setters. When an American on the minimum wage has to work 79,000 years to earn as much—$550 million—as Michael Milken did in 1987, to say one person, one vote and leave it at that is shockingly superficial. When the Berlusconis, Bertelsmans, and other Murdochs are extending their mediatic stranglehold over the whole globe, to talk of freedom of expression as if these tycoons were not "more equal" than any Tom, Hans, or Giovanni is hypocritical. And to add that the property of the Puerto Rican immigrant is protected in New York as much as that of Donald Trump is to reveal the class nature of this society and of its preachers. Genuine socialists were never against basic freedoms because these were *bourgeois*. They have always, as the words of Luxemburg testify, "revealed the hard kernel of social inequality and lack of freedom hidden under the sweet shell of formal equality and freedom," not to abolish democracy, but on the contrary to fill it with social content. This is the terrain on which common struggle must soon be resumed in Europe, across the fast-vanishing divide.

The main message from Eastern Europe is not the one frenetically drummed by the media. It is that when institutions do not correspond to needs, sooner or later they must yield; that people inspired by an idea can bring down walls; in other words, that radical transformation is possible. The philosophers from the State Department, Rand, and other corporations know better than they pretend. Their incantation about the end of history is merely designed to gain time for their masters. They know that a system torn by contradictions like capitalism, unless it first blows up the planet or poisons it through pollution, will also collapse in its turn. How soon? Admittedly it is now necessary to ask whether capitalism, universal in its aspiration like socialism, will invade the whole world before it leaves the historical stage. This is but another way of asking whether capitalism's gravediggers will come from the West or, after all and despite everything that is happening, from the East.

The time factor, however, is not without influence on our own mood. The thirty-seven years that have elapsed since Stalin's death are for the historian but a brief spell. For us they mark the passage from youth to nearly old age. It is in this contrast between historical perspective and humanity's natural political impatience that lies the reason why, in moments of despondency, when broken illusions, wasted lives, bloody sacrifices are vividly seen behind a shattered political model, one begins to doubt for a while, though only for a while, whether hope will ever create "from its own wreck the thing it contemplates."

Notes

1. Rosa Luxemburg, *The Russian Revolution and Leninism or Marxism* (Ann Arbor: University of Michigan Press, 1961), p. 80.
2. Personally I think that for a socialist there are no taboos dealing with the Soviet regime. But his or her judgment must assess the event in its historical context; draw a distinction between the early years and the Stalin era; and take into account the consequences of possible defeat and of surrender of power not to other left-wing groups but to the forces of reaction.
3. See Yevgenii Preobrazhensky, *The New Economics* (Oxford: Clarendon Press, 1965); also Alexander Erlich, *The Soviet Industrialization Debate, 1924–28* (Cambridge: Harvard University Press, 1960).
4. Karoly Grosz, leader of the Hungarian Communist Party at the time, has confirmed that in the spring of 1988 Mikhail Gorbachev had agreed in principle to a total

withdrawal of Soviet troops (*International Herald Tribune*, 23 January 1990). Hungary, with no NATO frontier, was a simpler case than, say, Czechoslovakia. Yet the only real problem is presented by the German Democratic Republic, where the quickening of the process of reunification could still spoil Gorbachev's East European gamble.

5. Luxemburg, *The Russian Revolution*, p. 71.

LUCIANA CASTELLINA

REMAINING AN ITALIAN COMMUNIST: REFLECTIONS ON THE "DEATH OF SOCIALISM"

To reflect on the European left in Italy means, first and foremost, to reflect on the Communist Party, since this is the largest party of the left. As of the last general elections, which were for the European parliament in 1989, the party had 1.4 million members and 28 percent of the vote; it was the second largest vote getter in the country; it was the largest in 1984.

For some time now, Communism in Italy has been an anomaly in the Western political panorama, where Communist parties have for decades either been grouplets without parliamentary representation, or—as in France, Spain, and Greece—once played an important role but have now been reduced to some 10 percent of the electorate. The one exception is the Portuguese Communist Party, which still has significant mass contacts and a substantial parliamentary representation despite its rigid Stalinist orthodoxy.

The Italian Communist Party (PCI) is anomalous not only because of its size, but also because of its nature and political line. It is deeply populist and national, and has acted with increasing autonomy with regard to Soviet discipline. It severed its ties with the Soviet and Eastern European Communist parties some ten years ago.

Yet in speaking of the PCI, I should conjugate my verbs in the past tense: in all probability, by the time this essay is published the PCI will have ceased to exist. In March 1990, at an extraordinary congress, the PCI decided by majority vote to begin discussions leading to a constituent assembly that will create a new political organization. This new organization will include other parts of the left, a concept previously foreign to the Communist tradition. There-fore, sometime between the end of 1990 and early 1991, the PCI will be dissolved. Although the decision was the result of a majority vote, one-third of the members *explicitly* rejected it, and many more did so implicitly—by silently distancing themselves from the party over a period of months. The proposal came from the party's secretary and was supported by most of the party apparatus, whose role has continued to be important even in the PCI, which is far more democratic than traditional Communist parties. In other words, it is a decision that is essentially irreversible.

It is not clear what the new force on the left will be like once the PCI is dissolved. But it is clear that what led to the decision was not the possibility of a fruitful exchange with other left forces capable of enriching and renewing the Communist tradition, or even the possi-bility of gathering and organizing those who are dispersed in the new social movements (ecological, feminist, peace) and have had trouble finding a place in a party. In Italy, we call these people the "sub-merged left," and although they are indeed dispersed, in recent years they have come closer to the PCI as the party has opened itself to new themes and new needs—particularly at the 18th Congress in March 1989—and has therefore become the center of a more, not less, radical opposition, one more capable of voicing the growing social antagonisms, antagonisms that are new in form and content. But the changes now underway give a totally different message, and are destined to disillusion those seeking an alternative rather than gather them together. In short, the changes, whatever their declared intensions, are in fact destroying the name of the party in order to facilitate its entrance into the existing political framework. In this context, this can only lead to the emergence of highly ambiguous corporate impulses, and this in turn risks the erosion of the demo-cratic structure itself.

But the main theme of this article goes beyond the recent activities of the PCI, although these had to be discussed first because they are part of the general crisis of the European left. The end of a party such as ours will profoundly modify not only (as is obvious) the Italian political scene, but also that of the entire continent. In the East, the end of the party deprives the forces liberated from the oppression of so-called actually existing socialism of a point of reference, of a left unstained by the errors of those regimes that have governed in the name of socialism. The existence of the PCI could thus have helped overcome the idea that only capitalism remains between heaven and earth. To the West, in the last few years the party has intervened forcefully in the struggles inside the social democratic bloc. The party has, in fact, despite a thousand ambiguities (and particularly thanks to Belinguer) stimulated the search for a possible "third way"—understood as an attempt to surmount existing problems through a critical reflection that should, and could, have led to a renewal of what was positive in the second and third internationals in the light of the new problematic posed by the mass social movements. This possible role—more talked about than practiced—will undoubtedly disappear with the dissolution of the PCI. This revision is part of the new left force and will bring with it a completely uncritical adherence to the second international.

It is important to note that this result should not—and I hope will not—mean the death of a tradition and of a theory (of the transition to a different social-political system), even if henceforth others are destined to carry it forward. Those PCI militants who opposed the majority decision are determined not to stop being Communists or to end their historic diversity. In an as yet undetermined way, these militants will be working in a new terrain, together with many who, even if foreign to our tradition, intend to remain an opposition force.

Those in Italy who choose this road must still explain why they will continue to define themselves as Communists given the dramatic collapse of the regimes that bore that name. It is necessary to understand the value, here and now, of this name, given that it has been rejected by so many, including many from the parties that governed in the East. It is necessary to show that the end of the PCI, the most important Communist Party in the West, is not the confirmation of a tendency prevalent elsewhere—namely, the historic decline of Communism, and with it every other force that still holds out hope for modifying the capitalist order—but continues to be part of a global process of transformation which, despite errors and limits, received its decisive thrust from the October Revolution and decolonization and was rooted theoretically in Marxism. Further, they must show the concrete possibility of such a force and culture being revived within the European left, part of the current struggles (in both East and West) to transform and launch a new opposition political force. Even if the specificity of the "Italian case" had not been weakened, there would still be the need to prove that it was not a phenomenon restricted to that one country but one capable of influencing the course of democratic socialist history on the European continent, since it is such parties that remain the home of those social forces that have the potential to transform society.

The events of the last ten years, and particularly those of 1989, could lead to a completely pessimistic conclusion. In the 1980s, in fact, there was a process of restructuring, for good reason termed epochal, that shook the premises on which the European left, including its social-democratic component, based its strategies. It affected the political bases, cultural and organizational, on which the left had grown in the postwar period. The process included the rapid acceleration of the international integration of markets, of finance, and of the command centers of production; the superceding of the Tayloristic organization of labor; the decline of the relative weight of industry and the consequent diminuition of the political role of the working class; the growth of marginalized groups, of irregular labor, of new intellectual professions strongly marked by individualism; the growing role of systems of information and training; and the ever increasing transfer of real decision-making powers to centers outside the control of democratic representative institutions and the consequent lessening of the role of the opposition, already beset by an increasingly effective manipulation of politics and culture.

In addition to these upsetting changes to which the left, in all its components, was not able to react effectively, there is now the crisis of the so-called socialist societies which has not occurred—as we might have hoped—as part of a move toward democratization brought on by a progressively better life and the reduction of Cold War tensions, but rather has been a sudden collapse. It has been followed by a recourse to the myths of the market without, thus far, any sign of restraint.

What has happened in the East has upset the balance of power both in that part of Europe and in the West, where the dominant classes are gaining strength from the newly offered possibilities of uncontested domination. This has opened the way for transforming the "popular democracies" into a colonial zone, and for a gigantic social "dumping," which is bound to weaken the organizations of the working class in the West. The labor force in the East is low cost and, in contrast to the third world, highly skilled, and rapid deregulation is taking place without the existence of a countervailing trade union presence. The old organizations have no credibility, while new ones have not yet been born. The perspective, therefore, is of a Brussels-centered Europe, dominated by financial capital, ever less restrained by the left, that will exercise its hegemony over the entire continent, gathering around the European Economic Commission in "concentric circles"—as EEC Commissioner Jacques Delors loves to repeat—all the other countries: in essence, a circle of satellites.

What has happened, and is happening, on the economic, political, cultural, and military levels—with the de facto dissolution of the Warsaw Pact, NATO's role as exclusive center of a new security system is reinforced—could lead to the conclusion that capitalism has won, and that, at least for a long time, there is no likelihood of any alternative. Not only must communism appear an obsolete theory, but so must every variant of reformist socialism as well, given the erosion of those factors that had allowed for the "Keynesian compromise" and the construction, in Europe, of the most advanced social welfare states in the world.

Hence, in these circumstances, what sense is there to again propose a Communist Party in Italy, to pretend that it has a role beyond the frontiers of this country? Certainly in Italy the name has a precise meaning: during this century, the PCI has provided the concrete image of a struggle for liberation from oppression, tightly tied to the defense of liberty and the development of political democracy. And since a great patrimony counts, and since historical memory is an essential part of collective life, this alone is enough to justify saving the name Communist. But there are other reasons, beyond those tied to the Italian past, which explain why so many of us continue to give force to that name. There is developing in contemporary society a need for things that cannot be measured in terms of money or judged by the criteria of the marketplace. There is a need for direct human contact and communication. There are demands for liberation from work that alienates us from ourselves, a need to return to labor its creativity and to give autonomy to our lifestyle. These needs cannot be fulfilled, anymore than justice and equality can increase, because they go beyond the equality that could exist in a society defined socialist.

To keep open the possibility of Communism means to recognize the value of these needs and to experiment with ways of communal life wherein they can find expression. It means to overturn certain rooted values—first among them that issue so tenacious, so continuously repeated, and so imprinted in contemporary societies: the differentiation between the weak and the strong. It means keeping alive the belief that the weak may have in them extraordinary resources that the strong do not have. It helps, in understanding this issue, to think about how women live out the experience of their sex, not as weak but as beaten. It will help to communicate with the stifled and squeezed worlds that will spring from the "continents of hunger"—such a large part of the human race. As a starting point for the transformation of society, Communism is a critique of production for the sake of production, of the absolute priority of accumulation regardless of its concrete ends, and hence of a social system that is uniquely devoted to the multiplication of things and needs. Communism is a critique of a conception of politics as the business of a professionalized elite and it is the assertion of democracy as a process that permeates every structure so that it finally overcomes the separation between the governed and the governors.

Communism also means—indeed, this is one of its essential meanings—that all of this is only possible with the gradual replacement of a social formation that places a priority on profits and markets, and can only be achieved through the conscious action and practice of those who are now being sacrificed by the system. Certainly it is true that the ideas and projects designed to eliminate the social restraints that impede human liberty must not lead to a totalizing conception of politics and life. Women, with their feminist theory and practice, were the first to affirm the partiality of politics and to produce the evidence for this. Thus it must be emphasized that the Communist project has not only been far removed from, but has been totally contradicted by, the despotic regimes of Eastern Europe, and that it remains more of a matter of belief than a blueprint for society. It must also be recognized that many elements provided by Marx in his analysis, or crystallized over time in Marxist currents, have not withstood the test of reality. We had hoped that stringent critical reflection would lead to substantial correction in the East and would open a new phase in the West. This did not happen: a break in continuity is at hand. Yet to simply accept that Communism must be discarded because of the crisis of the Stalinist model would preclude any search for a new vision.

When we speak of a vision, we have no intention of chasing after a utopia, of casting aside involvement in the present. On the contrary, it seems to us that without such a vision, it is impossible to operate correctly in the present, to interpret and provide a perspective on new contradictions, to understand and guide real movements which, however confused, are daily calling attention to the irrationality and oppression of the dominant structures and values.

Here a single, although partial, example is useful. In Italy in the past year there has grown up a new and extraordinary mass movement of students which led to the occupation—for months—of all the schools of higher education. The initial cause of the protest was a government plan to encourage private financing of university research, but it went well beyond a discussion of subordinating academic studies to the hardly neutral interests of corporations and took up more the fundamental issue of the uses of knowledge, the commercialization of culture, and the alienation of intellectuals. This was a very advanced position wholly within the framework of a radical opposition to the myths of capitalist efficiency and pseudomodernity.

Yet despite the extraordinary vitality and rich culture expressed by the movement, which translated its analysis into an academic counter-year managed by the students in the occupied classrooms, the students found themselves ultimately isolated: the left, enclosed in its myopic "realism," did not understand what the students wanted.

In fact, if one pays close attention to what is moving in the depths of the society, one sees that it is far richer in oppositional moods and potential than is generally acknowledged: new contradictions are producing an unwritten anticapitalist critique, in effect a recognition of the need for Communism, not as an idelogical construct but as the result of experience.

We could start by imagining a movement sparked by the discovery of the full dimensions of the ecological damage to the planet, which now worries both the vanished vanguards and the industrialized societies. How could such a movement act without first discussing those mechanisms that guarantee the dynamism of capitalism: the market as the sole criterion for orienting development, the enterprise as the sole subject of decision-making; profit as the sole motive behind, and yardstick for measuring, results? How is it possible to deal with the problem of ecological devastation without a long-term analysis, without an evaluation of social production as a whole and therefore without demanding the power to intervene in the productive process, to plan research, investment, and consumption—in short, a power totally different from that which exists under capitalism? Further, we need only to think of the problem of work, of the ever increasing distress among those who are employed as well as those who are not. How is it possible not to see that in regard to labor, whether from the standpoint of quantity (the tendency to reduce the workforce) or of quality (the polarization that is the result of narrow specialization on one side and deskilling on the other), the classic argument of the left is still valid, and indeed is even more pressing: the argument that salaried labor and freed labor must be superseded? Thus even in a postindustrial future, class conflict will continue to express itself. In sum, it is precisely the most radical aspect of the Marxian critique of capitalism—the liberation of labor from being a commodity—that is again relevant.

Further, how is it possible not to see that the classic tendency of capitalism, fought against by workers' movements from its inception—the tendency to inequality and poverty—has not weakened? On the contrary, it has grown, not only through the divergence between north and south but inside the developed countries, where poverty and inequality are not the residue of a backward system getting better but are the contemporary product of a selective modernity that is creating marginalization because it has broken the linear connection between development and well-being.

Finally, how is it possible not to see that the issue of democracy itself has become central—not only democracy as a system necessary to guarantee the liberty of the individual, but democracy as a political form that is capable of capturing the general will and the general interest. There is more and more evidence of the mystifying nature of democracy, and the fact that democracy cannot attack the ever more exclusive centers of real power, which is itself exercised in an ever more pervasive manner, in ever new sectors of social and individual life. At the same time that the importance and the value of difference is growing—not only the fundamental difference between men and women, but also the difference of individualization (which is not the same as individualism)—there is a contradictory increase in the heavy burden of uniformity. This makes people ever more subordinated, ever less free, ever more flattened and made passive by the dictatorship of consumerism, which the more it goes beyond the threshold of necessities (which at least represent some objective criteria), the more it arbitrarily shapes our values.

The evidence of these contradictions, which mingle old and new oppressions, should bring the European left not to the liberal-democratic binge which has swamped it and which has been made worse by a simplistic critique of Soviet totalitarianism, but to a rediscovery of the value of the Marxian—and Leninist—critique of the state.

Many other examples could be given, including the most significant, which is the problem of the third world. This alone shows that the present system cannot count on a global extension, if only because of ecological limits. What I am saying is that capitalist society, even with the transformations of the historic passage to a postindustrial society, will be shaken, even more than in the past, by material and ideological conflicts at the height of the modern capitalist operation. There is thus no reason to give in, to let ourselves be convinced that capitalism is living through a new springtime simply because new events have offered it unexpected justification.

It is certainly true that many of the contradictions now emerging cannot be summarily reduced to the conflict between capital and labor. New subjects and new needs are emerging, and their automony must be recognized. Yet even these new contradictions are deeply rooted in the existing structures and values of the capitalist mode of production: that is to say, these contradictions are setting forth, in ever more radical terms, the problem of overcoming the system while at the same time providing, in their ensemble, the basis—the subjects and movements—for doing so.

To capture this connection, a great renewal of theory and practice is necessary, because if the traditional capital/labor conflict does not find a new discourse of struggle, the working class will remain isolated and the new movements will remain mere expressions of distress. Unfortunately, what is happening today is that the European left, even when it sees the importance of these new contradictions and new needs, is unable to grasp the connection. Hence we are seeing an increasing separation: on the one hand, there is discussion of values and the great epochal contradictions (which fill the documents of all the parties, including the more pragmatic social democratic ones); on the other hand, the political project is ever more stuck in daily tactics, ever more operating within the system, ever more inspired by the "art of the possible" and so disposed to compromise. And then, when this is achieved, the result is a loss of internal consensus because experience deludes expectations, producing scepticism and depoliticization, until people can no longer distinguish between the left and the right.

These are the considerations that make us continue. Here is the basis for the conviction of those in Italy who reject the liquidation of the Communist Party and insist on the need to leap ahead and make a profound reevaluation. From this point of view, even the movements in the East may in the long run bring fresh air to our undertaking. Beyond their immediate outcomes, they have in fact a great positive value: they have set into motion great masses of people long stifled by the regimes of "existing socialism"; they have demonstrated to a world that seems to believe that nothing changes the enormous potential of non-violent popular mobilization. Thanks to this, in the medium-long term, processes of great relevance may develop. They may in fact allow for the reweaving of the torn cloth of the European left, the beginning of a joint reflection on our respective experiences, a uniting of our forces in an alternative project and an alternative movement to support it. The left may move beyond the divisive confines imposed by the Cold War.

This process will not develop automatically. Events can take a different road only if the Western left—the best positioned to provide a critical stimulus for the new project—proves capable of surmounting the present crisis of trust and identity. Nevertheless, the possibilities are there: the old divisions between reformers and revolutionaries are obsolete; national fragmentation will be lessened as the result of European unification; and there is no longer a social-democratic model to rebuild or a revolutionary model to replicate. Everyone is very conscious of this situation, and the abandonment of old divisions may well provide the basis for a new unity.

For sure, weighty differences remain, but these no longer operate within the confines of the old political claims of the left, but rather cut across them. We must distinguish between those who, while backing gradual transformation based on consensus, still envisage great changes and are convinced of the need for a fighting movement, a cultural battle, a unified political constellation in opposition to the dominant one. We must distance ourselves from those who, in calling themselves reformist, are not referring to the great experiences of past reforms, but are talking, nationally and internationally, of making marginal adjustments to moderate programs that are increasingly similar in content.

Finally, then, when we speak of a Western European left, we should keep in mind that we are not talking about a single reality, not even with regard to social democracy or the new green parties. Rather, the new contradictions are arising within a complex reality that includes, and is prompted by, events in the East. The changes in the PCI are therefore part of a fundamental confrontation that does not involve Italy alone, but is destined to characterize a long historical phase that is only now beginning.

—Translated by Carl Marzani

JOE SLOVO

HAS SOCIALISM FAILED?

Introduction

Socialism is undoubtedly in the throes of a crisis greater than at any time since 1917. The last half of 1989 saw the dramatic collapse of most of the Communist Party governments of Eastern Europe. Their downfall was brought about through massive upsurges which had the support not only of the majority of the working class but also a large slice of the membership of the ruling parties themselves. These were popular revolts against unpopular regimes; if socialists are unable to come to terms with this reality, the future of socialism is indeed bleak.

The mounting chronicle of crimes and distortions in the history of existing socialism, its economic failures, and the divide which developed between socialism and democracy have raised doubts in the minds of many former supporters of the socialist cause as to whether socialism can work at all. Indeed, we must expect that, for a time, many in the affected countries will be easy targets for those aiming to achieve a reversion to capitalism, including an embrace of its external policies.

Shock-waves of very necessary self-examination have also been triggered off among communists both inside and outside the socialist world. For our part, we firmly believe in the future of socialism; nor do we dismiss its whole past as an unmitigated failure. Socialism certainly produced a Stalin and a Ceaucescu, but it also produced a Lenin and a Gorbachev. Despite the distortions at the top, the

48

nobility of socialism's basic objectives inspired millions upon millions to devote themselves selflessly to building it on the ground. And no one can doubt that if humanity is today poised to enter an unprecedented era of peace and civilized international relations, it is in the first place due to the efforts of the socialist world.

But it is more vital than ever to subject the past of existing socialism to an unsparing critique in order to draw the necessary lessons. To do so openly is an assertion of justified confidence in the future of socialism and its inherent moral superiority. And we should not allow ourselves to be inhibited merely because an exposure of failures will inevitably provide ammunition to the traditional enemies of socialism: our silence will, in any case, present them with even more powerful ammunition.

Ideological Responses

The ideological responses to the crisis of existing socialism by constituents of what was previously known as the international communist and workers' movement (and among our own members) is still so varied and tentative that it is early days to attempt a neat categorization. At the risk of oversimplification, we identify a number of broad tendencies that we must guard against: (1) Finding excuses for Stalinism; (2) attributing the crisis to the pace of *perestroika;* (3) acting as if we have declared a moratorium on socialist criticism of capitalism and imperialism; and, worst of all (4), concluding that socialist theory made the distortions inevitable.

The term Stalinism is used to denote the bureaucratic-authoritarian style of leadership (of parties both in and out of power) which denuded the party and the practice of socialism of most of its democratic content and concentrated power in the hands of a tiny, self-perpetuating elite.

While the mold for Stalinism was cast under Stalin's leadership, it is not suggested that he bears sole responsibility for its negative practices. The essential content of Stalinism—socialism without democracy—was retained even after Stalin in the Soviet Union (until Gorbachev's intervention), albeit without some of the terror, brutality, and judicial distortions associated with Stalin himself.

Among a diminishing minority there is still a reluctance to look squarely in the mirror of history and to concede that the socialism it reflects has, on balance, been so distorted that an appeal to its positive achievements (and of course there have been many) sounds hollow and very much like special pleading. It is surely now obvious that if the socialist world stands in tatters at this historic moment, it is due to Stalinist distortions.

We should have little patience with the plea in mitigation that, in the circumstances, the Stalinist excesses (such as forced collectivization) brought about some positive economic achievements. Statistics showing high growth rates during Stalin's time prove only that methods of primitive accumulation can stimulate purely quantitative growth in the early stages of capitalism or socialism—but at what human cost? In any case, more and more evidence is emerging daily that, in the long run, the excesses inhibited the economic potential of socialism.

Another familiar plea in mitigation is that the mobilizing effect of the Stalin cult helped save socialism from military defeat. It is, however, now becoming clear that the virtual destruction of the command personnel of the Red Army, the lack of effective preparation against Hitler's onslaught, and Stalin's dictatorial and damaging interventions in the conduct of the war could have cost the Soviet Union its victory.

Vigilance is clearly needed against the pre-*perestroika* styles of work and thinking which infected virtually every party (including ours) and molded its members for so many decades. It is not enough merely to engage in the self-pitying cry, "We were misled"; we should rather ask why so many communists allowed themselves to become so blinded for so long. And, more importantly, why they behaved like Stalinists toward those of their comrades who raised even the slightest doubt about the "purity" of Stalin's brand of socialism.

In the socialist world there are still outposts that unashamedly mourn the retreat from Stalinism and use its dogmas to "justify" undemocratic and tyrannical practices. It is clearly a matter of time before popular revulsion leads to a transformation. In general, those who still defend the Stalinist model—even in a qualified way—are a dying breed; at the ideological level they will undoubtedly be left behind and they need not detain us here.

Most communists, of course, concede that a great deal "went wrong" and needs to be corrected. Some, however, fear that the corrective methods are so hasty and extreme that, in the end, they may do more harm than good. The enemies of socialism, so it is argued, are being given new powerful weapons with which to destroy socialism and to return to capitalism. The pace of Gorbachev's *perestroika* and *glasnost* are, either directly or indirectly, blamed for the "collapse" of communist political hegemony in countries like Poland, Hungary, East Germany, and Czechoslovakia.

In the countries mentioned, despite the advantage of over forty years of a monopoly on education, the media, etc., the parties in power could not find a significant section of the class they claimed to represent (or, for that matter, even a majority of their own membership) to defend them or their version of socialism. To blame *perestroika* and *glasnost* for the ailments of socialism is like blaming the diagnosis and the prescription for the illness. Indeed, the only way to ensure the future of socialism is to grasp the nettle with the political courage of a Gorbachev.

When things go badly wrong (whether it be in a movement or a country) it is inevitable that some who have ulterior motives jump on the bandwagon. When a gap develops between the leadership and the led, it always provides openings for real enemies. But to deal with the gap in terms only of enemy conspiracies is an ancient and discredited device. Equally, to fail to tackle mistakes or crimes merely because their exposure will give comfort to our adversaries is both shortsighted and counterproductive.

In general, it is our view that the fact that the processes of *perestroika* and *glasnost* came too slowly, too little, and too late in Eastern Europe did more than anything else to endanger the socialist perspective there. It is through these processes—and they must be implemented with all possible speed—that socialism has any hope of showing its essentially human face. When socialism as a world system comes into its own again—as it undoubtedly will—the "Gorbachev revolution" will have played a seminal role.

We are impressed with the contribution that crusading pro-*perestroika* journals (such as *Moscow News* and *New Times*) are making to the renovation of socialism. At the same time, we must not overlook the alarming tendency among many media partisans of *perestroika* to focus so exclusively on the blemishes of the socialist experience that the socialist critique of capitalism and imperialism finds little, if any, place.

Some Soviet journals have become so exclusively focused on self-criticism that the social inequalities within capitalism and the continuing plunder by international capital of the resources of the developing world through neocolonial manipulation, unequal trade, and the debt burden receive little emphasis. Middle-class elements, including many journalists within socialist societies, seem mesmerized by pure technocracy; the glitter of Western consumerism and the quality of up-market goods appear to overshadow the quality of life for society as a whole.

There is less visible than at any time a critique of imperialism's continuing human rights violations and its gross interference in the internal affairs of sovereign states through surrogates and direct aggression, and its continuing support of banditry and racist and military dictatorships.

The perversion of democracy in the socialist experience is falsely contrasted to its practice in the capitalist West, as if the latter gives adequate scope for the fulfilment of democratic ideals. The economic ravages caused by excessive centralization and commandism under socialism seem also to have pushed into the background the basic socialist critique of capitalism: a society cannot be democratic if it is ruled by profit and social inequality and if power over the most vital areas of life is outside public control.

Some communists have been completely overwhelmed by the soiled image of socialism, which they see in the mirror of history. They conclude that it reflects not only *what was* (and in the case of some countries, *what still is*), but, in addition, *what inevitably had to be* in the attempts to build a socialist society as understood by the founding fathers of socialist doctrine.

If, indeed, what happened in the socialist world *had to happen* because of some or all of our theoretical starting points, if the Stalin-type perversion is unavoidable, then there is no more to be said; we must clearly either seek an alternative to socialism or throw overboard, or at least qualify, some of its postulates.

We believe, however, that the theory of Marxism, in all its essential respects, remains valid and provides an indispensable theoretical guide to achieve a society free of all forms of exploitation of person by person. The major weaknesses which have emerged in the practice of socialism are the results of distortions and misapplications. They do not flow naturally from the basic concepts of Marxism, whose core is essentially humane and democratic and which projects a social order with an economic potential vastly superior to that of capitalism.

Marxist Theory Under Fire

Let us touch on some of the concepts that have come under fire in the post-*perestroika* polemics:

(1) Marxism maintains that the class struggle is the motor of human history. Some commentators in the socialist media are showing a temptation to jettison this theory merely because Stalin and the bureaucracy around him distorted it to rationalize tyrannical practices. But it remains valid both as an explanation of past social transformations and as a guide to the strategy and tactics of the struggle to win a socialist order, a struggle in which the working class plays the dominant role.

(2) The economic stagnation of socialism and its poor technological performance as compared to the capitalist world sector cannot be attributed to the ineffectiveness of socialist relations of production but rather to their distortion. Socialist relations of production provide the most effective framework for maximizing humanity's productive capacity and using its products in the interests of the whole society.

(3) Marxist ethical doctrine sees no conflict between the contention that all morality is class-related and the assertion that working-class values are concerned, above all, with the supremacy of human values. The separation of these interdependent concepts (in later

theory and practice) provided the context in which crimes against the people were rationalized in the name of the class.

(4) The great divide that developed between socialism and political democracy should not be treated as flowing naturally from key aspects of socialist doctrine. This approach is fueled by the sullied human rights record and the barrack-room collectivism of some of the experiences of existing socialism. We believe that Marxism clearly projects a system anchored in deep-seated political democracy and the rights of the individual which can only be truly attained when society as a whole assumes control and direction of all its riches and resources.

(5) The crucial connection between socialism and internationalism and the importance of world working-class solidarity should not be underplayed as a result of the distortions which were experienced. These included excessive centralization in the era of the Comintern, subordination of legitimate national aspirations to a distorted concept of "internationalism," national rivalries between and within socialist states (including armed confrontation). Working-class internationalism remains one of the most liberating concepts in Marxism and needs to find effective expression in the new world conditions.

In summary, we believe that Marxism is a social science whose fundamental postulates and basic insights into the historical processes remain a powerful (because accurate) theoretical weapon. But this is not to say that every word of Marx, Engels, and Lenin must be taken as gospel; they were not infallible and they were not always correct in their projections.

Lenin, for example, believed that capitalism was about to collapse worldwide in the post-October revolution period. It was a belief based on the incorrect premise that, as a system, capitalism had already reached the stage at which capitalist relations of production constituted an obstacle to the further all-round development of the forces of production. This was combined with a belief in the imminence of global socialist transformation, which undoubtedly infected much of the earlier thinking about the perspectives of socialist construction in the Soviet Union.

Also, it could well be argued that the classical description of bourgeois democracy was an oversimplification and tended to underestimate the historic achievements of working-class struggle in imposing and defending aspects of a real democratic culture on the capitalist state; a culture which should not disappear but rather needs to be expanded under true socialism.

In some cases, the deformations experienced by existing socialist states were the result of bureaucratic distortions which were rationalized at the ideological level by a mechanical and out-of-context invocation of Marxist dogma. In other cases, they were the results of a genuinely motivated but tragic misapplication of socialist theory to new realities that were not foreseen by the founders of Marxism.

The fact that socialist power was first won in the most backward outpost of European capitalism, without a democratic political tradition, played no small part in the way it was shaped. To this must be added the years of isolation, economic siege, and armed intervention which, in the immediate post-October period, led to the virtual decimation of the Soviet Union's relatively small working class. In the course of time the party leadership was transformed into a command post with an overbearing centralism and very little democracy, even in relation to its own membership.

Most of the other socialist countries emerged thirty years later in the shadow of the Cold War. Some of them owed a great deal to Soviet power for their very creation and survival, and the majority, for a great part of their history, followed the Stalinist economic and political model. Communists outside the socialist world and revolutionaries engaged in anticolonial movements were the beneficiaries of generous aid and consistent acts of internationalist solidarity. They correctly saw in Soviet power a bulwark against their enemies and either did not believe, or did not want to believe, the way in which aspects of socialism were being debased.

All this helps to explain, but in no way to justify, the awful grip that Stalinism came to exercise in every sector of the socialist world and over the whole international communist movement. It was a grip which, if loosened by parties (e.g., Yugoslavia) or individuals within parties usually led to isolation and excommunication.

We make no attempt here to answer the complex question of why so many millions of genuine socialists and revolutionaries became such blind worshippers in the temple of the cult of the personality.

Suffice it to say that the strength of this conformism lay, partly, in an ideological conviction that those whom history had appointed as the custodians of humankind's communist future seemed to be building on foundations prepared by the founding fathers of Marxism. And there was not enough in classical Marxist theory about the nature of the transition period to provide a detailed guide to the future.

Socialism and Democracy

Marx and Engels saw the future state as "a direct democracy in which the task of governing would not be the preserve of a state bureaucracy" and as "an association in which the free development of each is a condition for the free development of all" (*Civil War in France*). How did it happen that, in the name of this most humane and liberating ideology, the bureaucracy became so all-powerful and the individual was so suffocated?

To find the beginnings of an answer, we need to look at four related areas. (1) The thesis of the "dictatorship of the proletariat" which was used as the theoretical rationalization for unbridled authoritarianism; (2) the steady erosion of people's power both at the level of government and mass social organizations; (3) the perversion of the concept of the party as a vanguard of the working class; and (4) whether, at the end of the day, socialist democracy can find real expression in a single-party state.

The concept of the "dictatorship of the proletariat" was dealt with rather thinly by Marx as "a transition to a classless society" without much further definition. For his part, Engels, drawing on Marx's analysis of the 1871 Paris Commune, claimed that it indeed *was* a dictatorship of the proletariat. The Paris Commune was an exceptional social experience which brought into being a kind of workers' city-state (by no means socialist-led) in which, for a brief moment, most functions of the state (both legislative and executive) were directly exercised by a popular democratic assembly.

The concept of the "dictatorship of the proletariat" was elaborated by Lenin in *State and Revolution* in the very heat of the revolutionary transformation in 1917. Lenin quoted Engels approvingly when he said (in a letter to Bebel) that "the proletariat needs the state, not in the interests of freedom but in order to hold down its adversaries, and as soon as it becomes possible to speak of freedom the state as such ceases to exist." In the meanwhile, in contrast to capitalist democracy which is "curtailed, wretched, false . . . for the rich, for the minority . . . the dictatorship of the proletariat, the period of transition to communism, will, for the first time, create democracy . . . for the majority . . . along with the necessary suppression of the exploiters, of the minority."

Lenin envisaged that working-class power would be based on the kind of democracy of the Commune, but he did not address, in any detail, the nature of established socialist civil society, including fundamental questions such as the relationship between the party, state, people's elected representatives, social organizations, etc. Understandably, the dominant preoccupation at the time was with the seizure of power, its protection in the face of the expected counterrevolutionary assault, the creation of "democracy for the majority" and the "suppression of the minority of exploiters."

Rosa Luxemburg said, in a polemic with Lenin, "Freedom only for the supporters of the government, only for the members of one party—however numerous they may be—is not freedom at all. Freedom is always and exclusively freedom for the one who thinks differently . . . its effectiveness vanishes when freedom becomes a special privilege."

These words may not have been appropriate as policy (which is what Luxemburg argued for) in the special conditions of the phase immediately after the seizure of power in October 1917. Without a limitation on democracy there was no way the revolution could have defended itself in the civil war and the direct intervention by the whole of the capitalist world. But Luxemburg's concept of freedom is surely incontrovertible once a society has achieved stability.

Lenin clearly assumed that whatever repression may be necessary in the immediate aftermath of the revolution would be relatively mild and short-lived. The state and its traditional instruments of force would begin to "wither away" almost as soon as socialist power had been won and the process of widening and deepening democracy would begin. Lenin was referring to the transitional socialist state (and not to the future communist society) when he emphasized that there would be an extension of "democracy to such an overwhelming majority of the population that the need for a special machine of suppression will begin to disappear . . . it is no longer a state in the proper sense of the word [because] the suppression of the minority of exploiters . . . is easy, simple," entailing relatively little bloodshed, and hardly needing a machine or a special apparatus other than "the simple organization of the armed people (such as the Soviets)."

We know that all this is a far cry from what happened in the decades which followed. The whole process was put in reverse. The complete "suppression of the exploiters" was followed by the strengthening of the instruments of state suppression and the narrowing of democracy for the majority of the population, including the working class.

The anti-Leninist theory advanced (in the name of Lenin) to "justify" this process was that the class struggle becomes more rather than less intense with the entrenchment of socialism. In some respects this became a self-fulfilling prophecy; a retreat from democratic norms intensified social contradictions which in turn became the excuse for an intensification of the "class struggle."

One of the key rationalizations for this thesis was the undoubted threat, even after the end of the civil war, posed by imperialism and fascism to the very survival of the Soviet Union and the continuing Western conspiracies to prevent the spread of socialist power after 1945. But events have demonstrated that if the survival of the Soviet Union was at risk from the fascist onslaught it was, among other reasons, also the result of damage wrought to the whole Soviet social fabric (including its army) by the authoritarian bureaucracy. And if Western "conspiracies" have succeeded in threatening the very survival of socialism in places like Eastern Europe, it is the narrowing rather than the extension of democracy which has played into their hands.

The term "dictatorship of the proletariat" reflected the historical truth that in class-divided social formations state power is ultimately exercised by, and in the interests of, the class which owns and controls the means of production. It is in this sense that capitalist formations were described as a "dictatorship of the bourgeoisie" whose rule would be replaced by a "dictatorship of the proletariat" during the socialist transition period. In the latter case power would, however, be exercised in the interests of the overwhelming majority of the people and should lead to an ever expanding genuine democracy—both political and economic.

On reflection, the choice of the word "dictatorship" to describe this type of society certainly opens the way to ambiguities and distortions. The abandonment of the term by most communist parties, including ours, does not, in all cases, imply a rejection of the historical validity of its essential content. But the way the term came to be abused bore little resemblance to Lenin's original concept. It was progressively denuded of its intrinsic democratic content and came to signify, in practice, a dictatorship of a party bureaucracy. For Lenin the repressive aspect of the concept had impending relevance in relation to the need for the revolution to defend itself against counterrevolutionary terror in the immediate postrevolution period. He was defending, against the utopianism of the anarchists, the limited retention of repressive apparatus. But, unfortunately, practices justified by the exigencies of the earlier phases became a permanent feature of the new society.

The steady erosion of the powers and representative character of elected institutions led to the alienation of a considerable portion of society from political life. The electorate had no effective right to choose its representatives. Gone were the days when the party had to engage in a political contest to win a majority in the Soviets. The legislative organs did not, in any case, have genuine control over legislation; by their nature they could only act as rubber stamps for decisions that had already been taken by party structures. The executive and judicial organs were, for all practical purposes, under the direct control of the party bureaucracy. In practice the majority of the people had very few levers with which to determine the course of economic or social life.

Democracy in the mass organizations was also more formal than real. The enormous membership figures told us very little about the extent to which the individual trade unionist, youth, or woman, was able to participate in the control or direction of their respective organizations. At the end of the day these organizations were turned into transmission belts for decisions taken elsewhere and the individual members were little more than cogs of the vast bureaucratic machine.

The trade union movement became an adjunct of the state and party. Workers had no meaningful role in determining the composition of the top leadership which was, in substance, answerable to the party apparatus. For all practical purposes the right to strike did not exist. The extremely thin dividing line between management and the trade union collective on the factory floor detracted from the real autonomy of trade unions. Apart from certain welfare functions, they tended, more and more, to act like Western-style production councils, but without the advantage of having to answer for their role to an independent trade union under the democratic control of its membership.

Much of the above applied to the women's and youth organizations. Instead of being guided by the aspirations and interests of their constituencies, they were turned into support bases for the ongoing dictates of the state and party apparatus.

In the immediate aftermath of the October Revolution, the Bolshevik Party shared power with other political and social tendencies, including Mensheviks and a section of the left Social Revolutionaries. In the elections for the constituent assembly in 1918, the Bolsheviks received less than a third of the popular vote.

There may be moments in the life of a revolution that justify a postponement of full democratic processes. And we do not address the question of whether the Bolsheviks were justified in taking a monopoly of state power during the extraordinary period of both internal and external assault on the gains of the revolution. Suffice it to say that the single-party state and the guiding and leading role of the party subsequently became permanent features of socialist rule and were entrenched in the constitutions of most socialist states. Henceforth the parties were "vanguards" by law and not necessarily by virtue of social endorsement.

This was accompanied by negative transformations within the party itself. Under the guise of "democratic centralism," inner-party democracy was almost completely suffocated by centralism. All effective power was concentrated in the hands of a political bureau or, in some cases, a single all-powerful personality. The control of this "leadership" by the party as a whole was purely formal. In most cases the composition of the highest organ—the congress which finalized policy and elected the leadership—was manipulated from the top.

The central committee (elected by variations of a "list" system emanating from the top) had only the most tenuous jurisdiction over the political bureau. Within this latter body a change of leaders resembled a palace coup rather than a democratic process; invariably the changes were later unanimously endorsed.

The invigorating impact of the contest of ideas in Marxist culture was stifled. In practice, the basic party unit was there to explain, defend, exhort, and support policies in whose formulation they rarely participated. The concept of consensus effectively stifled dissent and promoted the completely unnatural appearance on unanimity on everything. Fundamental differences were either suppressed or silenced by the self-imposed discipline of so-called democratic centralism. In these conditions the democratic development of party policy became a virtual impossibility.

Socialist Economic Alienation

The unavoidable inheritance from the past and the most serious distortions of socialist norms in most of the socialist countries combined to perpetuate alienation, albeit in a new form. Private ownership of the main means of production was replaced by state ownership. Private capital, as an alien power, no longer dominated or exploited the producer. But without real socialization, the key condition for de-alienation continued to be absent.

The immediate producers were given very little real control or participation in economic life beyond their own personal physical and/or mental exertions. In general, the overcentralized and commandist economies of the socialist world helped to entrench a form of "socialist" alienation. At the purely economic level, this form of alienation often turned out to be the worst of both worlds.

Under capitalism, economic compulsion sanctified by the rule of capital (threatened unemployment, etc.) plays an important role in providing the "incentive" for rising productivity despite alienation by workers from the products of their labor. Capitalist economic levers based on the sanctity of private property are, at the end of the day, not overconcerned with the problems of alienation and more easily provide the incentive (in relation to the workers) that "he who does not work, neither shall he eat."

Under socialism guaranteed employment and the amount of re-muneration did not always depend upon quality, productivity, or efficiency, opening the way to parasitism at the point of production. Reward based on the socialist maxim of "to each according to his contribution" can obviously play a part in increasing productivity. But for socialist society as a whole to really come into its own requires an incentive based on the producer's real participation in the mecha-nisms of social control over the products of his/her labor; a feeling that the means of production and its products are his or hers as part of society. This incentive was too often absent and stood in the way of the process of de-alienation.

Episodes of direct compulsion against producers, such as the forced collectivization of the early 1930s and the extensive use of convict labor as a direct state and party exercise, made things worse. Like all forms of primitive accumulation, these episodes created a most profound sense of alienation whose negative consequences are still being felt. Pure exhortation and political "mobilization" did not, in the long run, prevent the onset of stagnation. Alienation, albeit in a different form, continued and inhibited the full potential of socialist economic advance.

There were, of course, other negative factors which require more extensive examination than is possible here. These include policies based on what has been called the "big bang theory of socialism" which ignored the historical fact that many of the ingredients of social systems which succeed one another—and this includes the changes from capitalism to socialism—cannot be separated by a Great Wall.

The economy of a country the day after the workers take over is exactly the same as it was the day before, and it cannot be trans-formed merely by proclamation. The neglect of this truism resulted, now and then, in a primitive egalitarianism (which reached lunatic proportions under the Pol Pot regime), the absence of cost-accounting, a dismissive attitude to commodity production and the law of value during the transition period, the premature abandonment of any role for market forces, a doctrinaire approach to the question of collectivization, etc.

But rectification of these areas alone would not establish the material and moral superiority of socialism as a way of life for humanity. Only the creation of real socialist relations of production will give birth to the socialist man and woman whose active participation in all the social processes will ensure that socialism reaches its full potential and moves toward a classless communist society. Under existing socialism alienation has persisted because of a less than full control and participation by the people in these processes.

In short, the way forward is through thorough-going democratic socialism, a way that can only be charted by a party which wins its support through democratic persuasion and ideological contest and not, as has too often happened up to now, by a claim of right.

SOCIALISM AND THE WORLD SYSTEM

CHRISTOPHER CHASE-DUNN

SOCIALISM AND CAPITALISM ON A WORLD SCALE

Recent developments in Eastern Europe, as well as marketization and privatization in the Soviet Union and China, have led to talk of the transition from socialism to capitalism and proclamations of the end of history, based on the final victory of capitalist and liberal democratic ideals. Socialists everywhere are looking for explanations and trying to determine the meaning of these events for their own theories and practice. The neo-Marxist world-system perspective provides a theoretical interpretation of the long-term interaction between the expansion and deepening of capitalism and the efforts of people to protect themselves from exploitation and domination. The historical development of the socialist states is explained as part of a long-run spiraling interaction between expanding capitalism and socialist organizational forms. This essay places the recent events in Eastern Europe, the Soviet Union, and China in this context and explores their meaning for the future of socialism.

The world-system perspective has stimulated a respecification of Marx's accumulation model of capitalism.[1] The analysis of capitalist development as a world system rather than as largely separate cases of national development reveals that capitalism is a system in which both firms and states compete with one another within an arena in which the core/periphery hierarchy is a necessary and reproduced feature. The core/periphery hierarchy is an institutionally structured system of inequality among "developed" (core) and "less developed" (peripheral) countries. Semiperipheral countries are those that display combinations of core and peripheral forms of capitalism.

67

Thus imperialism is not a stage of capitalism but is rather a necessary and permanent feature of the capitalist world system. It is this larger world system that develops, not national societies: what has been called national development is really upward mobility in the core/periphery hierarchy. The history and developmental trajectory of the socialist states is explained as socialist movements in the semiperiphery which have attempted to transform the basic logic of capitalism, but which have ended up using socialist ideology to mobilize industrialization in order to catch up with core capitalism.

The spiraling interaction between capitalist development and socialist movements can be seen in the history of labor movements, socialist parties, and socialist states over the last one hundred and fifty years.[2] This long-run comparative perspective enables us to see recent events in China, the Soviet Union, and Eastern Europe in a framework that has implications for the future of socialism. In order to use this perspective, I will need to first explain how the world-system theory reconceptualizes capitalism.

Commodification and Its Limits

One important aspect of the global expansion of capitalism has consisted of a deepening and widening of commodified relations. More and more aspects of life have become commercialized; more and more interactions are mediated by markets. And the spatial scale of market integration has grown to the point where local, regional, and national markets are strongly linked into a global network. There are clearly limits to the extent of commodification, however. As Karl Polanyi noted, the processes of commodification threaten certain things that are necessary or desirable in society, and this engenders the regulation of market forces.[3] Workers organize unions to protect themselves from capital and from competition with other workers. Capitalists often seek to limit market competition through state action. And states often control market forces and erect institutional barriers to the commodification of certain kinds of property and human relations. Much of politics in capitalist society is a seesawing struggle among different groups over the process of commodification and its limits. This struggle is a normal part of capitalist accumulation itself, although the resistance to commodification holds the possibility of challenging the basic logic of capitalism.

Some of the limits on commodification are erected by political groups operating explicitly in their own interest. Thus cartels, guilds, and trade unions are organizations that resist market forces in the name of "special interests." But the most extensive efforts to regulate market forces are carried out by states in the name of "society." Public health regulations, minimum wage legislation, national parks, and many other institutional features of capitalist society are legitimated in terms of state provision of "public goods" that market forces either do not provide or that must be protected from commercialization in the name of the "universal" interests represented by the state.

Polanyi sweepingly portrayed *The Great Transformation* outlined the growth of markets and the commodification of wealth, labor, and land in England and on the Continent. Polanyi also portrayed a societal reaction to commodification in which the negative effects of market forces were becoming subject to regulation by states. This reaction to the commercialization was understood by Polanyi as providing the basis for the emergence of socialism. The expansion of the welfare state, even though a long and uneven process, would eventually alter the logic of capitalism toward a more collective form of rationality.

Polanyi's analysis falters because he underestimated the importance of the fact that these struggles take place within a larger terrain formed by the world economy and the interstate system. Despite his focus on many international aspects of capitalist development, Polanyi did not see that the structure of the interstate system itself poses a major difficulty for his theory of the transition to socialism. The limits on commodification and the limits of collective rationality are set in a competitive struggle in which firms, classes, and most importantly *states* are the players against one another.

The myth of the "nation" as a transcendent solidarity is an important determinant of success or failure in this struggle. States must be able to legitimate their actions and to mobilize popular participation in order to survive or prevail in the world economy. Those that do this less efficiently or less effectively lose out in the competitive struggle. Thus both political mobilization and comparative advantage in the world market are important to the logic of capitalism.

The ideological mystification that holds that the state represents the "general will" or the "universal" interest is a falsehood for two major structural reasons: states are controlled more by capitalists than by workers *and* states represent only the interests of their own citizens, a subgroup in a larger socioeconomic system. Thus the "state" is simply a political organization in a larger arena of competing political organizations. Even if a state did represent all of its citizens, these would not be universal interests from the point of view of the socioeconomic system as a whole—the world system. The "society" represented by each state is a national society, a subgroup in a larger whole. And there is no world state to aggregate the interests of all participants in the world system.

The political structure of capitalism is not the capitalist state. It is the capitalist interstate system. This fact alters Polanyi's model of commodification and limits it as a process for the transition to socialism because there is no effective political organization to represent, even ideologically, the collective rationality of our species. This is why the limits that are placed on commodification do not easily add up to the transformation to socialism. As trends in the last two decades have shown, austerity regimes, deregulation, and marketization within the socialist states occur globally during certain periods, although not in the same way everywhere. The ability of any single national society to construct collective rationality is limited by its interaction within the larger system.

The expansion and deepening of commodification has always created reactions and stimulated the formation of political structures to protect political actors from market forces. Capitalists organize political institutions that limit market forces. Contrary to much ideology, most real living capitalists prefer monopolistic certainty to the vagaries and risks of market competition. Thus capitalist states have always tried to protect the capitalists who control them. States act either to protect their own capitalists or to destroy barriers to market competition when their own capitalists will benefit. The typical capitalist state is not *laissez faire* but is rather *interventionist,* and the trend toward "state capitalism" has long been a secularly increasing tendency, not a wholly new departure.

Workers and peasants have also tried to protect themselves from market forces through guild organizations, community structures, workers' co-ops, labor unions, and political parties. Marx's discussion of the struggle over the length of the working day shows how middle-stratum professionals became involved in welfare-oriented regulation of market forces. The abolition of child labor and slavery are additional examples of limits to commodification created by movements with complex class constituencies.

The constraints on market forces imposed within a particular state are often the most important driving forces behind the expansion of commodification to new areas. Successful labor organizing causes capital to look elsewhere for labor. Monopolies organized at the municipal or national level encourage consumers to try to gain access to outside markets where goods may be cheaper, and cheaper production in these outside markets is also encouraged. Thus commercialization and regulation interact in a spiral that drives a number of the long-run trends visible in the world system. Commodification causes political organizations to emerge, which then result in incentives for the further expansion and deepening of commodification. This may undermine earlier, smaller scale political organizations by pricing them out of competition or by encouraging them to impose new internal conditions of "market efficiency." Thus workers' co-ops are either driven out of existence or are encouraged to adopt the organizational features of more typical capitalist firms. So far the scale of market forces has always been able to escape political regulation, now even encompassing the socialist states and encouraging their movement toward deregulation and levels of social allocation more typical in the larger world economy.

The size of firms, the spatial scale of markets, and the depth of market integration increase partly in reaction to political efforts to regulate market forces. The "internationalization of capital" is partly explained by capital flight from political regulation and labor unions. A good portion of the trend toward ever greater state formation—the abrogation of power over more and more areas of life—can be attributed to state action *vis-à-vis* market forces. Increasingly, states not only react to market forces with regulation but they intervene to *create* market forces. As firm size and the spatial scale of markets has grown, state responsibility for economic development has increased. The state not only serves private entrepreneurs and tries to attract capital; sometimes it is itself the entrepreneur. This occurred first in several second-tier core and semiperipheral countries trying to catch up with British industrialization, but now peripheral capitalists regularly use the only organization they control that is powerful enough to compete in the global economy—the state. State capitalism is thus a trend, not of socialism, but of the increasing scale of production and market integration in the capitalist world economy.

What are the implications of the above for the reconceptualization of capitalism in the light of the historical patterns of development in the world system? For one thing, we need to reconsider the relations between forms of property and capitalism. The emphasis on commodification and the importance of markets in the context of multiple, competing, and unequally powerful states leads us to question a narrow interpretation of "private" property as the only appropriate form of ownership for capitalism. General Motors would still be a capitalist firm competing in the world automobile market if it were to become owned and controlled by its employees. Even state-owned firms are subject to constraints based on the ability of the state that owns them to compete in the larger global political economy. Capital is that sort of power which is able to combine the operation of profitable commodity production with the relatively efficient provision of those "public goods" that are necessary or advantageous to this profitability. Thus capitalists, in this sense, are neither just private owners of productive wealth, nor state managers. Rather capital is the combination of political and economic activities which produce success in the capitalist world system. I am not suggesting that we should abandon the distinction between privately held capital and the state; nor am I suggesting that these actors do not often have contradictory interests. What I mean is that "success" in the capitalist system requires both of these, whether or not the jobs are differentiated into "private" and "public" organizations or more integrated, as when states directly control commodity-producing firms. Thus states are part of the relations of production in capitalism, and capitalism cannot be understood as separate from the logic of nation-building, state formation, and geopolitics.

Socialist States in the World System

Socialist revolutions did not take state power in the core, but rather in semiperipheral and peripheral regions of the world system. The socialist states failed to institutionalize a self-reproducing socialist mode of production because of the strong threats and inducements emanating from the larger capitalist world system. The conflictual interstate system and the direct threats from capitalist core states encouraged militarism, authoritarianism, and "defensive" imperialism. The existence of a dynamic and competitive world market encouraged corruption, consumerism, and political opportunism by the "new class" of technocrats and bureaucrats who could bolster their own positions by mediating the importation of sophisticated technology from the core.

In 1982 Albert Szymanski proposed a "domino theory" of the transition to world socialism based on the large proportion of the world population then living in avowedly socialist states, and victories within recent decades of socialist national liberation movements in Africa, Asia, and Latin America.[4] Szymanski contended that the Soviet Union and Eastern Europe constituted a separate socialist world system with its own autonomous logic of development, and that world capitalism had been seriously weakened by the growing number of socialist states and their successes in building socialism.

I have disputed this contention. I believe that the socialist states have been significantly reincorporated into the capitalist world economy. Contrary to those who think that this reincorporation occurred only recently, the world system perspective on socialist states implies that these states were *never* outside of the capitalist world economy and that their political and economic development can only be understood as a response to the threats and inducements of the larger environment. Thus the political reincorporation of the Soviet Union began when it became apparent that the Bolshevik Revolution would have to survive in a hostile world and try to construct "socialism in one country." The realities of the interstate system demanded that the Soviet state create an apparatus that could defend against external political/military threats.

National economic planning, which was most highly developed in the socialist states, may be simply the most complete expression of the trend toward state capitalism. Though distribution has been more equal within the socialist states, this has not substantially changed the competitive logic upon which they interact with other states. Indeed, one of the most disconcerting features of socialist states has been their most unsocialist behavior toward each other.

The economic reincorporation of the socialist states began as the effort to mobilize autarchical industrialization using socialist ideology, an effort that was quite successful in terms of standard measures of economic development. The socialist states were increasing their percentage of world product and energy consumption up until the 1970s.[5] The Stalinist model of mobilization successfully urbanized and industrialized the Soviet Union and much of Eastern Europe, and the socialist states exhibited much better living conditions than other countries at similar levels of economic development.[6]

The economic reincorporation of the socialist states moved to a new stage of integration with the world market and foreign firms in the 1970s. Andre Gunder Frank has documented a trend in which the socialist states increased their exports for sale on the world market, increased imports from the avowedly capitalist countries, and made deals with transnational firms for investments within their borders. The economic crisis in Eastern Europe and the Soviet Union was not much worse than the economic crisis in the rest of the world during the global economic downturn that began in 1967.[7] The current deepening crisis is caused more by political uncertainties than by long-term insufficiencies of the command economy.

The recent moves toward further opening and marketization are simply the latest developments in a process that has long been underway. The big political changes are largely a matter of the superstructure catching up with the economic base. The democratization of these societies is, of course, a welcome trend for democratic socialists, but all socialists realize that democratic political forms do not automatically lead to a society without exploitation or domination.

Socialist and Nonsocialist Semiperipheral States

The world system perspective suggests that we should compare the socialist states with other semiperipheral countries.[8] The effort of the socialist states to mobilize import-substitution policies differed in form and extent from the state strategies employed by other semiperipheral countries (e.g., Brazil and Mexico), but all the developing semiperipheral countries shared certain broad features: State power was used to try to catch up with core capitalism. Protectionism was used to reserve the home economy for certain sectors, especially heavy industry. State firms were created in key sectors. And the stage of import-substitution industrialization was followed by a crisis in which this type of development reached its limits and needed to be replaced by a new type of economic policy. In Eastern Europe and the Soviet Union, this crisis has been described as the need to move from "extensive" to "intensive" economic development.[9]

The differences should be spelled out. The extent of state intervention in the socialist states was much greater than in the nonsocialist semiperiphery. A greater proportion of all production was carried out by state-owned firms and the concentration of these firms was usually greater. The involvement of foreign capital, on the other hand, was much greater in the nonsocialist semiperiphery. These differences affected the way in which the exhaustion of import-substitution industrialization came about, and the options for restructuring.

In the nonsocialist semiperipheral states, import substitution faced a problem of limited demand and overcapacity. Production for the home market soon saturates demand. This can be resolved in two fundamentally different ways: either the home market can be broadened by increasing wages and consumption, or export promotion for the world market can be combined with continued low wages. The political oscillations between populism and authoritarianism in the nonsocialist semiperipheral states partly reflect the tension between these very different paths of development.

In the socialist states, the options are somewhat different. The command economies do not produce a situation of weak demand because the "soft budget constraints" on state-owned firms in these economies ensure high demand for industrial output. But this demand is somewhat artificial and the problem of overcapacity relative to real use does exist. The development alternatives for resolving the exhaustion of import-substitution industrialization are analytically somewhat similar for socialist and nonsocialist semiperipheral states. In the Soviet Union, the command economy could be mobilized to support more varied and cheaper consumer goods, and indeed this has been happening over the last decades. It is not true that large-scale state firms or centrally planned economies are incapable of producing mass consumer goods that can satisfy workers and peasants. But the technocrats and bureaucrats of the Soviet Union and China, like the capitalists and technocrats of the nonsocialist semiperiphery, do not want to redistribute income because this would preclude their ability to import more expensive and elaborate technologies (and luxuries) from the core capitalist countries. Export promotion requires cheap skilled labor and the production of goods that can find a niche in the world market. This requires that subsidies on consumption goods be reduced and market discipline over labor be introduced.

Both socialist and nonsocialist semiperipheral countries face a situation in which they have successfully mobilized industrialization and created a type of production that was formerly the leading edge of production in the core. The effort to catch up with core capitalism has been frustrated for most of these countries, however, because the core has, in the meantime, developed new industries and new modes of regulation. Heavy industry has been sloughed off to semiperipheral producers and the highest rates of profit are now to be had in computers and biotechnology. Terry Boswell and Ralph Peters have recently argued that the socialist states face re-peripheralization because the Stalinist command economy is incapable of crossing the "new industrial divide," from Fordism to flexible accumulation.[10] I agree with this, but I would add the element of class power outlined above to the explanation. Workers and peasants in the Soviet Union and China do not need computers. They would be quite happy with cars and housing and the command economy could quite easily produce those.

The aptness of the above comparison between socialist and nonsocialist semiperipheral states is supported to some extent by the following anecdote. A U.S. sociologist who has many professional contacts in the Soviet Union has told me that most members of the

Soviet intelligentsia now support marketization and privatization in the context of a strong and repressive state that can control nationalist and labor resistance—*perestroika* without *glasnost*—and some of these same professionals have mentioned the relevance of the "Chilean model," by which they mean Pinochet's combination of Chicago school deregulation and political repression.

There are, of course, important differences among the state socialist countries that I have not discussed. The biggest difference is the legitimacy of the socialist state. In all of the countries of Eastern Europe which were dominated by the Soviet Union, the state itself was not legitimate. Most of the political upheaval in Eastern Europe is only understandable as a nationalist reaction to Soviet domination and has little to do with real socialism or capitalism. Unfortunately, the "dual dependency" of these countries on the Soviet Union and the West,[11] and their understandable rejection of socialist ideology as the state religion (imposed as it was by the Red Army after World War II) makes them very vulnerable to new exploitation by the capitalist core. Some of the former satellites have at least a chance of finding a niche in the next wave of capitalist expansion: certainly East Germany, perhaps Czechoslovakia and Hungary. Others will almost certainly be converted into the peripheral backyards of core capital, providing cheap skilled labor to transnational firms.

China and the Soviet Union both have a socialist state that derives its legitimacy from real indigenous socialist revolutions. But there are also several important differences between the two that are relevant to the problem of semiperipheral socialism. Despite significant industrialization of some regions, China still remains a largely agricultural country, while the Soviet Union is much more urbanized and industrialized. In China, the problem of subnations is much less threatening to the integrity of the central state than it is in the Soviet Union. The timing and sequencing of reforms has also differed between the two in ways that may produce very different outcomes. In China, marketization was begun earlier, largely in rural areas. Both political and economic reform have been halted and even reversed by the current reactionary gerontocracy. In the Soviet Union, some political decentralization and *glasnost* was implemented first. Marketization has been long discussed but not much implemented.

The Way Out

The discussion of "mixed economies" as a way out of the current crisis of the socialist states usually proceeds from the assumption that bureaucracies are inefficient and need to be subjected to market forces. Markets are described as "horizontal" institutions that promote equality, while bureaucracies and central planning are described as "hierarchical."[12] This characterization of the problem fails to consider both the nature of class relations in the socialist states and the potential for democratic control of planning bureaucracies.

I will not argue that markets are evil. It seems to me that a market sector can play a valuable role within a socialist mode of production. But I do mean to contradict the increasingly hegemonic ideology that the *only* antidote to bureaucratic inefficiency and oligarchical tendencies is marketization and privatization. First, bureaucracies themselves need not be hierarchical. There is an extensive social science literature on participatory and democratic organizational forms.[13] Second, central planning agencies can be controlled by institutionalized democratic structures. Proletarian democracy could be structured in the form of a popularly elected government that oversees the process of economic planning. In such a state the trade-off between efficiency and equality could be decided democratically. This might not be optimal for "success" in the capitalist world economy, but it could easily provide a good living for all citizens and a political situation free from repression. This is an institutional option that has not been tried in any of the state socialist societies, though it does partially exist in some social democratic core states.[14]

Mao used another method of attacking bureaucratic oligarchy. He mobilized the Cultural Revolution in order to combat the formation of a new Mandarinate in the party and the state. Though Mao's efforts failed, we should not dismiss this alternative mode of attacking oligarchy. But mass mobilization by a charismatic leader is too dependent on the leadership itself to provide a good solution to the problem of oligarchy formation. Revolutions may sometimes be necessary, but a more institutionalized political system would be better. A democratically controlled socialist government that is responsible for major investment decisions is an institutional solution that is superior, from the point of view of workers and peasants, to large-scale marketization and privatization.[15]

The Future of Capitalism and Socialism

The increasing number of socialist states did not weaken the logic of world capitalism. Rather, the political constraint on the free mobility of capital that these states created was one of the elements that pushed capitalist firms and states to further expand the scale of organizations and markets. This extensive expansion has been supplemented by intensive expansion, the conversion of more and more aspects of life to the commodity form and the expansion of profit-making opportunities in the provision of fast-food breakfasts, etc. The potential for further commodification is great, especially in the periphery, where a substantial terrain of production and consumption for use remains.

Increases in the extent and depth of commodification must eventually reach a limit, however. Only so much of human activity can be commodified, and the ability of markets and capital to expand beyond political regulation must decline as the density and scale of political regulation begins to catch up. Antisystemic movements create obstacles to the maneuverability of capital and place claims on profits. The see-saw, back-and-forth motion of capital generates consciousness and coordination among groups that have an interest in collective rationality at the world system level. Capital flight has pitted workers against one another for five hundred years, but the growing scale and density of political claims must eventually decrease the rate of profit. The equalization of profit rates across different regions of the world system decreases the incentive for capital flight. The little crises that accompany the Kondratieff wave, uneven development, and the expansion of commodification will eventually develop into a systemic crisis that will involve the creation of democratic and collectively rational control over investment decisions in a context in which "private" wealth no longer has the power or the motivation to continue directing the production process.

The growth of welfare states, decolonization of the periphery, and the emergence of states in which socialist parties control state power should be understood in this light. Despite the failure of these to fundamentally alter the capitalist logic of the world system, developments of this kind that manage to coordinate their efforts on a global scale can indeed transform that logic.

Political Implications of the World System Perspective

A central question for any strategy of transformation is the question of agency. Who are the actors who will most vigorously and effectively resist capitalism and construct socialism? Where is the most favorable terrain, the weak link, where concerted action can bear the most fruit? Samir Amin contends that the agents of socialism are most heavily concentrated in the periphery. It is there that the capitalist world system is most oppressive, and thus peripheral workers and peasants, who comprise the vast majority of the world proletariat, have the most to win and the least to lose.

On the other hand, Marx and many contemporary Marxists have argued that socialism will be most effectively built by the action of core proletarians. Since core areas have already attained a high level of technological development, the establishment of socialized production and distribution should be easiest in the core. And organized core workers have had the longest experience with industrial capitalism and the most opportunity to create socialist social relations.

I believe that both the "workerist" and "third worldist" positions have important elements of truth, but there is another alternative that is suggested by the structural theory of the world system: the semiperiphery as the weak link.

Core workers may have experience and opportunity but lack motivation because they have benefited from a nonconfrontational relationship with core capital. The existence of this labor aristocracy divides the working class in the core and, in combination with a large middle strata, undermines any political challenge to capitalism. In addition, the "long experience," in which business unionism and social democracy have been the outcome of a series of struggles between radical workers and the labor aristocracy, has created a residue of trade union practices, party structures, legal and governmental institutions, and ideological heritages that act as barriers to new socialist challenges. Nevertheless, it is true that even small victories in the core (e.g., further expansion of the welfare state, opposition to imperial policies, etc.) have important effects on peripheral and semiperipheral areas because of the demonstration effect and the power of core states.

The main problem with "third worldism" is not motivation but opportunity. Socialist movements that take state power in the periphery are soon beset by powerful external forces, which either overthrow them or force them to abandon most of their socialist program. Antisystemic movements in the periphery are usually anti-imperialist class alliances that succeed in establishing at least the trappings of national sovereignty, but not socialism. The low level of the development of the productive forces also makes it harder to establish socialist forms of accumulation, although this is not impossible in principle. It is simply harder to share power and wealth when there is very little of either.

Semiperipheral Socialism

These things are less true of the semiperiphery. Here we have both motivation and opportunity. Semiperipheral areas, especially those in which the territorial state is large, have sufficient resources to be able to stave off core attempts at overthrow and to provide some protection to socialist institutions if the political conditions for their emergence should arise. Semiperipheral regions have experienced more militant class-based socialist revolutions and movements because of their intermediate position in the core/periphery hierarchy. While core exploitation of the periphery creates and sustains alliances among classes in both the core and the periphery, in the semiperiphery an intermediate world system position undermines class alliances and provides a fruitful terrain for strong challenges to capitalism. Semiperipheral revolutions and movements are not always socialist in character, as we have seen in Iran. But when socialist intentions are strong, there are greater possibilities for real transformation than in either the core or the periphery. Thus the semiperiphery is the weak link in the capitalist world system. It is the terrain upon which the strongest efforts to establish socialism have been made, and this is likely to be true of the future as well.

On the other hand, the results of the efforts so far, while they have undoubtedly been important experiments with the logic of socialism, have left much to be desired. The tendency for authoritarian regimes to emerge in the socialist states betrays the notion of a freely constituted association of direct producers. And the imperial control of Eastern Europe by the Russians was an insult to the idea of proletarian internationalism. Democracy within and between nations is a constituent element of the logic of true socialism.

But it does not follow that efforts to build socialism in the semiperiphery will always be so constrained and thwarted. The revolutions in the Soviet Union and China have increased our collective knowledge about how to build socialism despite their only partial successes and their obvious failures. It is important for all of us who want to build a more humane and peaceful world system to understand the lessons of socialist movements in the semiperiphery, and the potential for more successful revolutions there in the future.

The latest stage of capitalist development in the core is based on flexible accumulation. Large-scale heavy industry, the classical province of strong labor movements and socialist parties, has been moved to the semiperiphery. This means that new socialist bids for state power in the semiperiphery (e.g., South Africa, Brazil, Mexico, perhaps Korea) will be much more based on an urbanized and organized proletariat in large-scale industry than the earlier semiperipheral socialist revolutions were. This should have happy consequences for the nature of new socialist states in the semiperiphery because the relationship between the city and the countryside should be less antagonistic.

Socialism in the United States?

What does world system theory imply about socialist political practice in the United States in the last decade of the twentieth century? The United States is a declining hegemonic core state. The processes of rapid growth and imperial success that have long undermined socialist politics in the United States are less salient now, and so there should be new openings for building socialism. On the other hand, if the United Kingdom is a relevant comparison, the remnants of hegemony do not pass quickly. The United States will certainly not experience a socialist revolution in which a working-class party seizes state power and socializes the major means of production. A revolutionary situation requires a weak and divided state, a weak and divided ruling class, and a strong and well-organized socialist party. All these conditions are lacking and are not likely to emerge soon.

Revolution, however, is not the only road to socialism. John Stephens has shown that important steps toward democratic socialism can be achieved by the route of political class struggle within capitalist core states.[16] In the United States, the eventual return of the liberals to presidential power in a context in which the old liberal ideology has been exhausted may be fertile ground for the struggle for a national industrial policy and economic democracy. While these reforms will not in themselves constitute a socialist mode of production, we should not underestimate their potential contribution to social justice, both in the United States and abroad.

Some critics of the world system perspective have argued that emphasis on the structural importance of global relations leads to political do-nothingism while we wait for socialism to emerge at the world level. The world system perspective does indeed encourage us to examine global level constraints (and opportunities), and to allocate our political energies in ways that will be most productive when these structural constraints are taken into account. It does not follow that building socialism at the local or national level is futile, but we must expend resources on transorganizational, transnational, and international socialist relations.

A simple domino theory of the transformation to socialism is misleading and inadequate. Suppose that all firms or all nation-states adopted socialist relations internally but continued to relate to one another through competitive commodity production and political-military conflict. Such a hypothetical world system would still be dominated by the logic of capitalism, and that logic would be likely to repenetrate the "socialist" firms and states. This cautionary tale advises us to invest political resources in the construction of multilevel (transorganizational, transnational, and international) socialist relations lest we simply repeat the process of driving capitalism to once again perform an end run by operating on a yet larger scale.

A Socialist World System

These considerations lead us to a discussion of socialist relations at the level of the world system. The emergence of democratic collective rationality (socialism) at the world system level is likely to be a slow process. What might such a world system look like and how might it emerge? It is obvious that such a system will require some kind of a democratically controlled world federation that can effectively adjudicate disputes among nation-states and eliminate warfare.[17] This is a bare minimum. There are many other problems that badly need to be coordinated at the global level, such as ecological difficulties and a more balanced pattern of economic development.

How might such a world state come into existence? The process of the growth of international organizations which has been going on for over one hundred years will eventually result in a world state if we do not blow ourselves up first. Even international capitalists have some use for global regulation, as is attested by the International Monetary Fund and the World Bank. These capitalists do not want the massive economic and political upheavals that would accompany the collapse of the world monetary system, and so they support efforts to regulate "ruinous" competition and beggar-thy-neighborism. Some of these same capitalists also fear nuclear holocaust, and so they may support a strengthened global government that can effectively adjudicate conflicts among nation-states.

Of course, capitalists know as well as others that effective adjudication means the establishment of a global monopoly on legitimate violence. The process of state formation has a long history, and the king's army always has to be bigger than any combination of private armies that might be brought against him. But while the idea of a world state may be a frightening specter to some, I am optimistic for several reasons. First, a world state is probably the most direct and stable way to prevent nuclear holocaust, a desideratum that must be at the top of everyone's list. Second, the creation of a global state that can peacefully adjudicate disputes among nations will transform the existing interstate system—the political structure that stands behind the maneuverability of capital and its ability to escape organized workers and other social constraints on profitable accumulation. While a world state may at first be dominated by capitalists, the very existence of such a state will provide a single focus for struggles to regulate investment decisions socially and to create more balanced, egalitarian, and ecologically sound forms of production and distribution.

Notes

1. This respecification is presented more fully in my book *Global Formation: Structures of the World-Economy* (New York: Basil Blackwell, 1989). I use the term "socialist state" to designate states in which Communist parties held state power because it has become common usage. As argued below, I do not believe that these states succeeded in institutionalizing a socialist mode of production.
2. This is the focus of Immanuel Wallerstein's discussion of "antisystemic" movements. See Immanuel Wallerstein, *The Politics of the World-Economy* (New York: Cambridge University Press, 1984) and Terry Boswell, ed., *Revolution in the World-System* (Greenwich, CT: Greenwood Press, 1989).
3. Karl Polanyi, *The Great Transformation* (Boston: Beacon Press, 1944).
4. See Christopher Chase-Dunn, ed., *Socialist States in the World-System* (Beverley Hills, CA: Sage Publications, 1982).
5. See John W. Meyer *et al.*, "Convergence and Divergence in Development," Table 2, *Annual Review of Sociology* 1 (1975): 223–46.
6. See Shirley Cereseto and Howard Waitzkin, "Capitalism, Socialism, and the Physical Quality of Life," *International Journal of Health Services* 16, no. 4 (1986): 643–58).
7. See Terry Boswell and Ralph Peters, "State Socialism and the Industrial Divide in the World-Economy: A Comparative Essay on the Rebellions in Poland and China," Table 1, *Critical Sociology* (1990).

8. While I emphasize the similarities more than the differences, Ellen Comisso's comparison between CMEA countries and NICs (newly industrialized countries) is an excellent presentation that emphasizes the differences while exploring the similarities. (See "State Structures and Political Processes Outside the CMEA: A Comparison," in Ellen Comisso and Laura D. Tyson, eds., *Power, Purpose, and Collective Choice: Economic Strategy in Socialist States* (Ithaca: Cornell University Press, 1986), pp. 401–22.

9. Ivan Szelenyi's excellent discussion of Eastern European reforms uses a comparative frame of reference that takes account of geopolitics and dependency relationships. See "Eastern Europe in an Epoch of Transition: Toward a Socialist Mixed Economy," in Victor Nee and David Stark, eds., *Remaking the Economic Institutions of Socialism* (Palo Alto: Stanford University Press, 1989), pp. 208–232.

10. Boswell and Peters, "State Socialism and the Industrial Divide in the World-Economy."

11. See Jozsef Borocz, "Dual Dependency and Property Vacuum: Social Change in the State Socialist Semiperiphery," paper presented at the Annual Meetings of the American Sociological Association, 13 August 1990.

12. For example, see Janos Kornai, "The Hungarian Reform Process: Visions, Hopes and Reality," in Nee and Stark, eds., *Remaking the Economic Institutions*, pp. 32–94.

13. See Joyce Rothschilde-Whitt, "The Collectivist Organization: An Alternative to Rational-Bureaucratic Models," *American Sociological Review* 44 (1979): 509–27.

14. Another alternative would be to decentralize economic planning itself. It is theoretically possible for all investment, production, and distribution decisions to be made by direct popular vote. This would be absurd, of course, but my point is that the falling cost of communications make direct participatory economic democracy much more feasible than it has ever been. Most people would rather delegate day-to-day decisions to hired administrators, while reserving the right to replace them if things go awry.

15. I do not mean to say that there should be no marketization. The Stalinist model overly centralizes and plans many things that could just as well be handled by market processes. But William Hinton's *The Great Reversal: The Privatization of China, 1978–1989* (New York: Monthly Review Press, 1990) shows what a disaster marketization has been for the Chinese countryside, and many of the earlier reforms have now been reversed.

16. John Stephens, *The Transition from Capitalism to Socialism* (Atlantic Highlands, NJ: Humanities Press, 1980).

17. Despite recent progress toward disarmament, it is necessary to remember that warfare continues to be a legitimate way of resolving conflicts as long as there is an interstate system. Joshua Goldstein's important study of Kondratieff waves, war cycles, and the rise and fall of hegemonic core powers concludes with the implication that the world system will enter another period of high risk of war among core powers in the 2020s. See Joshua Goldstein, *Long Cycles: Prosperity and War in the Modern Age* (New Haven: Yale University Press, 1988).

ANDRE GUNDER FRANK

REVOLUTION IN EASTERN EUROPE: LESSONS FOR DEMOCRATIC SOCIALIST MOVEMENTS (AND SOCIALISTS)

The course and speed of events in Eastern Europe, which have surprised everyone (including their protagonists), call for an agonizing reappraisal of widely held theories and deeply felt ideologies of socialism, of the nature of democracy and social democracy, and of the role of social movements in both. Moreover, both the economic causes and consequences of these sociopolitical processes merit more attention than has been usual in the euphoric reception of the 1989 revolution. Their analysis offers at least a dozen important lessons, which are explored below. Hopefully, they can embolden us all to face, and act in, the future.

The role of participatory social movements in social transformation requires reappraisal. It was, in initiating and carrying these events, perhaps greater than ever before. My previous writings about social movements referred to those in the East as pluri-class-based, but said little more than that they are growing massively and rapidly. Pluri-class participation in social movements seems to have continued in the East, while in the West participants are drawn predominantly from the middle class (especially the intelligentsia), and in the South social movements include these but are predominantly popular/working-class-based.[1] Leadership of the social movements in the East has also been drawn from the intelligentsia, but participation seems also to have included people from other middle-class backgrounds, as well as masses of working-class people. As elsewhere, women have participated more massively and in more important positions in these new social movements. This social composition of the movements may also help account for their less hierarchical and more anti-authoritarian character than in the traditional institutions whose power and legitimacy they challenged. This class and gender composition of the social movements, and their participation beyond all expectations in social transformation in Eastern Europe and parts of the USSR, now demands further analysis.

The peaceful character of the momentous social movements and political transformations in 1989 in Eastern Europe merits special attention. The movements themselves were deliberately peaceful, and little or no force of arms was used to repress them—except in Romania,[2] where armed repression by the Securitate was successfully countered by the army, which took the people's side in a (largely spontaneous?) uprising. Not only the role of the army, but also the spontaneity and suddenness of this popular uprising in Romania, should be distinguished from social movements elsewhere in Eastern Europe. These had much longer, deeper, and more organizational roots in the churches of East Germany, in Carta 77 in Czechoslovakia, in a multitude of peace and environmental movements in Hungary and, of course, in Solidarnosc and the Catholic Church in Poland. Bulgaria, perhaps, was between these and Romania. In the Russian parts of the USSR, social movements and a multiplicity of "clubs" have also been playing major roles in promoting *perestroika* and *glasnost*. Indeed, to permit "his" *perestroika* and *glasnost* to progress, the general secretary of the Communist Party, Mikhail Gorbachev, has had to appeal, over the heads of his own party, to social movement mobilization of people both outside and inside the party. The efficacy of all these different kinds of peaceful social movements in promoting social transformation requires reevaluation.

The demand for democracy was and remains so far reaching and deep as to expand the meaning of democracy itself. We must advance beyond parliamentary political and state economic democracy to include "civil democracy" in civil society. That is, democratic participation and demands include, but also extend far beyond, the institutional confines of parliamentary political democracy and of economic democracy, for example, to the rejection of the corruption and privileges of the *nomenclatura*. Street-level and local democratic participation and participatory democracy expresses itself through a myriad of other institutional (church, for example), more or less organizational and even spontaneous and rapidly changing forms. Our understanding of democracy, therefore, also requires revision and extension.

The role of party politics is downgraded, at least relatively, by these peaceful social movements and their demands for democracy. Many movements and their members reject and/or redefine exclusive or principal reliance on party politics. Not only do they mobilize and organize people and their demands through other forms, but the movements are also consciously and explicitly anti-party. Of course, they stand in particular against the communist parties, but they also reject (becoming) any other party. Several social movements rejected transforming themselves into political parties after achieving their immediate goals of liberation. At a national activist meeting of Neues Forum in East Germany, 80 percent of those present were against transforming the movement into a party for the coming national elections. Czechoslovakia's Civic Forum has a "loose organization" with "no master plan, no bylaws, and its strategy is not drafted by paid consultants."[3] A founder of the Left Alternative in Hungary declares that it is "a theoretical tendency, not a party. On the contrary it is an anti-party organization from the base of the society."[4]

However, the movements' memberships include people who were, or still are, in parties (even the Communist Party), and the movements expect some of their members to become active in new parties—but as individuals. The organizational independence of the movements, *qua* movements, was fought for too hard and is too precious to be easily sacrificed to party political demands and exigencies. On the contrary, the movements are very conscious of the contribution they must, and can only, make to democracy as social movements, and not as, or at least in addition to, political parties.

Nationalism and ethnicity were also factors in all of the social movements in Eastern Europe. Nationalism (if only anti-Russian) and ethnic issues helped mobilize people into these social movements and then to define some of their demands. In the Baltic republics of the USSR, nationalism is perhaps the major force in the social movements and the one which forms their demands. Other ethnic, national, and religious differences and demands are mobilizing people against Soviet power and against each other in ethnic/

nationalist (social?) movements in the Transcaucasian and Central Asian regions of the USSR. Of course, each of these movements is as different from the other as each ethnicity and nation, and their circumstances are unique. Moreover, the ethnic and nationalist demands of the moment are very much influenced by each group's more or less privileged class and geopolitical-economic position of dominance or subordination and by recent changes in these. Many of the more nationalist and ethnically based movements include, or even prioritize, demands for national state power. These demands also distinguish them from other social movements, which do not aspire to state power.

The problem of state power poses a difficult and partly novel challenge to the social movements and their relationship to political parties and to the state. The revolutions of 1989 were made by largely peaceful social movements that sought and achieved the downfall of governments and the crumbling of state power—which they mostly did not want to replace themselves. In the face of political state power vacuums, East European social movements have found themselves "obliged" to (re)organize to exercise state power. Lech Walesa declared that the greatest error Solidarnosc ever made was to assume government in Poland, but also that "it had no choice." Neues Forum in East Germany and Civic Forum in Czechoslovakia resist becoming parties, but cannot avoid intervention in rebuilding and running the state. Some of the social movements' membership must adopt a sort of double militancy, one in the movement and another in a political party. For example, the leading Czech dissident, Vaclav Havel, became state president.

Indeed, the most urgent political problem after "liberation" is widely presented as what to do about the state. Worries abound (at home and abroad) that the state is crumbling in East Germany, has already done so in Romania and—God forbid!—threatens to do so in a USSR that is armed to the teeth with nuclear weapons. Who will be "responsible" for managing the nuclear button in the no-longer-responsible superpower; who, even, will keep "public order" on the streets of East Berlin and Bucharest? The fear for stability is expressed abroad (for East Berlin "four-power" control has been proposed as a "solution," whilst all that is offered to Moscow is a prayer for Gorbachev). At home, however, the dilemma presents itself in more practical terms: if "we" do not act to assume positions of power, or at least to support our allies who have or want some, then others will so act and/or support our enemies. Thus, liberation or not, the "liberating" social movements are obliged more to conform to existing state institutions than to reform them. The hope for greater civil democracy lies in new social movements replacing those that succumb to existing institutions and their own institutionalization by them.

The institutionalization of movements into parties and state power is nothing new, of course. Many political parties started as social movements, and some ended up managing, even becoming indistinguishable from, state power. The now sixty-year-long all-powerful Mexican Partido Revolucionario Institucional (PRI) even incorporates this transition into its name. Indeed, some Communist parties in Eastern Europe, the USSR and elsewhere, could be said to have begun life as a social movement (albeit more of the "old," petty-bourgeois led, "working-class" kind). Even so, they or their "leader" unwittingly assumed the position, *"l'état c'est mois."*

The conflict between *fundi* (fundamentalist movement goals and procedures) and *realo* (realist party organization and state power compromises), which is splitting the Green Movement/Party in West Germany, is also built into the external (and perhaps internal) circumstances of the social movements in Eastern Europe. Thus, economic, political, and other exigencies may propel the social movements in Eastern Europe in the direction of state power, toward compromises of principle and the political cost of failure, in the face of impossible economic and other odds. In Poland, Solidarnosc now has to push bitter IMF medicine down its members' throats and administer shock treatment to the body public. Nationalist (and some ethnic) movements, however, often aspire to "independent" national-ethnic state power, or seek to share it in amalgamation with their ethnically homogeneous neighbor state. Hardly any seem to consider their own weakness in the face of the same economic crisis that is the motor of their movements.

The economic crisis, which has been expanding and deepening in Eastern Europe and the USSR, contributed materially to the desire and ability of these movements to mobilize so many people for such far-reaching political ends. The late 1970s and the 1980s are now called "the period of stagnation" in the USSR. It generated an accelerating economic crisis and an absolute deterioration of living standards in most of Eastern Europe, as well as in Latin America, Africa, and other parts of the world.[5] Significantly, especially in Eastern Europe, this period also spelled an important deterioration and retrocession in its standards of living and ability to compete, compared with Western Europe and even to the newly industrializing countries (NICs) in East Asia. Moreover, the course and mismanagement of the economic crisis generated shifts in positions of dominance, privilege, dependency, or exploitation among countries, sectors, and different social (including gender and ethnic) groups within the USSR and Eastern Europe. All of these economic changes and pressures generated or fuelled social discontent, demands, and mobilization, which express themselves through enlivened social (and ethnic-nationalist) movements. It is well known that economically based resentment is fed by the loss of "accustomed," absolute standards of living—as a whole or in particular items and by related relative shifts in economic welfare among population groups. Most economic crises are polarizing, further enriching the better off and further impoverishing those who were already worse off, especially women.

This change may also generate resentment and mobilization in both groups. The less privileged mobilize to defend their livelihood against the "system" and those who benefit from it. Such underprivileged ethnic groups include Turks in Bulgaria, Hungarians in Romania, Gypsies and others in Hungary, Albanians in Serbia, Serbians in Yugoslavia, Bohemians in Czechoslovakia, Azerbaijanis and a host of others in the Soviet Union, who have recently been plagued by massive unemployment, among other problems.

However, the more privileged also develop resentments against the "system," which obliges the richer to "carry" or "subsidize" their "good-for-nothing," "lazy," poorer neighbors. Moreover, these more privileged groups see even greener pastures for themselves on the other side of the border between socialism and capitalism. These include many Russians, Armenians, and others in the USSR, especially the Estonians, Latvians, and Lithuanians. They also include Slovenians and, to a lesser extent, Croatians in Yugoslavia. They include, of course, many Germans in East Germany (GDR), whose eyes (and feet!) are turned toward the economic magnet in the West. Whatever their current degree of privilege, thousands of "ethnic Germans" in the USSR, Poland, and Romania have suddenly discovered an age-old feeling of Germanity and a desire to partake of the German miracle in West Germany. The population at large (beyond its particular[ist] ethnic, national, and other groups) also mobilizes, or at least is more readily mobilizable in support of demands based on increasing economic resentment. These demands are easily politicized to extend to and be expressed by the participatory exercise of economic, political, and civil democracy—not to mention the ethnic and nationalist demands into which they can also be easily reformulated. These recently augmented, economically based resentments are indisputably a major factor in generating (and accounting for) widespread popular mobilization through the movements in Eastern Europe and the USSR.

However, strategic and political changes prepared new world and regional political circumstances, which also helped the social movements initiate, proceed with, and succeed (so far) in their social mobilization and political demands. Particularly important in Eastern Europe was the abrogation of the Brezhnev doctrine. Perhaps Gorbachev turned the Brezhnev doctrine on its head to exert pressure for political and economic change in Eastern Europe. For instance, the Hungarian foreign minister reportedly consulted the Soviet ambassador and received his approval before opening the border with Austria, which unlocked the floodgates from East Germany. During his visit to East Germany, Gorbachev literally planted the kiss of death on the cheek of Erich Honecker and then signalled that armed repression of the October 9 rally in Leipzig would be unacceptable. Some reports have it that he even threatened to place locally stationed Soviet troops between the demonstrators and any threatened attack by the East German state.

In the USSR itself, of course, *perestroika* and *glasnost* have paved the way for the mobilization of the movements; these in turn are both a necessary mobilizing factor to promote *perestroika* and *glasnost,* and a threat to the same should they get out of hand. Poland and China have already demonstrated that economic restructuring is subject to severely limited political reform, though possibly counterproductive without it. The Hungarian example has demonstrated that they can and must go hand in hand, at least so far. Perhaps also considering the experience abroad, Gorbachev has clarified that *glasnost* is a *sine qua non* of successful *perestroika* in the USSR. Successful *perestroika* is a *sine qua non* for the USSR maintaining any kind of power, let alone a superpower status in the competitive world political economy. Perhaps paradoxically, therefore, political abrogation of the Brezhnev doctrine and some "liberation" of the USSR from its economic burdens in Eastern Europe are also political-economic imperatives for the maintenance of strategic security and the promotion of economic development in the USSR today.

In short, these political and strategic changes are an important contributory factor to the mobilization and success of these social movements. Moreover, the world economic crisis and its particular manifestations in the USSR and Eastern Europe are contributing factors, both directly, through their generation of economically based resentments, and indirectly, through the economic imperatives they pose for political change. Of course, the importance of these economic, political, and strategic circumstances invites further elucidation.

The euphoria of democratic success and the honeymoon of liberation has relegated all these economic processes and polarizing problems to the last baggage car of the popular express train. Its locomotive seems to run on political steam alone and it is fuelled or even pushed along by the social movements themselves. The press, in particular (and all the more so in the West), has depicted almost the entire process as a jubilant joyride to freedom and democracy. But, whilst social change of this nature can be a euphoric process, the economic structure, process, and its problems are not transformed by political euphoria alone.

The bitter reality of worsening economic privation impresses itself daily upon the population in Poland and much of Yugoslavia. The situation is less harsh but also bites in Hungary, Czechoslovakia, Bulgaria, and East Germany, and worsens by the day in the USSR. Romania enjoys a temporary respite from the ravages of food exporting, but such problems will soon follow. Few people in these countries may know, or care to calculate, the importance of the economic reality underlying and guiding the directions of this political train. It is like the railway tracks and points, as well as the roadbed underlying them: it directs or at least limits the movement of the train.

In Poland already (and threatening elsewhere), it is as if the bulky economic baggage is moving relentlessly forward through the train, displacing more and more of the social movement passengers along the way. As a result, the anger of the passengers is increasingly displaced from political oppression to economic privation. The passengers' anger is also diverted against each other, against the more privileged passengers and cars to the fore (and by them against those in the back who are only "useless weight" to pull along), and by almost all the passengers and crew against the locomotive, the station masters, and perhaps against the whole railroad system. Of course, every passenger will insist on using the newly won democracy and the associated social movements to have his/her say on these matters of vital concern, and rightly so. Many passengers may soon wish to lend new (social movement) support to some populist, novice driver who promises final deliverance, especially from unwanted fellow passengers. The Serbian leader Milosevic and his support already offers a sufficiently terrifying example. Ethnic and national(ist) cars may well soon be detached from the train in Yugoslavia, the USSR, and perhaps elsewhere. The forward cars in the Baltics, in Slovenia, and in East Germany may find looser or firmer attachment to other more westerly directed locomotives. What (if any) alternative political-economic tracks—or sidings, more likely—may be available to the more rear cars is harder to say.

Thus the very social movements that first served as vehicles of liberation could threaten the political-democratic processes they had launched themselves. Indeed, in the throes of economic and political crisis, derivative or other social movements could become vehicles of ethnic, nationalist, and class strife and rivalries—with unforeseeable consequences, which could include dictatorial populist backlashes against the newly won democracy.

A historical comparison of the revolutions and their social (but not nationalist) movements of 1789, 1848, 1917, 1968, and 1989, and some comparative reflections on the place and role of Russia, may be in order. This can put the revolution of 1989 into some kind of historical context, in place of a conclusion to this review of an ongoing process in Eastern Europe and the USSR. The 1789 revolution was initially peaceful, but it turned violent and to counterrevolution after taking state power. It was a "bourgeois" revolution to pave the way for capitalist development, but it was not anti-feudal. (In the aftermath, on the winning side of the Napoleonic Wars and at Vienna, Russia became a European power.) The revolutions of 1848 were a combination of peaceful and violent assaults on state power, but all of them were violently repressed and condemned to failure. Thus these revolutions did not immediately impose liberal bourgeois principles over conservative ones, although many of their policies were eventually adopted, but with little thanks to social movements led by the working class. (Russia again lost influence in Central Europe in the face of German unification and economic development. After losing the Crimean War, Tsar Alexander II freed the serfs and introduced his own *perestroika* and *glasnost* with some, but insufficient, results.)

The 1917 revolution began peacefully in February, then resorted to more force to pass state power from the tsars to the Kerenski government. In October-November 1917, the initial aim was to exercise a peaceful threat to influence the existing government, but the revolutionary process accelerated into an armed assault on state power. It proved successful, but led to civil war and the subsequent power of the Soviet Communist Party. Working-class (social) movements failed everywhere in postwar Europe; even in Russia workers were a tiny percentage of the revolutionary forces, one which was further reduced by their decimation in the civil war. (During World War I, Lenin had made a separate peace at Brest-Litovsk and forfeited Soviet Russia's share of the spoils. However, as conqueror on the winning side of World War II and at Yalta and Potsdam, Soviet Russia assumed and was awarded a dominant role in Central—now "Eastern"—Europe and then world superpower status.)

The 1968 "revolutions" were largely peaceful social movements, often repressed by force of arms, even though none aspired to or seriously threatened state power. A particular distinguishing feature of the "new" social movements was that they were not working-class led or based. On the contrary, 1968 represents the acknowledgment that social movements must reach and appeal far beyond the "traditional," industrial working class and its communist party and/or unionized leadership. The Prague Spring, if it be included among 1968 "movements," contemplated a peaceful transfer of power within the existing state apparatus, but was reversed through the military invasion by the Soviet army. The 1968 Tet offensive in Vietnam was, of course, another matter. (Soviet power was challenged here and there, but survived.)

The revolutions of 1989 started peacefully as widespread and deep-going social movements. They succeeded, faster and more than even their protagonists expected, in putting civil democracy in civil society to work to achieve political liberation. Finally, the domino theory, which was feared on previous occasions but remained inoperative, worked this time—albeit rather unexpectedly. It did so in part because the social movements suffered no armed repression, either domestic or foreign (except in the more "independent" Romania, where, however, the army turned to support and save the popular uprising). The mild resistance by the regimes, of course, was conditioned by changes in circumstance and policy in the USSR. Their collapse, in some cases, in the face of these movements almost saw the destruction of state power and of those institutions that "guarantee public order," so much so that even commentators in the West took alarm. Perhaps this alarm reflects the failure—or let's hope it is only a delay—to appreciate the momentous de facto reformulation and extension of the democratic process when, to paraphrase Abraham Lincoln, it is extended "by, of, and for the people" beyond parliamentary political democracy to civil democracy in civil society.

At the same time, the economic structures and processes underlying these sociopolitical transformations have not received the attention that their importance merits. However, the hard knocks of economic life still threaten to divert, albeit hopefully not to revert, these social movements and political processes in dangerous directions. If, like 1789, 1989 will go down in history as a year of revolution, what portends for 1990 and its decade—analogous to the 1790s? Whether some kinds of counterrevolutionary Thermidors may still be in the offing (and when) we would not now like to predict. (Beginning with military failure in Afghanistan [another Crimean War?], the "imperial" reach of the USSR is under effective political challenge due principally to economic failure, and the "Union" may effectively break up. Russia, whether still "soviet" or not, may thereby be relatively weakened but perhaps absolutely revitalized and strengthened.)[6]

Actually existing socialism has undergone an important transformation because of these events and requires reconsideration. To account for these events and transformations, the prime determining factor has been the failure of actually existing (non)socialism in Eastern Europe and the USSR to compete economically with the West. It is well known that the centrally planned economies achieved relative success through forced absolute growth. Heavy industry and, in some countries, large-scale industrial agriculture boomed. Social services were provided and assured, but not individual services. It has become equally apparent that these inflexible economies were unable to promote intensive growth. It was precisely during the recent technological revolution, particularly computerization in the West and in the East Asian NICs that the centralized economies of the USSR and Eastern Europe were unable to keep pace. On the contrary, they lost ground both absolutely and relatively. This was the most determinant starting point of the social movements and revolutions. As an economic failure, moreover, "socialism" has proved to be no match for nationalism. First in Yugoslavia, Hungary, and (above all) in Poland, then in the Baltics, Transcaucasus, Central Asia, the Ukraine, and elsewhere in Eastern Europe, nationalism challenged the political-economic order and demanded democratic self-determination. With economic success neither these social and nationalist movements nor this (kind of) demand for democracy would have developed, much less this move to marketize the economies.

Such observations about Eastern Europe, however, require a brief, parenthetical, comparative glance at other parts of the world. It is noteworthy that economies throughout Africa, most of Latin America, and parts of Asia have recently suffered the same competitive failure, manifested in disastrously declining absolute living standards and relative marginalization from the world economy. Many of them have suffered even more than most economies in Eastern Europe. Perhaps Poland, Romania, Bolivia, Argentina (maybe Burma), and much of Africa top the sad list of greatest decline. Social movements have also developed in many of the other countries outside Eastern Europe, yet in none of them with similar results or such far-reaching goals. In Africa, the considerable *volte-face* in political-economic orientation, away from socialization and the East to support of ethnic and national independence at home, has been achieved without dramatic change. The return to political democracy in Latin America was only marginally carried by the many social movements, despite some of their claims to the contrary. The most dramatic process of democratization, in Argentina, was far less the result of the human rights movements (the Madres de la Plaza de Mayo and others) than it was of the defeat of Argentine military forces by those of Britain, with military aid from the United States and the political support of the whole Western world. In Burma, the social movement was repressed by force of arms. So it was to one degree or another in many other countries, from Chile to Mexico, Jamaica, Gabon, and Sri Lanka. In any of these countries social movements with the force and threat of those in Eastern Europe would have been drenched in blood.

Of similar significance is the fact that in none of these other countries has there been a serious attempt to replace the obviously failing economic system by another, radically different one, let alone to replace the failure of capitalism by socialism. On the contrary, in terms of economic organization there has been a move to the right, to marketization (privatization) everywhere. Moreover, the failure of "socialism" in Eastern Europe can only accelerate marketization elsewhere, no matter how socially costly run-away capitalism has already proved. None of the new democratic regimes in Latin America propose to reform, let alone to turn back, export-led growth (be it absolute growth as in Chile or absolute decline as in Argentina): the democratic opening is itself under threat from the repressive economic measures that democratic governments are obliged (not least by the intervention of the IMF) to impose on their populations.

Indeed, Iran has been the only notable exception to all these experiences. The armed-to-the-teeth regime of the Shah disintegrated, as its Winter Palace was stormed and taken by an unarmed peaceful crowd, the spearhead of a deep-going social movement. However, the movement was led by the exiled fundamentalist leader Ayatollah Khomeini, who returned in triumph and channelled this religion-led social movement into the construction of a Shiite Islamic theocratic state. It renounced and denounced Soviet communist and U.S. imperialist satans equally and, at enormous sacrifice to its population, fought a ten-year war against its Sunni Islamic neighbors in Iraq. (Both financed the war by their sales of oil on the world market.)

Thus the failure of socialist, but also of many capitalist and mixed, economies is marked above all by their inability to compete adequately on the world market. Of course, this has always been the case; it is in the "nature" of any competition that few can win and many must lose. This process of selection operates largely irrespective of the capitalist or socialist "system" that they use to compete, which is at best a contributory factor in the inevitable selection of winners and losers. Therefore, the economic failure and loss of "socialism" per se is relative to both the success and failure of "capitalism" to compete in the same ("capitalist") world market. The replacement of one "system" by the other is no guarantee that any economy will then compete more successfully; most will continue to lose the race.

The move away from "socialism" to the greater marketization of East European economies and their further integration into world competition comes on the heels of recently increased and still-growing economic weakness. Therefore, they pose great economic and political dangers, not the least of further economic failure and of popular political disillusionment and backlash.

The economic crisis in Eastern Europe and the USSR is almost certain to deepen further in the short run. Both deepening crisis and market response will result in greater shortages, new unemployment, rampant inflation, and disruption to the welfare state. All of these—particularly the latter—will increase the already disproportionate burden on women and children. In the USSR Gorbachev was ill advised by Abel Aganbegyan to push for *perestroika* and acceleration of growth in the economy at the same time. The result has been an economic (and political) disaster: restructuring temporarily reduces growth, instead of increasing it, and the simultaneous attempt to accelerate threw an additional spanner into the works.

In Eastern Europe, too, economic restructuring is bound to involve transitional economic dislocation in different degrees and forms. It will be the most absolutely severe in Poland, as well as in the south and east of Yugoslavia and the USSR, which have the weakest and most recently weakened economies. Romania was also weakened, especially by Ceaucescu's policy of exporting all to pay off the debt. Ceasing to export so much food can offer temporary relief and some resurrection of agriculture, but not of industry. East Germany faces the prospects of immediate *ausverkauf* to the West Germans who already come to buy subsidized consumer goods at 10 or 20:1 exchange rates between Western and Eastern marks. East Germany, which has long been a de facto silent member of the European Community through its privileged access to the West German market, also has the earliest prospects of full integration in the European Community. However, the weakening of the state in East Germany and its dependent confederation with or even integration into the West German state will also leave East Germany with scarce political-economic bargaining power in Germany, the European Community, and Europe. Czech and Hungarian state power may offer more competitive bargaining power and benefits to (parts of) their populations. Everywhere, however, the first steps toward productive integration are likely to be the sale of East European productive assets to West European firms and others, some of whom will engage in asset-stripping instead of real investment. In Eastern Europe itself, few have the money to successfully outbid foreigners for "privatized" assets. Only some small enterprises could be run as "cooperatives," in reality firms that must also compete in the market.

The political-economic move to marketization and privatization, whether "capitalist" or "socialist," which is engendered by the social movements in Eastern Europe, can at best replace one economic and social polarization by another. The corruption and privilege derived from Communist Party rule can be largely (but not entirely) eliminated, but marketization and privatization engender another, more automatic, economic and social polarization of income and position between the genders, among classes, ethnic groups, and regions. A minority will float to the surface of a, perhaps first ebbing and then rising, tide; the majority will sink even further below the surface. This polarization is likely to progress ethnically, nationally, and internationally. Therefore, it will further exacerbate ethnic and national tensions, conflicts, and movements within and among states. The more competitively privileged regions and peoples are likely to improve their positions further, perhaps by closer economic and political relations or even integration with neighbors to the west and north. Underprivileged minorities here, and underprivileged majorities in unintegrated places, are likely to become increasingly marginalized. The dream of joining Western Europe may thus be realized only for the few. At best, some parts of the East may become another southern Europe, albeit at the cost to both of competing with each other. (Fears have already been raised in the south of Europe.) However, many in Eastern Europe—and perhaps in the southeastern parts of the USSR—face the real threat of Latin Americanization, a fate which has already befallen Poland. East European countries face domestic inflation and foreign devaluation, and then currency reform, perhaps by shock treatment. The social costs are certain, but the economic successes are not, as repeated failures in Argentina and Brazil have recently demonstrated. In some cases, particularly in the USSR, even economic Africanization (or at least Mideasternization) and political Lebanonization is a serious threat. In the short run, any break-up of the Second World will permit some of its members to join the (capitalist) First World, but most will be relegated to the (also capitalist) Third World.

The question arises of a possible, different socialism for the future. How and what would it come to be? An oft-posed issue, at least by some who consider themselves socialists, is whether the USSR and Eastern Europe (indeed any other place) has been socialist at all. Since their answer is a resounding "no," they also argue that the long-standing failures and critiques of actually existing socialism, which finally gave rise to the revolutions of 1989, were not really of socialism, but of Stalinism or some other aberration of, or imposter for, true socialism. The ideological implication of this argument is, of course, that these failures do not compromise the true socialist cause and do not oblige real socialists to undertake an agonizing reappraisal. Real socialists, then, need only insist more than ever on their own critiques of actually existing (non)socialism to differentiate "us" (goodies) from "them" (baddies). The "practical" implication of this "theory" is that, experience notwithstanding, true socialism is still around the corner—or at least down the road.

However, the real practicality and even theoretical coherence of this, perhaps well-meaning, argument clashes with all world social-political-economic reality. To begin with, if ever there was an argument that only preaches to the already (auto)converted, then this is it. It could not possibly convert those who have already experienced actually existing socialism, even if it were really nonsocialism: those among them who reject most of the previously existing (non)socialism are likely to continue to reject any potential "real" socialism. Indeed, many of them are likely to put their faith in the magic of the market and some, alas, in far-right politics. On the other had, those who now lose the benefits of their previous experience will only yearn for the "good old days" of order and stability and the (non)socialist *ancien régime*. Among these, those who had little and now lose even that will recall their modest benefits and ask for renewed order, if not of the old "communist" variety, then perhaps of a new "fascist" one. Only those who received much from the old party may now, under a new democratic socialist guise, try to hang onto as much of it as possible. The social democratic argument will also lack appeal for those elsewhere who never wanted themselves or any one else to experience "socialism" or "communism," of whatever kind. Therefore, it is wholly unrealistic to think that the damage of the whole experience to the idea of socialism, of a democratic or whatever kind, can simply be wished away by latter-day professions of one's own purity against others' former sins.

Second, however anti-Stalinist the subjective intent of this argument, its objective consequence, is to stick to the guns of the Stalinist theory of socialism in one country (or even smaller community). Beyond disregarding the first problem and that of transition to this socialism in theory and praxis, this argument clashes with the same practical reality of having to compete in practice the whole world over. Yet the inability to do so was the fundamental failure and undoing of the Stalinist system, socialist or otherwise. Whatever the kind of socialism, capitalism, or mixed economy, Islamic political economy, or other system that people may "choose," they cannot escape worldwide competition; it is a fact of life. Cooperation as an "alternative" is all very well, so long as it is more competitive.

Third, the (only?) alternative interpretation of "real" socialism is "world" socialism. Beyond its unreality for any foreseeable future, it is difficult to imagine what this might ever mean. What would distinguish this world socialism from world capitalism, so long as competition reigns as a fact of life in the future, as it has for millennia in the past?

What of the chances for social democracy, if not democratic socialism? One time "socialists" in the West and the East, including

Mikhail Gorbachev himself, have found new appreciation for and interest in social democracy as the *desideratum* that best combines both "socialism" and "democracy." They, again including Gorbachev, look to Sweden, and sometimes to Austria, as the model for Eastern Europe and even for the USSR. In the architectural design for the new Common European Home, many socialists and social democrats would further provide for social democratic, if not democratic socialist, influences emanating from the East into the West. Thus the whole of Europe would become another Sweden writ large. As Gandhi answered when he was asked what he thought of European civilization, "It would be a good idea." Unfortunately, these good ideas take little account of some hard realities.

Thus, even disregarding the USSR, which is hardly realistic, the prospects for early Swedenization in Eastern Europe are not very bright. On the contrary, it will take much effort by all, including Western Europe and even the United States and Japan, only to lay some—indeed, even to protect already existing—economic (social democratic) foundations for political social democracy in Eastern Europe. It is at best uncertain whether, and how much, a West German/European Marshall Plan would promote social democracy in Eastern Europe. Nor is it certain that such an enterprise would advance the progressive version of social democracy (with small or large "s" and "d") and defeat conservative politics and parties in the West. Investment in good business (but not in unprofitable social investments) in the East could easily spell more polarization in the West as well. Really "new" social movements, East and West, could develop both to reflect and to propel such accelerated polarization.

Thus socialists are indeed obliged by the hard facts of life to rethink socialism if they insist on sticking to their socialist ideology at all. We would not pretend to do this rethinking here and now, let alone do it alone. To be realistic, however, any such socialism would have not only to take account of competition, but to rewrite the rules of the (competitive) game under which it takes place. Gender, class, national, ethnic, religious, community, as well as economic, political, social, cultural, ideological, and other interest groups and family or individual interrelations would have to have new participatory social (movement) expressions and institutional protection of and guarantees for the mutual respect of their democratic expression and for the peaceful resolution of their conflicts of interest beyond anything hitherto known. Realistically, the prospects for any such "democratic socialism," or otherwise, are still dim. Indeed, all the evidence is that things will, and will have to, get worse before they get better. However, things may get so much worse and so rapidly that mankind may face a common economic-ecological and/or military-political and, therefore sociocultural, crisis of such alarming proportions and absolute threat to physical survival that we will finally be moved to get ourselves together.

Notes

The author is grateful for comments on the first draft to Michael Ellman (especially on economics and history), to Marta Fuentes (on economics and social movements), and to Kim Hunter for editorial help beyond the call of duty.

1. M. Fuentes and A.G. Frank, "Ten Theses on Social Movements," *World Development* 17 (2 February 1989); A.G. Frank and M. Fuentes, "Social Movements in Recent World History," in S. Amin, G. Arrighi, A.G. Frank, and I. Wallerstein, *Transforming the Revolution: Social Movements in the World System* (New York: Monthly Review Press, 1990).
2. As this article goes to press Soviet troops occupy the streets of Baku, the capital of Azerbaijan.
3. *New York Times/International Herald Tribune,* 7 December 1989.
4. *International Viewpoint,* 11 December 1989, p. 13.
5. A.G. Frank and M. Fuentes, "Nine Theses on Social Movements." *Economic and Political Weekly,* 29 August 1987.
6. On the variety of social movements and their nineteenth and twentieth-century history, see S. Amin et al., *Transforming the Revolution.*

SAMIR AMIN

THE FUTURE OF SOCIALISM

It is surely time to raise the issue of the future of socialism once again. Since the beginning of the 1980s, the ideological offensive of the ultra-liberal right has forced the predominantly social-democratic elements of the Western left to fall broadly into line. In the third world, autonomous development has been systematically undermined in favor of the demands of world capitalism. Last but not least, the sudden collapse of the East European regimes may pave the way for the integration of these countries into the capitalist world system. Triumphant liberal ideology proclaims the definitive failure of socialism.

For those who believe, as I do, that socialism offers a system of values never fully achieved, and not a constructed model on display in any particular place, the issue is infinitely more complex. Quite frankly, today's real danger is that the illusions of the peoples of the West, East, and South can only mean that the inevitable failure of today's triumphant liberalism may be disastrous for the popular classes, once they are ideologically and politically disarmed. More than ever, I would argue that the choice lies between socialism or barbarism.

1

It might be helpful to begin this analysis with a critique of the three fundamental bases of the fashionable liberal thesis.

First liberal axiom: The "market" represents economic rationality

106

per se, outside any specific social context. (In its extreme version: Without the market, only chaos.)

This erroneous postulate expresses the economistic alienation essential for capitalist "legitimacy." Nothing more. The market does not in fact rationalize social relations. On the contrary, the framework of social relations determines how the market will operate. From an alienated, economistic standpoint, economic laws are analogous to laws of nature and exert external forces on every human action, and the economy is the product of determinate social behavior.[1] There is no economic rationality per se, but merely the expression of the demands of a social system at the level of economic management.

But no such social system is rational from a humanist point of view if it fails to meet the needs of the human beings subject to it. Unemployment, polarization in world development, and ecological waste are manifestations of the irrationality of this system which I call *really existing capitalism*. These negative phenomena are, purely and simply, necessary products of the market. The rationality of the market reproduces the irrationalities of the social system.

Second liberal axiom: Democracy equals capitalism. (Put more emphatically: Without capitalism, no democracy.)

This is mere trickery. Contemporary trends of opinion, broadly typified by Anglo-American evolutionism, impoverish the debate by treating democracy as a set of narrowly defined rights and practices, independent of the desired social result. This democracy can then stabilize the society by leaving the "evolution" to "objective forces." The latter are in the last resort governed by science and technology,[2] operating independently of the human will. Hence the functional role of the revolutionary process in history can be played down.

Socialist thought lies poles apart from this line of argument. The analysis of economic alienation provided by Marx, central to any scientific and realistic understanding of capitalist reproduction, rehabilitates the crucial function of revolutions, moments of qualitative transformation and crystallization of potentialities inconceivable without them. In each of the three great revolutions of the modern world (the French, the Russian, and the Chinese), the play of ideas and social forces at moments of radicalization succeeded in moving far beyond the requirements of historical, objectively necessary social transformation. Jacobin democracy did more than merely establish bourgeois power. Although the democracy operated in a framework of private ownership, its anxiety to establish power genuinely at the service of the people clashed with merely bourgeois needs. At this stage of social development the bourgeoisie looked for little more than a qualified democracy such as occurred elsewhere in the nineteenth century. They were furthermore willing to compromise with the monarchy and the aristocracy. The aspirations of the "people"—the crowd of peasants and artisans—went further. The people wanted something more than "free trade," to such an extent that during the convention, they launched the astonishingly modern slogan, "Liberalism is the enemy of democracy!" This was a foretaste of a socialist consciousness yet to come. In the same way, the USSR in the 1920s and China in the Maoist period expressed a communist vision well beyond the requirements of the national and popular reform on the agenda. Certainly these moments of radicalization are fragile. In the end, narrower concepts more consonant with "objective" needs win the day. But it would be quite wrong to underestimate their significance as an indication of the way the movement is bound to continue.

Bourgeois democracy is the product of the revolution that dethroned "tributary metaphysics."[3] It establishes "equal rights" and personal liberties, but not equality, except under the law. As late as the latter half of the nineteenth century, the labor movement could impose unqualified political democracy and seize social rights, but only in the framework of a compromise based on acceptance of capitalist management of the economy, itself made possible by world polarization to the benefit of the industrial centers. Western democracy is thereby restricted to the political domain, while economic management continues to be based on nondemocratic principles of private ownership and competition. The capitalist mode of production does not of itself *require* democracy, but its characteristic oppression is *in fact hidden* in economic alienation. By contrast, the socialist project of a classless society, free of economic alienation, *implies* a democratic structure. Once capitalist reliance on competition is broken, social relations based on cooperation among workers, and not on their subjection, are inconceivable without a full flowering of democracy.

If what are known as the third world countries have almost never seen their political systems in a genuinely democratic form, this is not a hangover from their "traditional culture."[4] What I call *really existing capitalism*, that is, *capitalism as a world system and not as a mode of production*, taken at its highest level of abstraction, has until now always generated polarization on a world scale. Unfortunately, this dimension has always been underestimated in socialist thought, including Marxism. The international polarization inherent in this expansion brings in turn a manifold internal polarization: growing inequality in income, widespread unemployment, and marginalization. Seeing the world system as the only ultimately meaningful unit of analysis is crucial to understanding what is at stake in the struggles, namely, that the essential reserve army of capitalism is to be found at the peripheries of the system.

Hence instability is the rule in the political life of the peripheries. The political norm of the vicious dictatorship (whether military or not), broadly amenable to the expansion of world capital, is occasionally shaken by explosions, which rarely lead to real political democracy. The most common response is the "populist" model. Such regimes genuinely address at least some aspects of the social problem and try to develop strategies to reduce the tragic consequences of peripheralization, but they do not break with capitalism.

Between the right-wing dictatorships and the popular movements there is a middle ground onto which "petty democracy" can sometimes sneak. Such regimes recognize the principle of multiparty elections and grant a measure of free speech, but fall short of addressing fundamental social problems and/or challenging relations of dependence and subjection to the world system. These "democracies" are little more than expressions of the crisis of the despotic system of capitalism. Latin America, Korea, and the Philippines provide examples of contradictions unresolved by such regimes. Democracy imposed in such circumstances faces a striking dilemma. Either the democratic political system surrenders to the demands of world "adjustment"—it cannot then consider any substantial social reforms, and democracy soon reaches crisis (as in Argentina); or the popular forces take charge of democracy and impose the reforms. But the political system then comes quickly into conflict with world capitalism and must shift from its national bourgeois project to a national and popular project.

The areas of the periphery most affected by capitalist expansion are in a more desperate plight. The historical record of capitalist expansion must own up to much more than the "development" it has engendered. Actually existing capitalism has a destructive side that is invariably omitted from its flattering self-portraits. Here the usual pattern of power is the *tontons macoutes* in Haiti, the Somozas in Nicaragua, and a disturbing number of dictatorships of the same stamp in contemporary Africa.

Third liberal axiom: A wide-open door to the world system is the *sine qua non* of any development. (Put more emphatically: Free trade, or no development.)

The underlying hypothesis is that "development" depends essentially on *internal* circumstances peculiar to each society, with integration into the world economy a *positive factor if only one knows how to use the opportunities it provides.* This thesis is not only contradicted by the history of five centuries of capitalist expansion—incessant polarization reproduced and intensified up until the present and for the forseeable future—but is also scientifically unsound. The "world market" in question is truncated and restricted to goods and capital; despite international migrations there has never been any suggestion of a "world labor market," and there is no prospect of one. Liberal economic theory demonstrates that mobility of a single factor of production (capital) while two other factors (labor and natural resources) are imprisoned by natural and political geography cannot lead to uniform world productivity and social conditions.

In such circumstances, the worldwide law of value can only produce and reproduce polarization. In this sense integration into the world system is by its nature unfavorable and becomes increasingly so. I have argued this thesis on intuitive evidence: a few decades were enough to allow nineteenth-century Germany to "catch up" to England. How long will Brazil need to "catch up" to the United States?

Undoubtedly the forms and content of the polarization have evolved over time.[5] From the Industrial Revolution to World War II it was a distinction between industrialized and non-industrialized countries. Accelerated industrialization of some areas of the third world does not, in my view, raise a question mark over polarization as such, but merely over its forms. The mechanisms of the new polarization are founded on various forms of domination: financial (new forms of worldwide finance capital); technological (in relationship to the new scientific and technological revolution); cultural (with the growing influence of the media); and military. In this context the "newly industrializing countries" (the NICs) are not semiperipheries on the way to becoming new centers, but the true peripheries of tomorrow.

By contrast, the countries of the so-called "fourth world" are not true peripheries, but are like the areas destroyed by capitalist expansion in its earlier forms. The perilous condition of the fourth world is not the outcome of a "refusal" to integrate within the international division of labor and a "failed" attempt to delink. In fact, the fourth world, which is talked of as something new, has been a consistent feature of capitalist expansion. A clear but lamentable example of this pervasive phenomenon is provided by the areas of slave labor in the Americas in the period of mercantilism: Northeast Brazil and the West Indies (including Haiti). These areas were regarded as prosperous in their day; and they were the heart of the periphery corresponding to the system of the time. Later, new structures of capitalist development marginalized them, and they are today among the most grievously wretched parts of the third world. Is Africa not now on the road to exclusion from the world division of labor by a system that has consigned the continent to specialization in agriculture and mining until the soils are exhausted, and by a technological revolution that provides substitutes for some of its still-plentiful raw materials? Fourth world societies that have been rejected by the system cannot, by definition, solve their problems through open-door policies.

From the standpoint of the various peoples of the earth, unification of the entire world system under the sway of the market is undesirable. It is not even the most likely outcome of the evolution now under way, so bitter are the conflicts provoked by the market in a world of "Darwinism." The ideological discourse of the West, which has chosen this strategy, aims to conceal the bitterness of these conflicts.

2

The values of socialism have scientific justification, not merely moral justification, in rejecting the three liberal theses—that economic rationality requires the market, that democracy requires capitalism, and that development requires free trade. All currents of socialist thought are primed to go beyond the philosophy of the Enlightenment, which sought to establish a "rational" basis that would serve society for all time. Socialism comes from an analysis of the historical limits of the "rationality" in question, namely its capitalist form. Socialism therefore offers the project of a qualitatively more advanced society, aiming at a more complete mastery over human destiny. Here again, the Marxist theory of alienation returns to center stage: the scientific and social project of socialism is to liberate humanity from alienation in its bourgeois economic form. The project cannot be defined more precisely in advance. Although it would be possible to be precise about what must be abolished (such as private ownership of the means of production), it would not be possible—in the absence of concrete social praxis—to delineate new methods of socialist management in advance. Any attempt to do so would militate against the liberation project itself, whereby the responsibility for shaping their destiny can lie only with the succeeding generations that will make their own history.

We are still faced with the fact that the so-called socialist societies of the East have abolished private ownership and established self-styled socialist systems of economic and political management. *These systems, particularly those in Europe, are collapsing.* Must we conclude that the socialist project itself is hopelessly utopian?

If we want to provoke a fruitful debate on these experiences, we must turn to the character of the so-called socialist revolutions in the East and the historical limits of the capitalism from which they emerged. Two approaches are possible. One is to focus on what defines capitalism at its highest level of abstraction—namely the contradiction between capital and labor—and defines the historical limits of capitalist society by the boundaries imposed by its characteristic economism. This viewpoint inevitably leads to a "stageist" vision of the evolution of society: the backward (peripheral) capitalist societies must "catch up" with the advanced societies before they are in turn faced with the challenges of a possible (or perhaps necessary) supersession of the limits of those advanced societies. Or one can place more emphasis in the analysis on what really existing capitalism, which in its actual worldwide expansion has given rise to a centers/peripheries polarization impossible to overcome within the framework of capitalism itself. Nearly all currents of socialist thought have underestimated this dimension of capitalism, as I have said.

A challenge to the capitalist order on the basis of revolts on its periphery requires a serious rethinking of the issue of the "transition to socialism" and the abolition of classes. The Marxist tradition, however subtly interpreted, is handicapped by an initial theoretical vision of *worker* revolutions, on the basis of advanced forces of production, initiating a fairly speedy transition, marked by democratic power for the mass of the people—a power that is more democratic in principle than that of the most democratic of the bourgeois states. By contrast, I would suggest that the profoundly unequal character inherent in capitalist expansion has brought onto history's agenda a revolution by the peoples of the periphery. This revolution is anticapitalist, in the sense that it stands up against a really existing capitalist development that has become unbearable. But for all that, it is not socialist, even though it rises up against capital in its cruelest manifestation. It has by force of circumstance a complex character.

These postcapitalist societies are now faced with the demand for substantial development of the forces of production. It is illusory to imagine basing an "alternative development" on poverty, even if one rejects the consumer lifestyle of capitalism in its advanced centers and takes into account its real waste and inhumanity.

A recognition of this does not mean accepting the thesis that an initial passage through a phase of capitalist accumulation is inevitable. Such a "bourgeois revolution" is a most unlikely outcome of a mass movement that is led by political parties with an openly anticapitalist ideology and view of the future. A capitalist expansion fostered by the local bourgeoisie but open to the world system will here be challenged by the mass of the people, for whom it could only be a form of oppression.

This specific and new contradiction, not envisaged in Marx's classic concept of the socialist transition, gives the postcapitalist regimes their real quality of a national and popular construct in which there is a conflictual mix of aspirations and achievements of a socialist kind and aspirations of a capitalist kind called for by the need to develop the forces of production.

This contradiction, inherent in the long transition imposed by the unequal development of capitalism, can be defined by three fundamental elements, the inverse counterparts of the three liberal axioms criticized in Part 1 of this essay: bureaucratic planning (rationality without the market); anti-democratic political monopoly of a ruling party-state (no democracy to go with no capitalism); and total delinking from the capitalist world system, almost to the point of autarky (development with a closed door). This last has been more an imposition by the West than a desire on the part of the East.

It is certainly significant that this so-called socialist construct has worked through a nondemocratic political system and bureaucratic planning. The complex explanation includes social and cultural-historical determinants and the limits of the ideologies of the countries' revolutionary intelligentsia—Leninism and Maoism. I believe that national and popular hegemony could operate differently from the way they have operated in the past, that there is room for political democracy and market forces. These, after all, cannot in socialist societies any more than in capitalist societies operate outside the boundaries of the social base on which they rest. Indeed, I would go further and say that for this national and popular hegemony to progress it must move in these directions.

In these circumstances, the magnitude of the crisis of the societies of the East should come as no surprise to us, even if like everyone else we have been astounded by the suddenness with which it has manifested itself. These societies now face a triad of options that I briefly summarize under three now-familiar headings:

(1) Evolution toward a bourgeois democracy, *or* progress beyond it, by strengthening the social power of the workers in the management of the economy.

(2) Restoration of an out-and-out "market economy," *or* progress through carefully controlled resort to market forces guided by democratic planning.

(3) An unguarded door open wide to the exterior, *or* guarded relations with the surrounding world, albeit directed toward increased trade.

The confused theoretical debates and political disputes that are sending shudders down spines in the East arise in part because the ideological label "socialist" has imparted confusion as to the status of the genuinely national and popular character of the revolutions that established some of the regimes in question. But more pertinent is the fact that the conflictual forces of capitalism and socialism are meeting within genuine national struggles. The forces anxious to restore capitalism propose unilateral acceptance of the market as a springboard for the restoration of private ownership, and of an "open door," with or without democracy in the Western sense, according to the tactical requirements of their project. If the socialist forces dither in their resistance to this project, if they find it difficult to articulate a coherent alternative along the lines sketched above, it is because the lack of democratic debate and the ideological confusion over the status of the present governments have proved to be major impediments to action. Need I add that the Western ideological offensive, orchestrated through powerful media, is massing entirely on the side of the pro-capitalist (and antidemocratic) forces?

A political response to the three options posed above would lead to intensive internal class struggle, already (silently) under way. A significant minority in the East—perhaps 20 percent—might benefit from the restoration of capitalism. But in light of the inadequate levels of development and international competitiveness achieved by the socialist countries, this minority could never attain the Western standard of living that fuels their aspirations *without grinding down the mass of the people*.

In this struggle, the peoples of the various countries of the East start with unequal weapons. Intuitively, one can grasp why peoples who have by force of arms made their own socialist, nationalist, and popular revolutions (the USSR, China, Yugoslavia, etc.) have an ideological weapon that may enable them to put a progressive complexion on their struggles. By contrast, those of the East European countries with no comparable historical achievement run the risk of being bewitched by the attraction of annexing themselves to Western Europe.

In the current crisis, assertions such as "recourse to the market" and "an open door to the exterior" remain ambiguous because they unite those who seek a launching-pad to capitalism and those who seek a progressive social approach to the political and economic management of their society, and thus a genuine social advance. It is interesting to note that social surveys in the USSR show that the privileged classes prefer the "pluralist democracy and a market open to the exterior" formula, whereas the popular classes remain attached to the achievements of socialism (full employment, social services, national independence, and public ownership). The latter favor "planning" along with democratization of the political system. Gorbachev apparently straddles these antinomian currents, allied only in their opposition to the "conservatives," who have always hoped for a standstill. One notes similar cleavages in Yugoslavia.

In China, Deng Xiaoping has opted for an open door to both internal and external capitalism, an option, it should be remembered, that is supported eagerly by the West.* The democracy movement has (remarkably) recruited forces both from the well-off classes, which openly hope to restore capitalism and from the majority (some claiming to be Maoist), which complains that it has been harmed by capitalist developments during the Deng Xiaoping era![6] The Western media, by describing repression of the democracy movement as a return to "Maoism" mixed with "Stalinism," have certainly not contributed to clarity. They have played a leading role in supporting the reactionary option of restoring capitalism, even if it must be carried out to the total detriment of democracy.

The situation is quite different in those East European countries that have no revolutionary past. Here the social achievements, although real, *have not been won* but have been handed down in a paternalist manner by Communist parties installed by the Soviet Union. It is quite "obvious" to an expert from the World Bank that the Polish problem is very simple: wages must be cut in half (without regard for the impact of this on productivity) and an unemployment level of 2 or 3 million accepted. The situation, remarkably similar to that of Argentina, is obscured by the illusions of the Polish people, to whom nobody has explained that in the world system they desire to join, their place is closer to that of the NICs of the third world than to that of the Western societies whose advanced democracy they admire! One must also be wary of a drift from transitional democracy to an authoritarian regime (of the Pilsudski sort, based on the Catholic church) as the only one capable of imposing the "discipline" that capitalism demands. Evolution of this kind is also to be feared in

---

*The society to which this option logically leads would be South Korea or Taiwan.

Hungary, for example. It is difficult at this moment to say more, especially about East Germany, where internal struggles are mixed up with the desires of the German people for unification, and with the initiatives that the Bonn government will take.

Generally speaking, one is struck by the incredible political naiveté that has grown up among the people of the non-democratic regimes of Eastern Europe. Their attacks on the *nomenklatura*, which are intended as an indictment of "privilege" under actually existing socialism, ignore the fact that the class aspiring to form a bourgeoisie will inevitably be composed of just this *nomenklatura*, that the privileges it has enjoyed are as nothing in comparison with the social inequalities under actually existing capitalism.

The initiative for change in the East has in fact been taken by the ruling class itself. This is constituted on the basis of a "statism" that has been the way of dealing with the capitalism/socialism contradiction within the national and popular construct. It hopes now to be rid of the constraints of the popular classes and to opt four-square for capitalism. The scuttling of the system (to which it lends itself to a degree astonishing to Western commentators) is not really surprising at all: it is the logical terminus of its evolution, and was perfectly foreseen by Mao. This class in attacking its own system repeats all the outworn prejudices of the critique of socialism by bourgeois ideology, but refrains from pointing out that the system it is abandoning has been marvelously effective in making possible its own constitution as a bourgeoisie!

3

The question of the future of socialism is not limited to possible advances or retreats on the part of the countries of the East. One must look also at the countries of the third and fourth worlds—true peripheries, and societies destroyed by capitalist expansion, where development that can meet the material needs of all social strata is impossible within the framework of capitalism, and where it becomes necessary to consider alternative development outside capital's bounds. This is the meaning of the expression *delinking*. It is not a recipe, but a fundamental and principled choice: that of divorcing the criteria of rationality in economic life from those that govern world capitalism, freeing oneself from the constraints of world-capitalist value, and substituting a law of value of national popular reference.

If the bourgeoisie is incapable of delinking, and if only a popular alliance must and can be persuaded that this is required for any development worthy of the name, the social dynamism must lead in a direction that we can only describe as socialist. It is understood that the socialism in question remains a prospect for society well in the future, and not a ready-made model that has merely to be copied.

The current changes in the world economy and political and cultural situation cannot alter the polarizing character of really existing capitalism, but can only heighten the contradictions through which it is expressed. The policies of surrender to world unification through the market—described as "adjustment" for the peripheries, although one speaks of "restructuring" when the centers are concerned—do not in any way "neutralize" its effects. Such policies are not therefore acceptable alternatives to national and popular "breaking away," which is necessary now more than ever. The national bourgeoisies of the third world, who have coopted national liberation to their own advantage, have already become compradors, under the laws of evolution of the world system. They are therefore incapable of mediating the new worldwide phenomena to the advantage of their own country. The popular classes are still confused and indecisive following the exhaustion of the former national liberation movements. Hence it is difficult to forecast the precise next step in an uninterrupted popular revolution that still threatens upheavals in the peripheries of the global system.[7]

In the short term, the responses of the peoples of the third world are generally inadequate, as in the past. The revival of fundamentalist religious movements here and there is itself a symptom of the crisis, and not an adequate response to its challenge.[8] But insufficient reflection has been given in the West to the significance of the failure of the Islamic fundamentalists in Afghanistan, presented in the media as "freedom fighters" (although they propose to close the schools opened by the "atheists in the pay of Moscow," beginning of course with the girls' schools). They were expected to make an undisputed entry into Kabul on the morrow of the withdrawal of Soviet troops.

There is no reason, of course, to exclude the West from the debate on the prospects for socialism. One must neither discount a labor movement that has made possible the achievements of social democracy nor overlook the democratic victories of the West. But standing still means falling back. Socialist advance in the West requires that the people free themselves from alienation and idolatry as they appear in societies whose major means of communication are all in the hands of the dominant classes. The intense communication campaign that operates within really existing capitalism does nothing to contribute to liberation or democratization. Quite to the contrary. People who are not permanent residents of the West on a day-to-day basis are always struck by the incredible saturation by the dominant media—a veritable carpet bombing of the public consciousness. From one country to another, from liberals and conservatives to socialists, an ideological consensus forces near-unanimity on many of the central issues. The pluralism that is so vaunted as synonymous with democracy is stripped of all real content, and minor, provincial differences among competitors of the political class are blown up to bizarre proportions. At a time when "the end of ideology" is being proclaimed again, the West has never before been as subject to so exclusively ideological a discourse.

In a reference elsewhere to the remarkable breakthroughs in social consciousness that are exemplified by the women's movement, I did feel it necessary to express reservations about the real *extent* of these breakthroughs. They can be *absorbed* by a system that remains basically capitalist and imperialist in its relations with the periphery, or, to the contrary, be nodes of positive change.

The intra-Western contradictions since 1945 have never gone beyond the limits of mercantile competition. The Japanese and the Europeans have never dared to take a stand that might really displease the United States. Will this necessarily be the case in the future? The question remains open. According to some views, these conflicts must worsen and lead in the end to a breakup of the world market into spheres of influence around the dominant axes (the United States, Europe, and Japan). The strengthening of détente in East-West relations should enhance this possibility, as the U.S. military umbrella becomes meaningless. But one must be doubtful about the eventual consistency of a common neo-imperialist policy for Europe, which is cornered between competition from the industrialized peripheries (the NICs) that are better placed relative to traditional industries, and from Japan and the United States, both of which may be better equipped in the fields of new technology. In this context could Europe possibly come to the fore? Furthermore, renewed German expansionism will weaken Bonn's solidarity with its EEC partners and further complicate intra-Western relations. In any event, one might ask whether the pursuit of the European construct, the EEC's single market by 1992, could withstand the absence of any common social policy. I doubt it. It seems to me that the social conflict could become very severe.[9]

In fact, the most likely scenario seems to be the following. Either Europe presses on with the common capitalist market, with or without the East; or the more progressive forces in the West understand that an alternative Europe (that of the "Common European Home" envisioned by Gorbachev) would imply a greater social autonomy of all partners—Westerners, Germans, and Easterners.

The future of socialism in Western Europe will therefore depend heavily on the evolution of intra-European relations. Undoubtedly, the ideological polarization that emerged from the socialist revolutions since 1917 would vanish if capitalism were to be restored to the countries in question. A change of this kind, unhappily desired by a high proportion of the anti-Communist West, would have the consequence of a lasting retreat for Western socialist aspirations. It would redound not to the benefit of social democracy, of course, but to that of the right. In the event of greater national and popular evolution in the Eastern countries, everything would depend on the resonance of this for the peoples of the West. The change might leave things as they have been—Cold War attitudes—if the workers of the West continue to think that with their higher living standards they have nothing to learn from their counterparts in the East. But it could also provoke a revival of socialist consciousness among workers in the West. This would be the most favorable outcome for the cause of socialism, and it seems to me to be the implication of Gorbachev's "Common Home."[10]

But the crucial axis for the future of socialism in the West is that of North-South relations. I am not saying anything new here, my main argument being based on the decisive part in history that is played by the polarization inherent in world capitalism. The bitterness of the

East-West conflict for a while obscured the more fundamental conflict arising from this polarization, just as the interimperialist conflict was in the forefront just before 1914. The lessening of intra-Western and East-West contradictions is accompanied by a renewal of hostility toward the peoples who are the prime victims of capitalism—those of Asia, Africa, and Latin America. There are many signs today of this regressive evolution: the recrudescence of racism and colonial arrogance, even in the detail of the "realignment" of NATO bases, whose guns are henceforth to be trained on the southern shore of the Mediterranean.[11]

4

The contours of a new globalization of capital remain quite vague. The configuration that materializes will follow from conflicts that will inevitably occur despite the liberalism common to the nations of the capitalist center. Hence the future remains open to various possibilities and there is no justification for abandoning the thought and struggle to promote a better world project. This is no plea for "voluntarism," since the political options that delimit the possible futures are historically objective. Exploring these options calls for examining alternatives along three axes of evolution: (1) the centers/peripheries contradiction, governed by the logic of world capitalism; (2) West-East relations; and (3) intra-Western competition. I have attempted to do so briefly, from the starting point of unilateral unification by the market that constitutes the essence of the Western project.

More than ever, the forces of the left have a duty to promote a credible alternative to this disastrous option. I shall not dwell here on the possible features of this alternative, some aspects of which I have discussed elsewhere.[12]

First: The only strategy that is meaningful for the progressive forces on a world scale, on the basis of which the peoples of the West, East, and South can together draw new breath, must envision a "polycentric" world. The various component areas must be articulated in a flexible way, allowing the implementation of specific measures required by their varying levels of development and by other objective circumstances. It must be acknowledged at the outset that the problems that the peoples of the world must solve differ from one area to another. It is therefore essential that the world system permit peoples the autonomy to promote their own interests. There must be a balance between general interdependence and this legitimate concern for autonomy. The logic of mutual and reciprocal adjustment must be substituted for unilateral "adjustment" by the weakest and expansion for the exclusive benefit of the strongest.

Second: Polycentrism means that the countries of the East and South pursue development policies that are delinked in the sense I have given to this word. This strategy looks to advances toward socialism (democratization and strengthening national and popular trends) and not to a "restoration of capitalism" in the countries of the East, and to a refusal by the countries of the South to become compradors. It must likewise allow progressive advances in the countries of the West, through the opening of nonmarket social spaces and through other reforms based on socialization of economic management.

Third: With particular reference to the third world, this strategy favors progress in the organization of the productive forces even to the detriment of "international competitiveness." It puts at the top of the agenda an agricultural revolution marked by the maximum of equality, and transformation of the informal sector into a popularly managed transitional economy. It calls for an effective combination of planning and market forces as the foundation for economic and social democracy. The vision of polycentrism it inspires gives the countries and regions of the third world a measure of autonomy that is denied them under world unification by the market.

Fourth: As regards international cooperation for interdependence, the strategy aims to encourage embryos of a democratic world government and, for example, a world tax to be spent on environmental measures. It also aims to reduce the arms race, notably by the superpowers. It aims finally to breathe new life into the democratic institutionalization of world management through the United Nations.

Let me say in conclusion that the construction of a polycentric world with new prospects for socialism implies acute awareness of the cultural universalism of humanity's project. On this point I have put forward elsewhere a critique of the Eurocentrism and cultural nationalism that form the obverse image.[13]

—*Translated by Michael Wolfers*

Notes

1. See Samir Amin, *Eurocentrism* (New York: Monthly Review Press, 1989); Samir Amin, *Unequal Development* (New York: Monthly Review Press, 1976), Ch. 2; Karl Polanyi, *La liberta in na societa complessa* (Turin: Boringheri, 1987); and the works of the Frankfurt school.
2. Science and technology is a major topic in the work of the Frankfurt school.
3. Amin, *Eurocentrism*, pp. 15–59.
4. See Samir Amin, "La question démocratique dans la tiers monde contemporaine," *African Development* (1989). See in particular my critique of neo-Weberian theses in Richard Sandbrook with Judith Baker, *The Politics of Africa's Economic Stagnation* (Cambridge: Cambridge University Press, 1985). See also Giovanni Arrighi's theses on the world distribution of active and passive labor armies and my contribution, "The End of National Liberation?" in Samir Amin, Giovanni Arrighi, Andre Gunder Frank, and Immanuel Wallerstein, *Transforming the Revolution* (New York: Monthly Review Press, 1990).
5. See Samir Amin, "Réflexions sur le système international," forthcoming in a collective work edited by Peter Golding. See also Samir Amin, *Delinking: Towards a Polycentric World* (London: Zed Books, forthcoming).
6. Samir Amin, *The Future of Maoism* (New York: Monthly Review Press, 1983).
7. See *Delinking*, Ch. 1 and 4; Samir Amin, *Maldevelopment: Anatomy of a Global Failure* (London: Zed Books and The Third World Forum, forthcoming), Ch. 6; and my contribution to *Transforming the Revolution*.
8. My writings on these movements are mainly in Arabic, but see "Existe-t-il une économie politique islamique?" *Peuples Méditerranéens* 21 (1982), and *Eurocentrism*, pp. 124–35.
9. Samir Amin, "In Favor of a Polycentric World," *IFDA Dossier 69* (1989).
10. Samir Amin, "La maison commune Europe," *IFDA Dossier 73* (1989).
11. Observation by Alberto Santos of the CEDETIM study group, Paris. See Samir Amin, "Conditions for Autonomy in the Mediterranean Region," in Faysal Yachir, *The Mediterranean: Between Autonomy and Dependency* (London: Zed Books and Tokyo: The United Nations University, 1989), pp. 1–24, esp. p. 11.
12. Samir Amin, "Une autre configuration des relations internationales Ouest-Est-Sud: est-elle souhaitable, probable, possible?" *Forum de Delphes* (Paris: Harmattan, 1989); "L'Europe et les rapports Nord-Sud," *L'évènement européen* 7 (1989).
13. *Eurocentrism*, pp. 124–52.

RESPONSES TO CHANGES IN THE COMMUNIST STATES

HARRY MAGDOFF AND PAUL M. SWEEZY

PERESTROIKA AND THE FUTURE OF SOCIALISM

The facts on the severity of the crisis that emerged in the Soviet Union in the 1970s and 1980s are clear. The puzzling question is why regression set in after so many years of social progress and impressive achievements in industrialization.

Bourgeois economists have an easy answer to this question. They have claimed all along that central planning of an economy would come a cropper: it couldn't deliver the goods and was bound to fail. In recent years, quite a few prominent economists in the Soviet Union and Eastern Europe have joined the bandwagon in blaming central planning for the economic woes of their societies. It is now common for critics in the Soviet bloc to argue that even though national planning was serviceable in the past, it long ago outlived its usefulness. Not only is an administered economy intrinsically inefficient, they maintain, but its failures inevitably loom larger the more it attempts to extend its functions from basic industrialization to the satisfaction of consumer needs.

It seems to us that this kind of blanket condemnation of central planning is based on the implicit assumption that Soviet practice reveals the essential nature of a centrally planned economy. What is missing and what needs to be understood is that the Soviet way of running an economy evolved under very special historical circumstances. There was pitifully little experience to rely on, nor was there time or opportunity for the trial-and-error experiments essential to the rational construction of a new economic system. Furthermore, what was at stake was not only a desire to build socialism but the

127

simultaneous need to industrialize the nation—each a formidable enough task in its own right. And both were undertaken under the continuing actuality or threat of invasion by one or more hostile capitalist powers.

Not only were the blueprints for a new order missing, so were trained and experienced administrators of a socialist persuasion. In large measure, the available personnel with administrative knowhow came from the old state apparatus, ridden with bureaucratic and semi-feudal traditions. All in all, the Soviet planning system was designed and introduced under economic and social conditions that bordered on the chaotic.

The Soviet Union did not have to embark on central planning and massive industrialization when it did in the late 1920s. An important part of the leadership, led by Bukharin, advocated a slower and more gradual course. But once the decision was made, it was inevitable that certain consequences would follow from the initial goal of an incredibly rapid acceleration of economic growth under unusually strained conditions: a vast increase in the economic role of the state, extreme centralization of decision-making, harsh regimentation of the population.

The state and the economy thus became fertile ground for the emergence of a huge bureaucracy which in turn shaped and controlled its members, teaching them ways of operating and giving them jobs and special privileges they soon became masters of extending and protecting. Although changes were later made from time to time in some aspects of organization and planning, the system inherited by Gorbachev and which he set himself the task of overhauling remains essentially the one forged under Stalin in economic and social conditions very different from today's.

It was not only the bureaucracy and its way of functioning and protecting its interests that survived from the time of Stalin but also the ruling ideology which developed to rationalize its existence and that of the system it served. Planning was elevated to the status of a science, invented in the Soviet Union and available for adoption by the rest of the world. Planning was guided by alleged laws of socialism—actually rationalizations of existing practices but proclaimed as eternal truths. This was part and parcel of a general tendency to project all aspects of Soviet society—the Communist

Party, its monopolization of state power, the planning system—as inherent in socialism and the necessary model for any country taking the road to socialism.

For purposes of the present discussion it is crucial to keep this background in mind and to reject any notion that Soviet practice during this stormy period and central economic planning are one and the same, with its logical corollary that the present crisis of the Soviet economy and society is also a crisis of economic planning. The truth is rather that what led to the present plight of the Soviet economy is precisely those aspects that are peculiar to the Soviet experience and not any inherent characteristics of planning as such.

The forced-draft industrialization of the Soviet economy set in motion by the First Five-Year Plan would of course have been impossible if the necessary human and material resources had not been available within the borders of the Soviet Union. They were there, a rich potential supply of fuel, minerals, other raw materials, and a large pool of unutilized and underutilized labor. But none of these reserves was inexhaustible, and there was never any guarantee that needed inputs called for by the planners would be available in the right proportions at the right times. Unless this aspect of the planning process could be developed and steadily improved, there was always a danger of crises and/or slowdowns in the overall performance of the economy. And it was in fact precisely in this complex of problems that the tendency to declining growth rates had its roots.

The slowdown in the growth of the labor force is a case in point. During the early stages of industrialization, a huge potential labor reserve was available. Women were drawn into the labor force and surplus farmers recruited for industry. From 1928, the start of the First Five-Year Plan, to 1940, employment of wage and salary workers increased at the rate of 9.5 percent a year. But once the main pre-existing labor reserves were tapped, the rate at which the workforce could be expanded depended on population growth and further redundancy of agricultural workers. Population growth, however, slowed down. The birth rate declined from 31.2 per thousand of the population in 1940 to 18.3 in 1980. And even though the death rate also fell, the natural increase of the population (births minus deaths) in 1980 was less than half what it had been in 1960.

The net effect of the drying up of existing labor reserves, heavy wartime losses, and lower birth rates has been an unavoidable slowdown in the rate of increase of employment. Instead of the 9.5 percent a year increase during the first two five-year plans, the annual growth rate was 3.8 percent in the 1960s, 2.2 percent in the 1970s, and only 0.9 percent between 1980 and 1985.

The declining rate of growth in employment is hardly a full explanation of the downward trend in the national income growth rate that began in the late 1950s. Theoretically, an increase in labor productivity could have made up for a lag in labor inputs. Productivity did indeed rise, but not enough to fill the gap. And the problem was compounded by the changing needs of a rapidly urbanizing society: the expanded need for services drew workers away from construction and industrial production.

These and other problems arising from the slowdown in the rate of growth of the labor force are certain to become more acute in the period ahead. Already the less than 1 percent growth rate of 1980–1985 has dropped, and Leonid Abalkin, one of Gorbachev's top economic advisers, warns that in "the next fifteen years the national income and the output of all branches of material production will grow without an increase in the workforce."[1]

A similar hindrance to growth showed up in the extraction of minerals. Blessed as the USSR is with ample natural resources, it is equally true that these are nonrenewable and subject to exhaustion. Thus, Abel Aganbegyan, another key economic adviser to Gorbachev, points out after discussing the difficulties arising from the declining labor force:

> Yet more striking are changes in the *extraction of fuel and raw materials*. In the 1971–75 period the volume of output of the mining industry increased by 25 percent but only by 8 percent in 1981–85. This decline in growth by a third was mainly connected with the worsening of the geological and economic conditions of mining. With its large-scale mining industry, currently the largest in the world, the Soviet Union is rapidly exhausting the most accessible of its natural resources. To maintain levels of extraction it is necessary to dig deeper, to discover new deposits and to transfer to less favorable fields. The fuel and raw material base in the inhabited regions of the country is already unable to meet our requirements and in many of them the volume of

extraction is declining. It is necessary therefore to discover new deposits in the north and eastern regions, to construct transport links, to create new towns and develop territories and attract population there.[2]

Problems relating to the production of raw materials are matched by others no less serious on the side of their utilization. Comparative international statistics strongly suggest that there is a great deal of waste and inefficiency in the use of material inputs in the Soviet Union. How else explain why the Soviet Union, with a much smaller industrial output than the United States, produces twice as much steel and consumes about 10 percent more electricity in industry? Equally puzzling is the situation in agriculture where the Soviet Union with a much smaller total output that the United States turns out about 80 percent more mineral fertilizer and at least three times as many tractors. These are only a few examples among many that could be cited: they point to the conclusion that Soviet planning practice from the beginning was focused on expanding production in the various separate sectors of the economy without paying adequate attention to their necessary interrelations.

Among the "laws of socialism" enshrined in Soviet textbooks was the supposed necessity to expand production of the means of production more rapidly than the means of consumption. It is therefore not surprising that planners, when faced with increasing problems of labor and material supplies, should seek a way out through expanding production in plant and equipment. Whatever the problem, more investment in means of production was the solution.

The trouble with this is that it flew in the face of experience dating back at least as far as the 1960s. As Moshe Lewin, one of the West's most insightful historians of the Soviet period, pointed out in 1974:

> Unnoticed for some time [in official circles] were those self-defeating features in the economic mechanism that had appeared in the early 1960s. Growing means devoted to accumulation and investment ironically led to falling returns on investment and a dwindling growth rate. . . . Research showed that the growing cost of the operation slowed down the whole process, and that the strategies employed had become blatantly counterproductive and urgently needed revision. The unilat-

eral devotion to priority of investment in heavy industry, which was supposed to be the main secret of success, together with huge injections of labor force and coercive political pressure, appeared as factors in this slowdown. Yet dogmas and the practices behind them were tenacious. Heavy industry still continued to be lavishly pampered, at the expense of consumption, with relatively more products serving heavy industry rather than benefiting consumption. "Production for production's sake" certainly expressed the position of the Soviet economy, and neither the standard of living nor the national income adequately benefited from it.[3]

One of the most serious consequences of investing in new plant and equipment as a remedy for all ills was neglect of existing industry. Normally, as an economy becomes industrialized, a larger and larger proportion of its capital investment is used to replace worn-out equipment. Because of the strong emphasis on creating additional capacity, this generalization does not apply to the Soviet Union, where on the average only about 2 percent of machinery and equipment has been replaced each year. "Under these circumstances," according to Leonid Abalkin, "it would take forty years to completely modernize [machinery and equipment] in industry, and in the engineering [and metal-working] industries it would take around fifty years."[4] Depreciation reserves have been used in the main to patch up worn-out equipment, with little being done to replace inefficient or obsolete machinery. By far the lion's share of investment goes to expanding the country's gross capital stock, a fact that goes far toward explaining why the ratio of capital to industrial output declined by almost 40 percent between 1960 and 1985. Workers have to operate inefficient and obsolete equipment, with frequent time out for breakdowns. Furthermore, to the extent that the new equipment is added with a view to compensating for inadequate supplies of labor, raw materials, and parts, it may only add to an already existing problem of unutilized productive capacity.

Clearly, the social and economic crisis that preceded Gorbachev was not an accidental phenomenon. As constituted, the Soviet economic system could produce growth as long as there were ample resources that could be mobilized. But with the exhaustion of the resources, the "magic" of the command economy evaporated.

By the late 1970s and early 1980s it had become apparent to important segments of the ruling elite that the well-trodden path was leading to a precipice. The stagnation of national income was alarming enough. But taken together with the incredibly steep drop in capital productivity, it looked as if the economy might be on the verge of going over the precipice and landing in an abyss.

Once this was understood—as it clearly was by Gorbachev and his circle of supporters and advisers when they came to power in 1985—the way out of the impasse seemed relatively straightforward. Much could be achieved by economizing on the use of energy and raw materials; the well-developed machine-building industry could be devoted to modernizing existing industry instead of continually expanding it; the accumulated knowledge and skill of the working class could be mobilized. And it was around a core of such measures as these, and in an atmosphere of excitement and optimism, that Gorbachev's ambitious program of *perestroika* (reconstruction) was launched.

The results, however, were far from what was expected. Not only was the crisis not overcome, it actually deepened. What needed to be done, in general if not in detail, was obvious. The trouble lay elsewhere in the very political and economic processes that produced the crisis in the first place: the repressive political system, the strategy of economic development, an overcentralized and cumbersome planning apparatus, above all a deeply entrenched bureaucracy jealously guarding its turf to protect jobs and privileges. In short, what was needed was not bright ideas but a radical overhaul of the entire political-economic structure.

To a certain extent, of course, *glasnost,* which accompanied *perestroika* from the beginning, was itself a move toward such an overhaul. Open discussion in areas previously hidden from the public view was not only allowed but encouraged. The dark side of the history of the Communist Party and Soviet society began to be revealed in a fresh wind of truth-seeking and truth-speaking. Exposés of current ills (corruption, alcoholism, prostitution, etc.) appeared in the media, along with harsh criticism of high officials and leading institutions. Censorship of literature, drama, and film was in large measure lifted. All of this freeing of speech was a necessary prelude to the reconstruction of the political system: an ongoing process aimed at a separation of the government from the Communist Party, revitalization of the state by empowerment of the soviets, and elections of delegates to these bodies at all levels from slates of candidates selected independently of the *nomenklatura.*

In an important sense this thrust toward democracy is consistent with the ideals that inspired the Bolshevik Revolution and very much in keeping with the socialist vision of Marx and Engels. Their views of the Paris Commune are especially relevant in this respect. In his introduction to the 1891 German edition of Marx's *The Civil War in France,* Engels hailed the Commune as a model of the dictatorship of the proletariat in action. Crucially important was the need for safeguards against corruption of state officials and the danger of their becoming masters instead of servants of the people:

> From the very outset the Commune was compelled to recognize that the working class, once come to power, could not go on managing with the old state machine; that in order not to lose again its only just conquered supremacy, this working class must, on the one hand, do away with all the old repressive machinery previously used against itself, and, on the other, safeguard itself against its own deputies and officials, by declaring them all, without exception, subject to recall at any moment. What had been the characteristic attribute of the former state?. . .
>
> Against [the] transformation of the state and the organs of the state from servants of society into masters of society—an inevitable transformation in all previous states—the Commune made use of two infallible means. In the first place it filled all posts—administrative, judicial, and educational—by election on the basis of universal suffrage of all concerned, subject to the right of recall at any time by the same electors. And, in the second place, all officials high or low, were paid only the wages received by other workers. . . . In this way an effective barrier to place-hunting and careerism was set up, even apart from the binding mandates to delegates to representative bodies which were added besides.

It should go without saying that the Soviet Union is very far from meeting the standards set by Marx and Engels in this and other writings. Yet in *glasnost* and related political reforms, it seems thus far to be at least facing in that direction.

Encouraging, important, and necessary as these moves toward democracy are, they still do not directly address the stubborn problems of the economic crisis in which the Soviet Union finds itself mired. Why?

As discussed earlier, structural problems in the supply of labor and materials brought about a long-run decline in the rate of growth of the economy, and the traditional panacea of Soviet planners—increasing the stock of capital goods—had lost its effectiveness and even become counterproductive. Here, perhaps more than anywhere else, the bureaucratic structure of the party and the state served as a protective shield against change. The administrative apparatus had plenty of ways to sabotage innovative reforms. Officials had little reason to be concerned about whistle blowers and other critics as long as the means of repressing trouble makers were at hand. Incompetence and corruption were covered up in an intertwined and interdependent network in which patronage played an ever present role. There was no way the counterweight to bureaucratic inertia inherent in the creative potential of the masses could express itself. The political turning to democracy was thus a necessary but not a sufficient condition for the reawakening of the economy.

Against this background, it is hardly surprising that Soviet economists, including Gorbachev's closest advisers, should conclude that the country's economic problems were attributable to the planning system and that the way out would be to substitute a system of economic regulation through markets as practiced under capitalism. This would involve freeing the various units that make up the economy from bureaucratic restraints and directives and allowing them to operate in the manner of competing enterprises in the market economies of the West. The results would presumably be elimination of shortages and waste and a greatly increased efficiency in the utilization of labor and materials.

This way of viewing markets and market economies is not wrong, but it is greatly simplified and can be seriously misleading. Markets have many purposes and consequences, and in any given context it is important not to omit or unduly neglect those that are of greatest relevance. In the kind of debates that are taking place today in both capitalist and noncapitalist societies, there are three functions of markets that are particularly important: (1) as a means of distributing goods and services to consumers; (2) as a mechanism for allocating productive resources among various uses; and (3) as a way of deciding how much individuals and groups get paid for their labor and/or other assets they own.

In capitalist societies, markets typically perform all three of the functions—modified to a greater or lesser extent (depending on the differing histories of the countries concerned) by state intervention of one sort or another. In planned societies of the Soviet type, on the other hand, only the first of these functions (distribution to consumers) is entrusted to the market (again with modifications), while the other two are for the most part discharged by executive organs of the state (presumably guided by the planners).

Capitalist markets of course operate on the principle of profit maximization. Competition supposedly forces all suppliers to sell at the same price. The more efficient gain higher profits and expand their share of the market. The less efficient stagnate or fall by the wayside. Capital (followed by labor) moves into industries with higher profit rates and out of those with lower, creating a tendency toward a uniform average rate of profit across all industries. Everywhere, in these circumstances, a system of competitive markets generates unremitting pressure on enterprises to produce at lowest possible costs and to gain advantage over rivals by introducing new products and new methods of production.

This is the textbook theory of a market economy which since the days of Adam Smith has dominated bourgeois ideology. It is easy to understand its enormous attraction for Soviet economists, confronted as they are by the rigidity, inefficiency, waste, and palpable failures of their own system of central planning and economic management. To the architects of *perestroika* nothing could have seemed more logical or appealing than substituting the elegant "magic" of the market for the discredited Stalinist "laws of socialism."

The trouble is that capitalist reality has never conformed with the textbook model, even under the most favorable conditions, while under less favorable conditions—such as exist in most of the third world today—the resemblance is close to nonexistent. The reasons are many and hardly need elaboration: the universal tendency of competition to turn into monopoly, the tendency of capital accumulation to generate wealth and income at one pole and deepening poverty at the other (not only within nations but between rich nations and poor nations as well), the system's periodic crises of overproduction and mass unemployment—and much, much more.

Are the *perestroika* reformers unaware of the manifold evils produced by market economies? It hardly seems likely. While most of them have had only limited contact with capitalist reality, they surely have had ample opportunity in the course of their studies to acquaint themselves with the history of capitalism and the contemporary problems and crises of the system, especially its third world underside. But if this is so, we may wonder that they would still embrace a comprehensive marketization of the kind described in the following statement by Abel Aganbegyan, considered by some to be the chief architect of *perestroika:*

> Let us now sum up what is meant by the extension and the intensification of the socialist market. We can safely say that the market will encompass the key sections of the economy and will play a very important, indeed crucial role in the further development of our country's economy. It will be in the marketplace that the goods and services produced by enterprises to satisfy money-backed demand will acquire their social value. It will be the market that balances production and demand in the country. And it will be through the market that production will start to depend more on consumer demand and will begin to satisfy social needs.[5]

Two possible explanations of this seemingly unconditional enthusiasm for the market suggest themselves.

First, the economic crisis that gave rise to *perestroika* has shown no signs of abating: on the contrary, it seems to have gotten worse. By the time of Aganbegyan's statement (and many similar pronouncements by his reforming colleagues), one can sense the emergence of a mood of desperation. Something has to be done quickly lest the situation get out of hand, and as far as the Soviet economists are concerned, the only measures they can conceive of are a more rapid and more intensive resort to marketization. True, this would run the risk of bringing with it the evils capitalist experience has shown to be associated with marketization. But the risk must be assumed, leaving the evils to be dealt with later.

A second possible explanation puts the attitude of the reformers in a different light, i.e., that they, reflecting the values and aspirations of the relatively privileged stratum of Soviet society to which they belong, feel in their heart of hearts that their place in the world is with the better-off, more privileged intelligentsia of the West. Capitalism, whatever its faults and shortcomings, has created in a few of its most advanced units a standard of living and a degree of security for its more fortunate citizens far beyond anything available in any other form of society, whether earlier or contemporary. Among these fortunate citizens are many in the arts, sciences, and professions whose status in their respective countries is below that of the ruling establishments but who live well, are influential in their own communities, and enjoy a wide latitude to dissent and criticize. Politically, most of these people are liberals or social democrats who believe in more or less basic reforms. Most Soviet reformers would doubtless like their own country to develop along similar lines, and they tend to see marketization as a necessary step in that direction. That it is also a step toward the restoration of capitalism may or may not be recognized; that degree of understanding may only come further along the road to capitalism.

Pressure for marketization is not the only indication that the Soviet reform movement has a capitalist orientation. Others are the strong preference for integration of the Soviet economy into the global capitalist network of trade and finance, and the great admiration for the high-tech culture of the advanced countries of the West, both of which permeate the Soviet reform literature. In evaluating these tendencies, it is important to preserve a sense of balance and to avoid falling into a sterile dogma of either condemnation or uncritical enthusiasm.

No sensible person believes that a socialist country should eschew economic relations with the capitalist world, but it is a time-honored tenet of socialist thought (and indeed of heterodox bourgeois thought as well) that a country with a weak economy that wants to maintain its independence and the possibility of charting its own course needs to protect itself against being overwhelmed and economically subjugated by stronger countries. The form this protection takes can vary according to circumstances, but what is essential is that the weaker country should have control over what it buys and sells abroad and the terms on which foreigners do business within its borders.

History records many cases of weak countries that have successfully defended their independence and have grown strong in the process (the United States and Japan are perhaps the two most outstanding examples). On the other hand, there are even more cases of weak countries shunning protective measures in the belief that laissez-faire in matters of trade and investment would be in their best interest. Most of these have ended up as dependents of their stronger partners, with their economies being shaped for the benefit of others rather than their own citizens. In the present international context there is no doubt that the Soviet Union is a weak economy vis-à-vis the advanced capitalist countries it wants to integrate with, and the *perestroika* literature certainly suggests a willingness to do so on terms very favorable to the capitalist side. If things actually develop along these lines (so far there is not much concrete experience to go by), it is hard to see how the Soviets can avoid increasingly adapting and adjusting their institutions and policies to the needs and preferences of their stronger partners.

With regard to the Soviet Union's relation to the high-tech culture of the West, no sensible person believes that in developing their economy the Soviets should avoid taking part in and deriving maximum benefit from today's ongoing scientific-technological revolution(s). But there are different ways of going about it. One is to be guided at all times by the needs and priorities of a huge country suffering from the grave problems and deprivations: the need to supply running water to hospitals, toilets for schools, sewers for villages, silos to save grain from going to waste, country-to-town roads, and much, much more.

How can the latest technology contribute to solving these problems? How can computers that make possible the exploration of space be adapted to the equally complex and challenging problems of national economic planning? How can modern industry and technology be reconciled with and harnessed to the task of saving the environment? How convert the monstrous engine of death and destruction that is the legacy of the Cold War to satisfy the urgent needs of liberated humanity? These are just examples of the infinite number of problems science and technology can help to solve.

But there is another way of taking part in the high-tech culture, and that is to become dazzled by the fads and fashions of upper-class Western consumerism; to see the accumulation of computers, automobiles, and gadgets of all kinds as the purpose of life; to elevate the quantity and style of personal possessions over the quality of life for society as the criterion for development and progress. These are the hallmarks of late capitalism and the frightening symptoms of its degradation and decay. There are unfortunately all too many indications that the Soviet reformers share the same values and aspirations and hope to see their own society join the club.

So far in our discussion of *perestroika* we have been dealing mostly with theories and blueprints. Apart from the very positive moves toward openness and democracy discussed above, very little has changed. Five years into *perestroika,* the structure of the economy and its working principles remain as they were. All the talk about marketization and what is supposed to go with it is just that—talk. Attempts to introduce private enterprise under the guise of cooperatives have yielded meager results and by all accounts have aroused more negative than positive feelings among the public. Meanwhile, the poor performance of the economy is not very different from the conditions that gave rise to *perestroika* in the first place.

There is nothing surprising in all this. Up to now the reformers have had little to offer except their marketization panacea. Their message seems to be: take from capitalism what has worked and hope that somehow the bad side effects will be absent or manageable. The trouble is that this is utopian thinking in the worst sense of the term. The conditions for a functioning, market economy in the capitalist world quite literally took centuries to evolve, and in some parts of it are still far from fully developed. Not only were suitable property relations necessary but so was a sophisticated legal system to regulate and enforce them. Perhaps even more important was the shaping of a "human nature" fit to operate such a system. The possessive individuals of classical political economy did not just appear one fine day to run the new economy. It took generations to create them. A similar process was under way in Tsarist Russia, but it was cut short by the revolution. Neither the institutional framework nor the human material needed for a functioning market system exists in today's Soviet Union, and bringing them into being can only be the work of decades, not months or even years. This is what we mean when we say that the idea of comprehensive marketization as a way of combatting the present Soviet economic crisis is hopelessly utopian.

If this argument is accepted, it follows that any realistic program for coping with the country's economic crisis has to start from the situation that actually exists. If the present system is not working—and it isn't—it has to be changed from within, not discarded in favor of another system which, whatever its supposed merits, is simply not a practical option in the relevant time frame. And change can only mean a massive infusion of new people with energy and ideas into the existing institutional framework.

How can this be achieved? To our way of thinking, the answer is: only through streamlining and speeding up the processes of democratization already under way. The assumption has to be made that there are human resources out there in the Soviet population, especially among the working people who constitute the vast majority, who, aroused and motivated, have the capability to turn things around.

As we write, crucially important elections at the local and regional levels are about to take place. They could be the beginning of a fundamental process of political change that clearly is a necessary condition for economic revival.

Necessary of course does not mean sufficient. New ideas and strong leadership are also needed. But they won't appear out of the blue. In fact, if they are to develop at all, it is likely to be in the course and as a result of an ongoing but still far from finished political revolution.

Socialists all over the world have not only an interest but a personal and political stake in what happens in the Soviet Union in this coming and decisive phase of the process that began with

Gorbachev's accession to office in 1985. We can only hope that the outcome will be positive and that it will set the stage for a following phase of economic recovery.

Notes

1. Leonid Abalkin, *The Strategy of Economic Development in the USSR* (Moscow: Progress Publishers, 1987), p. 21.
2. Abel Aganbegyan, *The Economic Challenge of Perestroika* (Bloomington: University of Indiana Press, 1988), p. 8.
3. Moshe Lewin, *Political Undercurrents in Soviet Economic Debate* (Princeton: Princeton University Press, 1974), pp. 132–33.
4. Abalkin, *Strategy of Economic Development,* p. 57.
5. Abel Aganbegyan, *Inside Perestroika* (New York: Harper and Row, 1989), p. 47.

WILLIAM HINTON

WHY NOT THE CAPITALIST ROAD?
THE TIANANMEN MASSACRE
IN HISTORICAL PERSPECTIVE

At five o'clock when I got back into the city I had a chance to go down to the Beijing Hotel, where a close friend of mine had a room on a high floor, and I went up there to see what was still going on at the square. The square was completely secure; there were two rows of soldiers blocking Chang An Street, and behind them a row of tanks, and behind those a whole rectangle of personnel carriers. The people kept coming from the east and getting as close as they dared to the troops and shouting at them, most of them trying to persuade them to cease and desist from killing people. Whenever 200–250 people gathered there the soldiers fired point blank and mowed them down. I only witnessed the last time this happened, but my friends who had been there all day and kept notes said it happened at least six times. Just about every hour on the hour it was time to shoot down the people, and they counted fifty bodies carried out of there assumed dead, not to mention the wounded. The army wouldn't allow any ambulances to go in, so the people who brought the bodies out were these pedicab men, some of whom have little freight bikes. They would rush in even while the firing was going on and pick up the casualties. At the time I saw this happen, the firing was absolutely intense and it lasted five minutes. How anyone survived it, I don't know. The only warning the victims had was that when the soldiers were about to fire, they ran forward a few steps, then aimed and fired. So during that second when they ran forward, people could drop to the ground. But each time, of course, people were killed, people were wounded, and some who ran away were shot in the back. It was a

143

most gruesome sight. The killing was absolutely unnecessary because the whole of Chang An Street was under control. The army had cleaned out the square and there was no reason to think that two hundred people, most of whom had come only to talk, could in fact threaten armed men. The response from the people that last time was to set fire to the last bus that still sat unburned in front of the Beijing Hotel. Flames and smoke billowed out and blew down in the soldiers' faces and obscured the people who were shot, so it was hard at that time to tell how many were killed or wounded.

I think the purpose of the assault didn't have so much to do with the students. It was pretty clear that if the government had waited another week or so there would have been almost no students in the square. They had done just about all they could do to raise issues and organize and mobilize. They had welcomed colleagues from all over the country, but more people were leaving every day than were arriving and the numbers were dwindling. If the authorities had waited another week, probably the square would have been quiet, and if the square had been quiet, the people would not have been mobilizing at night to prevent the army from coming to clear the square. There would have been no need for a military assault. But I think that Deng was extremely upset by the mobilization of people, by the millions that went into action. He was frightened by them, and he set out to punish them. You know, Deng is a man who likes to teach people a lesson. He sent the army into Vietnam to teach the Vietnamese a lesson, and of course, the Vietnamese taught the Chinese army a lesson. It wasn't necessary to use military force, but he wanted to send a strong signal to the people of China concerning who was boss, so he moved with force.

You may ask what I think the future holds. I think this government is very shaky, that Deng Xiaoping has really lost his mandate. Deng and his colleagues have alienated a large part of the army, a large part of the party, and the vast majority of the Chinese people—they really have no leg to stand on. They're ruling only with the gun and with terror.

There are differences among the people in this ruling group, but the differences relate to the pace and scale of privatization, to the mix of planning and free market, and so on. They are certainly not trying to build socialism—they're *all* capitalist roaders. And they've developed beyond that to the point of being bureaucratic capitalists with strong comprador tendencies. The one thing that united China in this movement was the disgust at corruption. The level of corruption in China has reached proportions similar to those that overwhelmed the Guomindang back before 1949. What made it possible was, on the one hand, the development of a free market, and on the other, state-controlled prices and quotas and a big state intervention. People with clout, people in high office, have been able to use their influence to buy commodities at low prices from the state and turn around and sell them at high prices on the free market. In this way they have been able to make huge fortunes which everyone in China believes are being salted away in Swiss bank accounts, in real estate deals, and so on. I think that this is certainly true. And the people who are doing this are mainly the sons and daughters of the top people. Zhao's sons are deeply involved, Deng Xiaoping's sons are deeply involved, though apparently Li Peng's sons are not. Yang Shangkun's whole family is involved and they're deeply involved in the army as well.

So you have what could be called the development of bureaucratic capitalism, government officials who are taking over hugh chunks of industry and combining them as private fortunes and then making comprador deals with external capitalists.

The surprising thing to me is the speed with which these reforms brought China to the crisis it's in today. The crisis is the direct outcome of reform policies, of the privatization of agriculture, the attempted privatization of industry, of the free market and of the decentralization which threw important economic decisions to regions, particularly coastal regions that then, making money fast and loose, bid against interior China for scarce goods, particularly raw materials. Conditions developed that brought the country close to economic chaos. The government could not guarantee supplies, power was cut down so much that factories worked two or three days instead of six, prices soared out of control, corruption became endemic, and all the moral degradation of the old society started to come back.

You have open prostitution, you have begging (you actually have the return of child mutilation so children can beg better), you have a huge pool of unemployed—last winter there were 50 million people uprooted from the countryside, who had no employment in the cities. In order to combat inflation the government shut down 10,000 construction projects and created 4 or 5 million more unemployed. You have these enormous contradictions all arising directly out of the reform. You have the virtual collapse of the birth control, family planning program. The birth rate is now much higher than China has acknowledged. You have a crisis in education, particularly in rural areas but also in the cities where funds are so short that they can't pay teachers adequately. They say if your money isn't enough, you should moonlight on another job. You have this weird situation where teachers in the classroom are running ice-cream concessions and soda pop stands, and trying to find second jobs and third jobs and of course neglecting their teaching. And then of course you have the privatization of health care, particularly at the grassroots level. There is an across-the-board decay of normal services and normal service standards, so that everyone is becoming angry.

The peasants have figured Deng out quite well. They have the impression that every time a problem arises, Deng will make a snap decision as to what to do about it and then, of course, the results often turn out less ideal than they should. Then he makes another snap decision which turns out even worse than the preceding one—a whole series of pragmatic decisions. So the peasants say "You no sooner think of it than you say it, you no sooner say it than you do it, you no sooner do it than it's a mess." And so it seems to be in one area after another. I believe that this massacre of the people of Beijing is exactly one of those terrible mistakes which Deng has made. In an effort to solve one problem he has jumped into much, much worse problems.

Of course, the Western media is presenting this as the last gasp of Communism and the ultimate result of having carried out a revolution, but it is not that at all. It's the ultimate result of having betrayed the revolution ten years ago. I haven't had the time to go back and search out those very cogent statements that Chairman Mao made about Deng, Liu Shaochi, and other capitalist roaders. On many separate occasions he said that if these people come to power our party will change color and we will end up with a fascist regime, and then the Chinese people will rise up and will again conduct revolution and change this. The only surprising thing to me is how fast this happened. Ten years ago Deng was a very popular man. Ten years ago he was supposedly saving China from the debacle of the Cultural Revolution and putting China back on its feet by introducing a measure of freedom and discussion, a free market and other liberating innovations. And here, ten years later, there is absolute military dictatorship, everyone is being forced to agree that a counterrevolutionary insurrection broke out, that the army did exactly the right thing, and that the organizers of this movement should be persecuted and punished.

One of the last things that happened to me in Beijing before I came home was that an old friend who is a party member came to me and said, "Yesterday we had our party meeting and we all had to *biaotai* (that is, express an attitude) and we had to say the army had acted justly in suppressing a counterrevolutionary insurrection. I also said those words, and I was lying and I've been lying so often, so many times and I'm sick of it, but I have to live here, I have to support my family. I have to lie in this circumstance, but I'm only hoping that you will be able to go home and not lie about what happened here."

The truth is, the students were not conducting an insurrection at all. They were not trying to overthrow the government. They were demanding Deng's resignation because he is eighty-four years old, corrupt, and his policies are jeopardizing China's future. And they are demanding the resignation of Li Peng primarily because he imposed martial law. Prior to the martial law decree they were asking for dialogue, a freer press, more democratic rights, public disclosure of high officials' assets. This is not equivalent to demanding the overthrow of the government; nor is calling on certain leaders to resign insurrectionary. This happens frequently in other countries, most recently in Japan, twice. But Deng regarded it as a terrible affront, as turmoil, as chaos, and he punished them for it.

Many people on the left in this country worry about the politics of the students: Aren't they rightists? Aren't they making bourgeois demands? Aren't they attacking socialism? Well, there is a lot of political diversity among the students; many of them look to Western capitalism as a model. They have rediscovered Adam Smith and the market and they harbor serious illusions about both. But the students are not the right wing in Chinese politics. The right wing consists of Deng and his group. The students are part of a huge progressive coalition—people in the middle, people to the left of the middle, and even some to the right of the middle—that is attacking the real reactionaries. Furthermore, as the movement develops it has to move to the left, and it is moving to the left. The students, on their own, do not have the power to transform China. To do that they have to go to the people, and when they go to the people they have to start dealing with the nitty-gritty issues of peasants' rights and workers' rights. They have to defend land-use rights and protect peasants against adverse price scissors. They have to stand with the workers against surrendering all prerogatives to management. They have to defend the "iron rice bowl," the job security workers won through revolution.

Some people in the United States are calling for the establishment of a new revolutionary party in China and the launching of a new revolution. My estimate is that there are large numbers of dedicated Communists in the Chinese Communist Party and also in the army. I foresee the possibility of change brought about by the mobilization of such people—perhaps through an army coup led by radical officers who can rally all the revolutionary elements in the army, in the party, and in society.

The Tiananmen Square massacre made clear to the world the corruption of the Chinese leadership. But to understand these events and their meaning a longer perspective is needed.

In the 1930s Chairman Mao declared that the capitalist road was not open to China in the twentieth century. The Chinese revolution against internal feudalism and external imperialism, he said, could not be a democratic revolution of the old type like the British or the French, a revolution to open the road for capitalism, but must be a democratic revolution of a new type, one that would open the road to socialism. In the first place, the imperialist powers would not allow China to carry out any transformation aimed at autonomous capitalist development if they could possibly help it. Every time any section of the Chinese people rose up to challenge traditional rule the powers intervened singly or in unison to suppress the effort by force of arms. This predictable response led Sun Yatsen to ask, "Why don't the teachers ever allow the pupils to learn?" The answer was, of course, that the landlord class as a whole and the compradors in business and government served as the main props of imperialist power in China; hence the latter used all its financial and military might to support, inspire, foster, and preserve these feudal survivals.

Moreover, capitalism was not an option, because as Mao said, "Socialism will not permit it." By this he meant that without allying with and winning support from all the socialist forces in the world—first of all the Soviet Union and second the working classes and working-class movements of Japan, Britain, the United States, France, Germany, Italy, and other countries—and the backing these provided through their own struggles against capitalism and imperialism, the Chinese revolution could not possibly succeed. In the modern era, defined by Mao as an era of wars and revolutions in which capitalism was unquestionably dying and socialism was unquestionably prospering, such an alliance and such support would come only as a response to a Chinese revolution of a new type, a Chinese revolution clearing the ground for working-class power and socialism and not for a Chinese revolution clearing the ground for bourgeois class power and capitalism.

Finally, China's independent national bourgeoisie was weak and vacillating. It could not possibly take on both the Chinese landlords and the imperialists and their Chinese comprador partners without fully mobilizing both the working class and the peasantry. But mobilizing the working class meant putting certain limits on managerial power and meeting certain working-class demands, while mobilizing the peasantry meant carrying out land reform. This could not be done without confiscating the wealth of the landlord class from which the bourgeoisie had, in the main, arisen and to which it still maintained myriad ties. Furthermore, the confiscation of property in land threatened the foundations of all private property and caused the capitalists, much as they desired liberation from feudalism and imperialism, to vacillate. Over and over again the national bourgeoisie proved incapable of firm national leadership against the people's enemies, foreign and domestic. Leading the Chinese democratic revolution thus shifted, by default, to the working class, more numerous by far and older and more experienced than the bourgeoisie, and to the Communist Party that established itself as spokesman for all the oppressed.

New Democracy Proposed

With the Communist Party assuming leadership in the revolution, mobilizing both workers and peasants by the millions, and threatening to confiscate not only all the land of the landlords but all the property of the imperialists and their comprador and bureaucratic allies, the first goal of the revolution could hardly be capitalism. Mao projected a new national form, a mixed economy heavily weighted on the side of public and collective ownership with the joint state-private and wholly private enterprises of the national capitalists playing a minor supporting role. Hence the concept of a New Democratic revolution, a New Democratic transitional period, and a New Democratic state founded after victory with a mandate to carry land reform through to the end and to nationalize the wealth (industrial, commercial, and financial) monopolized by the four ruling families. Once these projects had been completed, the overriding task would be to launch a socialist revolution.

Given the world situation of the 1930s with capitalism in crisis, the Soviet Union booming with new construction, regional wars merging into all-out global war and the third world on the brink of revolution, Mao argued convincingly that China had no choice but socialism. Now fifty years later, at a time when resurgent capitalism demonstrates temporary stability while socialist construction flounders and the "four tigers" of the Pacific Rim (Hong Kong, Taiwan, South Korea, and Singapore) take off, the seers are writing off Mao's compelling logic as anachronistic, irrelevant, even quaint.

In full agreement with the West on the castigation of Mao, China's leaders, after ten years of national and civil war, thirty years of socialist construction, and ten years of capitalist-road reforms, still talk socialism. But they practice massive privatization as they integrate their country as fast as possible into the world market. Optimistic, confident, even arrogant as they were at the start, however, their policy has had enough appalling consequences to place its whole orientation in doubt. And so, like it or not, the old question of whether China can achieve the goal of becoming a strong, modern, independent nation by taking the capitalist road is shouldering its way back onto the agenda.

My view is that autonomous self-generating national capitalism for China is no more viable an option today than it was in 1930, 1950, or 1970. Numerous obstacles stand in the way, some of them extensions of long-standing historical phenomena, others newly created in the course of revolution, land reform and thirty years of socialist construction. Crucial among them are the state of the world economy, the nature of the Chinese state, working-class resistance, and peasant self-sufficiency, the ability of the rural poor to survive on subsistence plots.

In regard to the world economy the strategy of the reformers is to build China into a genuine NIC (newly industrialized country) by following the path pioneered by South Korea, Taiwan, Hong Kong, and Singapore—that is, by taking advantage of the country's cheap labor to solicit foreign capital and start up large-scale manufacture of labor-intensive commodities—primarily textiles but also electric and electronic appliances—for the world market. To this end China created free-trade zones, invested billions in infrastructure, borrowed billions more, and entered the export arena full of hope. But so far China has failed to consolidate an appropriate market share.

This failure has two main causes. First, the expansion of the world market, which once soaked up most offered goods, is now slowing up. As the 1980s wind down, glut not scarcity plagues the globe. The window of opportunity that South Korea and the other "tigers" leaped through is closing fast. Furthermore, they never would have been in a position to make that leap without the economic muscle provided by two protracted American wars for mainland staging grounds against China, wars that called forth decades of heavy U.S. spending on China's open flanks. While many Chinese now look with envy at Taiwan and South Korea and conclude that China took the wrong road, what they fail to understand is that without the challenge which the Chinese revolution posed to the American Century there would be no "tigers" on the Pacific Rim today.

Second, even if the window were still open, even if the market was as lively as ever, it could not hope to absorb the output of a country the size of China. It is one thing for small countries with workforces numbering in single digit millions to tool up for labor intensive exports, but quite another for a Chinese workforce numbering in tens, even hundreds of millions to do the same. It never was reasonable to expect that China could duplicate what small Pacific

Rim countries had done. Only a few ever succeeded at it and even those are now moving toward crisis. Other contenders, such as Brazil, Mexico, and India, have run into serious problems without finding any viable road to solvency.

The World Bank strategy of opening third world economies to international market forces by privatizing, liberalizing, making concessions to foreign investors, and concentrating on exports has sharply escalated their dependency on world markets and foreign bank loans. Unable to service their rapidly mounting debts, most of the countries involved have frozen wages, devalued currencies, and cut spending, including spending on vital inputs. Living standards have dropped precipitously. At the same time the cutbacks undermine the economies of the exporting countries, deepening the glut on the supply side of the market. The entire strategy is now clearly bankrupt.

In the final decade of the century the only viable strategy for the third world is to reverse the whole process, diversify, develop internal markets for domestic goods and services and thus reduce dependence. To do this third world countries have to carry out land reform, set up progressive taxation, guarantee workers' rights—all things that China did, was doing, and was doing well prior to the reform. Yet China's leaders still harbor illusions about the NIC model of development, and pin their hopes on a strategy whose time has passed and which for China, given the size of the country and the labor pool available, never could provide an adequate framework for development.

Rice Bowls: Bright, Hard, and Brittle

The internal barriers to capitalist road development in China are today as formidable as the external ones. They can be summed up as (1) the "golden rice bowl"; (2) the "iron rice bowl"; and (3) the "clay rice bowl." The "golden rice bowl" refers to the prerogatives exercised by bureaucrats in office at all levels in the state system over the economy under their control and management and, as a consequence, over their own substantial salaries, fringe benefits, and illicit windfall profits.

The power they wield is essentially feudal, with roots in the highest development of Chinese ancient society, the centralized bureaucratic state where power adhered not to wealth, landed or otherwise, but to government office. Now that, as a consequence of revolution, the government owns most of the economy, official position confers immense and unprecedented economic power. For this reason some young economists have begun to characterize the Chinese system as a "position-power economy." Hua Sheng, Zhang Xuejen, and Luo Xiaoping, writing in the magazine *Economic Research,* used this term recently to describe the present system, one that cannot move toward free market regulation because of government intervention. They bemoan China's failure to establish a functioning national market: "The root cause lies in our failure to separate political power from economic management. The Chinese economy today is, to a significant extent, manipulated by political power. . . . True price reform demands that the country's political as well as economic infrastructure be overhauled." They conclude that "genuinely market oriented reform requires the state to cede its power and responsibility over almost all economic fields to economic bodies. It should allow market participants with full control of their assets to oversee pricing and other economic decisions."[1]

But one may ask: How can these omnipotent bureaucratic powerholders be expected to liquidate their own historical prerogatives and surrender control to technocrats and entrepreneurial upstarts operating under the vagaries of the market? History has no precedent for such behavior. Indeed, this point is argued well in another recent article: "However much the reformer-bureaucrats want to utilize market forces to break through bureaucratic immobilism, they cannot do so," writes Richard Smith, "because to permit real market forces to prevail would destroy the bureaucracy's means of existence and reproduction as a class."[2]

So far the reform in China has ceded some central state power to lower levels such as provinces, major municipalities, and special trading zones, but this has only encouraged lower level bureaucrats to escalate self-enrichment by exercising their local monopoly of power. This often means protecting and advancing regional and sectional interests at the expense of neighbors and the nation. If the reform has dispersed some "position power" it has certainly not dissolved the power system as a whole. Meanwhile, the independent kingdoms where devolved power has come to rest are virtually immune to central control.

How to create a national market in the face of such powerful bureaucratic intervention is a big unresolved problem. No one familiar with Chinese history can be too sanguine about blunting, not to mention abolishing, traditional bureaucratic prerogatives. The whole phenomenon poses as big an obstacle to developing socialism as it does to developing capitalism—which is one major reason why Mao launched the Cultural Revolution.

The "iron rice bowl" refers to the guaranteed lifetime jobs and benefits to which all regular workers in state enterprises are entitled. The reformers view these guarantees as the major stumbling block to raising labor productivity and modernizing the economy. "Working slowly is fairly common in state-owned factories," write Hua, Zhang, and Luo. "In return for their dependence [on the state] people actually monopolize the work posts they fill. . . . They are guaranteed lifelong tenure and needn't worry about unemployment or bankruptcy."

Reformers long to apply the "stick" of job competition and enterprise failure to these people. They want to transform the relations of production in ways that will force tenured workers onto the labor market and turn their labor power into a commodity—as it must be in any capitalist country.

But from the workers' point of view lifelong job security and its accompanying prerogatives are among the primary accomplishments of the revolution. They are something to cherish and defend. They are what gives meaning to the phrase "the workers are the masters of the factories." If bosses can hire and fire at will, if the reserve army of the unemployed waits to swallow all those rendered redundant for whatever reason, what is left of workers' rights? What is left of socialism?

"Focusing on the lack of free and independent trade unions and the right to strike, [outsiders] assumed that the working class was a helpless controlled victim of the party apparatus," writes James Petras.[3] "A closer view of Chinese factory reality, however, reveals that the Chinese working class operates within a tight network of relations that protect workers from firings, speedup, and arbitrary managerial initiatives, job safeguards that far exceed those found in most Western democracies and would be the envy of many unemployed steel workers." Petras concludes that the reforms are "not only economic reforms but can be more accurately described as socio-political measures designed to restore managerial prerogatives and dismantle the dense network and norms that have been in place since the Revolution."

Viewed realistically, the slowdown on the plant floor is not the inevitable result of the "iron rice bowl," the wonderful job security the revolution has provided for workers, but a response to the "golden rice bowl" of the officials, the managers, the bosses. When cadres take advantage of "position power" to enrich themselves and their offspring "to establish connections to get rare goods, desirable apartments, opportunities for going abroad, promotion and so on,"[4] why should wage workers break their backs? In the past those state leaders who were motivated by socialist norms could mobilize the working masses for socialist competition. They could inspire socialist production enthusiasm and achieve "better, faster more economical results." But to do this they had to apply the same set of standards to all. They could not practice self-enrichment up above and expect serve-the-people, build-the-country commitment down below. Unfortunately such officials were far too few in the past and all but nonexistent today.

The reformers, however, do not address the "golden rice bowl" problem. Just the opposite. While paying lip service to socialist morality, they put their faith in making management prerogatives preeminent across the board at the expense of workers' rights and entitlements. They insist on confronting workers with the threat of summary dismissal or job loss due to bankruptcy. They place their faith in fear as the prime source of diligence.

This attitude will inevitably lock the reformers into a showdown battle with a working class that has experienced three decades of socialist relations of production and will not surrender any hard-won right easily. It is a battle that has only just begun, and one which the reformers have no assurance of winning.

Small-Plot Security

The "clay rice bowl" refers to the use-rights to the land, which the peasants still retain as the legacy of their land acquisitions during land reform. I call it a clay bowl because the income derived from this source is fragile. Unlike the wages of workers and the salaries of officials, returns from the land depend, in great measure, on sweat, pests, and the weather. Peasants fertilize, till, plant, hoe, and harvest but what they reap will always be, for the most part, beyond their individual control. Their clay rice bowl may reward them bountifully or return nothing at all. Unlike gold or iron it is vulnerable to outside forces and at the mercy of "heaven."

In order to establish capitalism and make the market supreme, China's rulers must create conditions for primitive accumulation, which means, first and foremost, separating large masses of peasants from the land and making sure they have nothing to sell but the skills of their hands—in short, turning their labor power into a commodity.

But during the New Democratic revolution in the early 1950s every peasant got a share of that most precious and basic means of production, the land. During the cooperative period they pooled their plots, village by village, to form collectively owned and tilled fields. Decades later the state began to treat collective ownership as public ownership. Thus, when the reform began, what each peasant got was a renewable right to use small plots of publicly owned land for a limited period of years. Quite commonly, during the reform drive, communities first allocated per capita shares, what could be called subsistence plots, to every man, woman, and child, then contracted whatever land remained to those families interested in farming for a living, to those who were willing to raise grain for sale—quota grain for sale to the state at contract prices and surplus grain for sale to the market at whatever price it might bring. Under this system a substantial proportion of the cropland in China lies outside the sphere of commerce. It provides a food source of last resort to the rural masses regardless of conditions in the general economy. The underemployed and ill-equipped peasants, given good weather, can probably survive on these miniscule holdings. To prosper, however, the ablebodied laborers among them must set up nonfarm sidelines or seek work beyond the village. Either way, they tend to neglect the land, farming it indifferently, even letting it lie idle when wage work expands, transport booms, and peddling pays, then skimming off whatever crop they can coax from the neglected soil when the downturn comes.

The reformers hoped and planned that after the break-up farming specialists would be able to contract use-rights from less committed neighbors and create holdings of scale suitable for mechanization and scientific management. But since most small holders regard their plots as social insurance against unemployment, enterprise failure, or other personal disaster such as illness or old age, few have been ready to yield up their per capita use-rights to others even when they do not exercise them themselves. What this means overall for Chinese agriculture is that a substantial part of the nation's scarce cropland, all of which ought to produce to the utmost, will produce at far below its potential for a long time to come.

Recent developments—the sudden withholding of credit, the shutting down of thousands of construction sites, the failure of thousands of small rural enterprises—threw millions of peasants out of off-farm work. This demonstrated as nothing else could that peasant reluctance to part with per capita land-use rights was shrewdly grounded. But this same reluctance also means that the conditions for primitive accumulation in China cannot easily be satisfied. The reforms cannot easily reduce peasant labor power to a commodity in the usual sense, nor can they easily make all land marketable. Per capita land use rights as distinct from contracted rights, though theoretically subject to lease or purchase, are not often surrendered. In the long run food production suffers serious erosion. Those who control the use-rights, the peasant masses, cannot and do not utilize them to the full, while those who might develop their potential, the crop-raising specialists, cannot get their hands on them.

Crop specialists, on their part, contracting only the land that is left after the per capita distributions, also work only scattered strips of land, the pathetic "noodle strips" that now characterize Chinese farmland; hence their labor productivity is extremely low. Few can make as much money by farming as they can by leaving the land. Consequently, to keep people farming community after community has to subsidize the contractors with free materials and services.

Privatization has thus created a situation that all but guarantees agricultural stagnation. Without a sound agricultural base there is little chance for the rest of the economy to prosper. Beijing authorities are blaming this year's chronic power shortages on lack of coal, which in turn they blame on lack of transport, which in turn they blame on lack of power. But if one looks more deeply into the problem one finds that Shanxi coal has been in short supply all winter because the itinerant miners who staff the private and the collective mines responsible for half the province's production have quit in droves because they could not afford grain at this year's inflated free market prices. So the power shortage really stems from the grain shortage. All the above phenomena—the glut on the commodity markets of the world, especially in labor-intensive industrial goods, the "golden rice bowl," the "iron rice bowl," and the "clay rice bowl"—none of which are easy to exorcise—make the capitalist road a very arduous and uncertain one for China to take.

Even if China could somehow overcome the barriers en route, it would still only achieve, as Petras has pointed out, an economy plagued as other third world economies have been by "short-term growth punctured by long-term stagnation; foreign dependence, leading to capital inflow in boom periods and outflow during crises; and management controls that maximize competitiveness but provoke adversarial class relations."[5] These are hardly consequences that favor the creation of an autonomous self-generating economy capable of providing a reasonable level of prosperity for a majority of the Chinese people.

Notes

1. Hua, Zhang, and Luo, cited in "Top Economists Look Back Over Decade of Reform," *The China Daily*, four-part series, December 1988, p. 1.
2. Richard Smith, "Class Structure and Economic Reform," paper presented at the Columbia Seminar on Modern China, 12 September 1987, p. 7.
3. James Petras, "Contradictions of Market Socialism in China," unpub. ms., 1987, pp. 5–6.
4. Hua, Zhang, and Luo, *The China Daily*.
5. Petras, "Contradictions," p. 1.

MICHAEL BURAWOY

MARXISM IS DEAD,
LONG LIVE MARXISM!

Marxism is dead. So we are told. It has shown itself to be morally, politically, and economically bankrupt: it justified the gulag, the Soviet-Nazi pact; it provided the foundation of totalitarianism, the decimation of the peasantry, the denial of civil rights to its working class and oppressed nations, as well as armed invasions of its colonies in Eastern Europe; through its advocacy of planning it promoted proverbial inefficiency, waste, shortages and low standards of living. The bankruptcy of Marxism as ideology spells its death as science. The prediction of a socialist future is its most fundamental flaw. The failure of Communism proves that there can be no future after capitalism. Communism is only a nightmarish detour: the longest road from capitalism to capitalism. The scourge of Marxism has finally been laid to rest.

So speak the jubilant apostles of Marxism's demise. But what form of idealism is this that attributes such demonic powers to an ideology, to a system of ideas? And, if Marxism is so all-powerful, why would it so calmly wither away? Their claim that Marxism is responsible for the failure of "Communism," while flattering to the power of Marxism, receives little substantiation from historians who also call attention to the conditions of the Soviet revolution—the legacy of backwardness, the encirclement by industrially more advanced nations, fighting first a civil war and then bearing the brunt of a world war, the arms race, and so it goes on.

As to Marxism's status as a science, far from being a refutation of Marxism, Soviet Communism's failure to realize the promises of socialism is a powerful vindication of Marxism. After all, the social-democratic wing of Marxism, in the tradition of Eduard Bernstein, George Plekhanov, or Karl Kautsky, was forever condemning the Bolsheviks for usurping history. Even the revolutionary Rosa Luxemburg, while ardently supporting the Bolshevik seizure of power in 1917, warned them not to make a virtue out of a necessity: premature seizure of power is a necessary part of the world revolutionary process, and the Bolsheviks had been compelled to do so under the most difficult of circumstances, but they should not turn the peculiarities of the Russian Revolution into a model for subsequent revolutions. Moreover, she added, without parliamentary assemblies, without freedom of press and association, without free expression of opinion, "life dies out in every public institution" and the dictatorship of the proletariat becomes the dictatorship of bureaucracy.

Except for postrevolutionary Marxism-Leninism, Russian Marxism was no more optimistic about the prospects of socialism in one country. As early as 1906 Trotsky was anticipating both the inevitability and the degeneration of a Russian revolution. He was destined to become a carrier and then a victim of the very forces he predicted would ensnare the revolution—forces he would analyze in great detail when later cast into exile. Like Trotsky, Lenin insisted that without revolution in the West the Russian revolution was doomed. His foreboding and fear of bureaucratization and his embrace of state capitalism through the New Economic Policy are too well known to need recounting here. Even Marx and Engels themselves were unequivocal: "The development of productive forces is an absolutely necessary practical premise because without it *want* is merely made general, and with *destitution* the struggle for necessities and all the old filthy business would necessarily be reproduced." If communism was to be, it would come only after the entire world had been conquered for capitalism.

The "Marxism is dead" school would do well to confine its self-congratulation to the burial of Marxism-Leninism, if only for reasons of self-preservation. They violate history when they reduce all Marxisms—the writings of Marx and Engels, the German Marxists, the original Russian Marxism, and the Frankfurt School, and third world Marxism—to Marxism-Leninism. More sophisticated anti-Marxism recognizes the plurality of Marxisms but claims that Marxism-Leninism is but their logical culmination, their highest expression. The dogma of Marxism-Leninism is read back into all Marxism. It is the pure form of the cancer which afflicts all its varieties. These conclusions rest less on careful analysis of the history of Marxism and more on the religiosity of anti-communism.

I too am celebrating the death of Marxism-Leninism, but as the death of a ruling ideology which, in the name of Marxism, sought alternately to hide and justify class domination. Petrification besets any ideology which is used to deny or rationalize the violation of its core commitments. What we are witnessing, therefore, is not the death of Marxism but the death of its most degenerate branch. Or to put it another way, we are witnessing the *liberation of Marxism* from forces which have often distorted and stunted its growth. The winds of *glasnost* may spread the seeds of new revitalized Marxisms, but can they meet the challenge of *perestroika*—the transformations of the Soviet Union and Eastern Europe?

The Rise and Fall of State Socialism

According to the "death of Marxism" school, the end of communism spells the rise of capitalism. It is assumed there are only two possibilities—communism which has been discredited and capitalism which has been vindicated. But to assume this choice it to make the same mistake as Marx and Engels, who thought the end of competitive capitalism spelled the end of all capitalism. Why should the end of barracks communism, or what I prefer to call "state socialism," be the end of all socialism? Indeed, in an ironic twist on Marx and Lenin's theories of the transition from capitalism to communism, history now poses not just the question of the transition from *communism to capitalism* but also from *communism to socialism*. But irony takes a further twist for, as I shall argue, Marxism's theory of transitions works even better for state socialism than it does for capitalism.

Before examining the transformation of state socialism let me recapitulate how Marx's theory was supposed to play itself out for capitalism. Historical materialism treats history as the intersection of class struggle and the law-like unfolding of social relations which are both indispensable and independent of an individual's will. With respect to capitalism, privatized appropriation first advances and then fetters socialized production, galvanizing the working class into revolutionary action. More specifically, capitalists compete in the marketplace for profit by lengthening the working day, intensifying labor, and cutting wages, but above all by introducing new technology which simultaneously deskills work and increases the reserve army of unemployed. Once one capitalist finds new ways to extract more surplus, every capitalist must follow suit on pain of extinction. The results follow just as inexorably: mounting production of goods which can no longer find buyers, the destruction of forces of production, and the accumulation of waste. These same economic processes create a class structure polarized between the concentration of capital and a working class made up of homogenized deskilled labor whose struggles, first in the economic arena and then in the political, intensify as its position deteriorates. Thus, as capitalism creates ever deeper economic crises so it creates its own gravedigger in the form of a revolutionary working class.

There are, of course, many flaws in this theory and Marxists have devoted much energy to reconstructing the original analysis by developing theories of imperialism, underdevelopment, combined and uneven development, monopoly capitalism, state intervention, ideological hegemony, capitalist patriarchy, capitalist democracy, dual labor markets, contradictory class locations, and so on. Indeed, the vitality of Western Marxism has resided precisely in the bold and imaginative theories that turn apparent refutations of Marxism into illuminating confirmations.

How might historical materialism be applied to the transformation of state socialism? The defining attribute of state socialism is state appropriation and redistribution of surplus. The forces of production, while owned by the state, are managed in enterprises which have a discrete organization. Historically, the state begins by directing enterprises to produce specified products, ones necessary to build the infrastructure of an industrial society: energy, transportation, education, communication, steel. In laying the foundations of industrialization, Soviet planning can claim considerable success—if at great human cost. Central ownership created obstacles to economic development as goods became more specialized, catering to consumer needs. Central control was relaxed to give greater autonomy to enterprises which would now compete for resources from the center in order to enhance the political position of their managers. Bureaucratic competition, every bit as fierce as market competition, gives rise to its own irrationalities. To paraphrase Marx, from a form of development of the logic of production, the logic of investment turns into its fetter.

This perspective on the continued vitality of Marxism as it applies to state socialism comes from my experiences in Eastern Europe over the last seven years. The Hungarian steel industry, where I worked as a furnaceman between 1985 and 1988, illustrated the contradictory forces that enmeshed the entire society. As in other socialist countries, the production of steel was the rallying cry and emblem for socialist development in the 1950s. Resources poured into the steel industry. A new Stalin Steel Works (now known as the Danube Steel Works) was created and two other steel works in the north were expanded. In the 1950s, what mattered most was the volume of steel produced. This amount could be laid out in planned directives from the central authorities. But with the growth of industry, the production of diverse steels became imperative. New investment was planned in the 1970s which would introduce modern technology and afford the production of quality steel. Leading these developments was the construction of a new combined steel mill within the huge complex of the Lenin Steel Works at Miskolc, recently renamed the Diósgrör Technical and Metallurgical Works. It combined a German basic oxygen converter, Japanese continuous caster and electric arc furnace, and a Swedish vacuum degaser. The Combined Steel Works came on line in 1981 at the very height of the international crisis in steel production. Instead of making a profit and producing steel for export as expected, the Lenin Steel Works went further into the red, so much so that its director committed suicide. Having battled for scarce foreign currency against the two other steel enterprises, he had to deliver but failed.

The Lenin Steel Works outlived its director to begin to produce quality steel for the manufacturing industry. But only with difficulty. It was surrounded by a sea of more backward technology which produced unreliable inputs. Outdated blast furnaces produced pig iron of inconsistent quality; another major ingredient, scrap, was not even graded. The rolling mills which process the molten steel were also from another era. This uneven development of technology is not a function of error or corruption but of the "rationality" or "irrationality" of a bureaucratic bargaining in which resources are distributed according to political criteria. Instead of all new investment being concentrated in the renovation of one steel mill, it was divided among three steel mills, leading to partial renovation and therefore uneven development within each.

Within the Combined Steel Works itself, the production of quality steel tended to be a hit-or-miss affair. Having visited other steel mills I know that these problems are endemic to steel production in Western countries, particularly the United States. But under state socialism problems of internal coordination are acute because of shortages. In a centrally directed economy, paternalism governs the relations between state and enterprise. Enterprises are rarely closed down, although their managers may be removed. In order to protect and advance their interests, enterprise managers seek to garner more resources , particularly investment resources, from the state. Their demands become insatiable, equalled only by the intense bureaucratic rivalry for those resources. Inevitably this leads to shortages, which in turn leads to hoarding and the further exacerbation of shortages. Shortages and the unreliable quality of inputs are very disruptive to any complex production process. Such uncertainty has often generated distinctive flexible and autonomous forms of work organization on the shop floor. For a time these even became formalized in types of inside contracting systems—self-organized, self-selected groups of workers would bid for specialized tasks to be completed in extra hours. But there were definite limits to their expansion as they threatened the political interests of middle managers.

With increased demand for variegated products, Marx's theory of the fettering of the forces of production by the relations of production is vindicated. But what about history as the history of class struggle? Marx distinguished between changes in the material conditions, that is the evolving conflict between forces and relations of production, and the ideological forms in which people become conscious of this conflict and fight it out. To understand the ideological terrain we must first turn to the distinctive form of politics engendered by centralized ownership.

From Painting Socialism to Painting Democracy

Within the Marxist framework private appropriation provides its own legitimation—ownership of the means of production bestows individual rights of control over what is produced by workers. There is a close correspondence between capitalist relations of production and the ideology of individualism and individual rights. Class relations are thereby mystified. With state socialism, on the other hand, centralized appropriation and thus class relations are transparent: there are conceivers (planners) and executors (direct producers). Because it is palpable, central appropriation has to be legitimated, which makes state socialism vulnerable to immanent critique—to the discrepancy between ideology and reality. State socialism promises justice and equality but produces injustice and inequality. State socialism promises efficiency, but all around we find waste and inefficiency. Its ruling class continually "paints" socialism, that is, presents it in a light that is clearly falsified by day-to-day experience. This painting of socialism is not simply the bombardment of political messages, it is also embedded in compulsory rituals—in campaigns, production conferences, marches, and brigade competitions.

This immanent critique, this condemnation of existing socialism for not living up to its promises, can lead to either an endorsement of "true" socialism or a cynical rejection of socialism altogether. The adoption of one or another of these alternatives varies over time and between classes. During the first twenty years of "communist rule" in Eastern Europe, revolutionary movements challenged the social order in the name of socialism. They sought a renewal of socialism. This was true of Hungary in 1956, among the followers of Imré Nagy, among leading intellectuals, as well as among workers who set up elaborate networks of workers' councils. In Czechoslovakia in 1968, intellectuals led the search for a socialism with a human face, followed by independent workers' struggles. By 1981, Polish discourse had become increasingly anti-Marxist and often antisocialist, yet Solidarity's project was still a socialist one in which the direct producers would reappropriate control of civil society within the shell of a socialist state. Solidarity has now been hijacked by intellectuals hungry for the market and Western capital, all in the name of democracy.

The convulsions we have been witnessing for nearly a year now have shifted the discourse from an immanent critique of state socialism to the celebration of democracy. The vocabulary of socialism has lost all credibility among all classes of Eastern Europe. It has become the currency of an aggressive war of delegitimation. *Painting socialism* has been replaced by *painting democracy*. Ideology and reality are as far apart as ever. Ritual affirmations of the magic of democracy are sowing the seeds of its destruction. For the moment it binds people on the basis of what they reject. But as a positive program it portends intense class war. Let me sketch the class forces that are colliding on the terrain of Hungarian democracy.

While never denying the progressive attributes of bourgeois democracy, Marxism has always been skeptical about its claim to freedom, particularly as it relates to the working class. That view finds substantial confirmation in Hungary. When I ask my workmates in the Lenin Steel Works about politics and democracy they shrug their shoulders. They can't figure out the difference between the parties. They all promise a better future, they all condemn the past. So when workers discuss politics they talk about the corruption of the party leadership and the latest scandal that has erupted in Budapest. They talk about the bonuses their bosses receive and their continuing misuse of resources. I ask whether the investments by foreign capital have made much difference and they laugh. Cynicism is widespread, not just at the workplace, but at home too. A widowed pensioner, hardened by working in industry all her adult life, now has to find odd jobs because rampant inflation makes it impossible to live off her pension. She complains that it doesn't matter who is in power, Hungarian leaders have always looked after one another. "Why don't we put some of these people on trial like they are doing in East Germany? They tell us such show trials would be bad for foreign investment!" For the working class, democracy is only meaningful if it gives them some real control over those who run society, over what happens to the products of their effort.

They have good reason to be skeptical of democracy and electoral politics. What, after all, does democracy mean to the *apparatchiks* of the state and the managers of industry? For them democracy means the freedom to assume private ownership of state property. It means the freedom for the *nomenklatura* to turn itself into a class of capitalists. Democracy affords a legal route to the transformation of property relations without a change in class membership. New legislation allows erstwhile managers and *apparatchiks* to write off their taxes if they accept (!) privatization loans from the government to buy up either their own or other state enterprises. Egged on by U.S. bankers, the state is trying to divest itself of all its property as quickly as possible. Foreign capital is invited to buy up state enterprises for a fraction of their book value. It turns out that there are always capitalists ready to buy property, even socialist property, for peanuts. As Lenin once wrote, the omnipotence of wealth is more certain in a democratic republic.

But why should managers get the enterprises rather than workers? You may well ask. Others asked this too and so legislation was proposed which would allow workers to buy up shares in their companies. However, it was argued that workers don't understand the meaning of risk so they, unlike managers, have to pay for their shares out of their personal savings! The legislation seemed designed to make worker buy-outs impossible. The struggle goes on, for some do realize that turning state property over to managers and foreign capital could court political disaster, particularly since the project is being financed by increasing taxes (most recently on private mortgages) and by eliminating state subsidies on some basic items while reducing it on others (such as rent). Thus, for example, subsidies for workers' dormitories were withdrawn and so homelessness for the first time became a public issue in January of this year. Inflation is expected to be 40 percent in 1990—unimaginable under the previous regime.

What are the unions doing? One of my friends who works for Miskolc City Transportation has just been elected, against her will, to shop steward. The union, she says, is a "big nothing." All talk and no action. The bosses still decide everything. In a few isolated enterprises workers have thrown out their unions and established their own councils, but it is not clear what to do next. There is no party that speaks specifically to workers. The communist party transformed itself from the Hungarian Socialist Workers' Party to the Hungarian Socialist Party, as if the very mention of worker was even more of a political liability than the word socialist! Even the World Bank is uneasy about the lack of interest in social policy, in retraining unemployed workers, in strengthening trade unions. Even the World Bank is to the left of the present Hungarian government!

For the most part workers wait and see the "quiet before the storm," as my ex-shop steward told me last summer. Massive unemployment has yet to come. For now they say, "You can't recover from forty years of communism overnight. The next few years are going to be tough. But strikes are definitely not the solution. Just look at Poland." But for how long will they be patient? As inequalities intensify, as their standard of living continues to erode, as unemployment increases, will they sit back and watch? After all, state socialism, despite itself, did create a working class which was assured a certain minimal security and standard of living. Rights of employment and welfare are simply taken for granted. What happens when these customary rights are profoundly disrupted, as surely they will be when capitalism comes to Hungary?

There is one class which has a clear insight into the virtues of a market economy. They are the emergent petty bourgeoisie who for over a decade have been expanding their ranks, hiring out their services, setting up shops, boutiques, restaurants, bars. They know where their interests lie and they are organized. In January they undertook a two-day national strike for commerce and against administration, a strike against the bureaucratic red tape that still straps their entrepreneurial energies. For them democracy means freedom from the state, it means autonomy. Booty capitalism for the *apparatchiks* and boutique capitalism for the petty bourgeoisie— they both share a distinctive understanding of democracy, namely democracy for the few.

What about that other fraction of the petty bourgeoisie, the celebrated "new class"—the intellectuals? They are the true devotees of democracy, its publicists and propagandists. As intellectuals they depend on basic civil liberties to ply their trade, to communicate, to develop their "culture of critical discourse." They too seek autonomy from the state, autonomy from censorship, the freedom to write and speak their mind. They are the new politicians, the leaders of the dozens of political parties that have mushroomed in Hungary in the last year. They are there on the radio, on the television and on the newsstand, spewing out their condemnation of communism, Bolshevism, socialism, the state, trade unions, the party.

While the Hungarian Socialist Party continues to run the government, the two major contenders for power are the Free Democrats and Hungarian Democratic Forum. They replay an old Hungarian battle between National Populism, advocating a Third (Hungarian) Road, and the Westernizers who seek to construct Western liberal democracy based on Chicago economics. Rather than developing their platforms and taking them to the people, they aggressively abuse each other as being worse than the Bolsheviks or being anti-Semitic and chauvinistic. This orgy of words and slander doesn't mean much to those outside their ranks. That yawning chasm between intellectuals on the one side and workers and peasants on the other—a chasm of mutual suspicion and contempt—cannot, after all, be bridged overnight.

If the Third Road is unclear, perhaps leading toward some form of Peronist rule, the capitalist road involves the coercive imposition of the market, what Boris Kagarlitsky has aptly termed "market Stalinism." This is the road to disaster. Forty years of communism has unleashed a simply-minded faith in the magic of the market. When Hungarians think of capitalism they think of Germany or the United States or Japan or perhaps South Korea. They don't think of Peru or Bolivia or Kenya. They expect the West to bail them out with loans and gifts, perhaps even write off part of the $20 billion debt, as if capitalism owed them a new lease on life. Selling state enterprises to foreign companies is seen as the dismantling of socialism, not as the creation of new forms of subjugation, not as a headlong rush into rampant deindustrialization. Having faced the party state for forty years, the world capitalist market is seen as liberator, not as exploiter. Even the great Hungarian economist János Kornai, no fan of socialism, considers the present trajectory to be suicidal. He advocates state subsidies for the private sector rather than the immediate sale of public enterprises.

If money is not already flowing in, the free marketeers claim that this is because the West is waiting until after the elections. Then the final remnants of socialism will be swept away and democracy will establish a new stability conducive to free markets and capitalist expansion.

Will reality be so kind? Marxism teaches us that electoral democracy does not give rise to a thriving capitalism. To the contrary, electoral democracy requires as its precondition an expanding capitalist economy. As Gramsci taught us long ago, capitalist democracy is only stable if it can engineer real material concessions to its constituency. More than likely, the elections on March 25 will be followed by deepening chaos in which one unstable coalition will follow another. Representing a common opinion, one president of a collective farm and member of parliament assured me that to turn chaos into order Hungary needs a "sheriff." Hungary may get one too. Let us not mistake the rhetoric of democracy for its substance.

Prospects for the Future

What is clear from this brief sketch of the social forces at work in Hungary is that they follow class lines. I would expect this to be also true of the other Eastern European societies, particularly where civil society is still rudimentary. At the same time, these societies exhibit very different constellations and balances of forces. Even under the iron fist of communist rule these countries assumed very different paths of development. Hungary, for example, early on dismantled central planning, created a thriving legal second economy alongside the state sector, and realized a successful collectivization campaign in the early 1960s. But in each country the transition to capitalism seems to be activating a contest of classes on the terrain of democracy. I am reminded of Marx's commentary in *Class Struggles in France:* "But if universal suffrage was not the miraculous wand for which the republican duffers had taken it, it possessed the incomparably higher merit of unchaining class struggle, of letting the various middle sections of the petty-bourgeois society rapidly live through their illusions and disappointments, of tossing all the fractions of the exploiting class at one throw to the head of the state, and thus tearing from them their treacherous mask." One shouldn't forget that it ended with the coup d'état of Louis Bonaparte. Kadarism may yet represent a radiant past!

If, for the time being, the socialist vision is dead in Eastern Europe, is it also dead in the Soviet Union? Travelling between Budapest and Moscow gives one the impression that, whereas Hungary embraces capitalism as its natural destiny, the Soviet Union (or should I say Russia) provides a most infertile soil. The visible contrasts are extreme. Next to the Soviet Union, Hungary is a consumer paradise. One can buy anything one wants, from oranges and bananas to AT computers, all in ordinary shops and with local currency, provided one has enough. In the Soviet Union the shops are empty, and only graft and cunning secures one's daily bread. Western entrepreneurs seeking joint ventures are continually frustrated by Russian failure to grasp the profit motive, much as they are fascinated by Hungarian ingenuity. If capitalism cannot grow in Russia, there may be no alternative to socialism.

So much for the negative forces inhibiting capitalism—what about the positive forces for socialism? The Soviet democratic revolution has already unchained national struggles on the periphery of the Soviet empire. But even if these republics were to secede, there still remains the heartland of the Soviet Union, the Russian Federation, with 50 percent of the population, 76 percent of the land area, 70 percent of the national production, and the bulk of the natural resources. Here class struggle could still advance toward the renewal of socialism, much as Solidarity was advancing in 1981. Here the collapse of the party state and the construction of political pluralism could engender a democratic socialism. There was, after all, a revolution in Russia. Its nationalism may not be closely tied to the fate of the party but it is still tied to the future of socialism. What such a democratic socialism might look like is unclear but it is likely to be more attractive than a peripheral, clientalistic, booty capitalism.

Shed of Marxism-Leninism, Marxism remains a vital tool to comprehend not only the trajectory of capitalism but also the demise of state socialism and a possible socialist future. Other frameworks have been so driven by their hostility to communism that they got no further than static models of totalitarianism and inefficiency. They proved blind to the dynamics of these societies. Marxism provides a framework within which to learn from the last seventy years of Soviet history. Rather than repress it as a catastrophe or celebrate its despotism as socialism's essence, those committed to a viable future beyond both capitalism and state socialism may want to understand how the Soviet society survived as long as it did—how its economy worked at all. With that understanding we can proceed to construct alternative models of socialism. The end of communism, far from being the end of socialism, opens up debate in the West and the East, in the North and the South, about what we might mean by socialism.

Socialism will remain, we can be sure of that. Even where its reality fails, its promises will live on as long as there is capitalism. Just as the irrationalities of state socialism generate utopian visions of market capitalism, so the abiding irrationalities of advanced capitalism will continue to generate utopian visions of socialism. And after all utopias are what move people to make a better world, to hold out the possibility of a better future—one which guarantees greater material security, gives greater scope to the realization of individual needs, and provides the means for collectively shaping the society in which we live. Capitalism continually generates problems for which it has no solutions. So, the death of socialism, like that of Marxism, comes only with the death of capitalism.

Notes

I should like to thank the Bay Area *Socialist Review* editorial board, and particularly Brian Powers, for comments on an earlier version of this paper.

PHIL HILL

THE ALTERNATIVE IS DEAD, LONG LIVE THE ALTERNATIVE!

Der Kleine, der mit Lammsgeduld
sich durch den Dreck der Grossen quält,
und trotzdem nicht die Grünen wählt,
ist selbst dran schuld.

The little guy who's always seen
Waste-deep in the crap of the rich man's game
And still refuses to vote Green,
Has only got himself to blame.

—Campaign poster at Samariterstrasse subway stop,
East Berlin, 1990

The scene: The Socialist Scholars' Conference, annual tribal gathering of the intellectual left from whatever radius around New York they can be attracted. The main topic: Eastern Europe. The interest, clearly, is more than merely academic. This is not only that something big has happened. We are socialists and so it happened to us, at least in some sense. It wasn't just in the paper. It was in the family.

The room is full of cousins who claim to have barely known the deceased. He was, after all, the black sheep. After a token mourning gesture, we can smile in a self-satisfied way and assure ourselves that now everything will be okay, he's not around to give us a bad name anymore. A view of the history of socialism prevailed that was at the least curious, that seemed to find little worth discussing between the first signs of the crumbling of Stalinism in 1956 (Hun-

173

gary, Khrushchev's secret speech) and the current collapse of that system. The 1960s, with all that went with them internationally—cultural revolution (not just the orchestrated Chinese version), the new role of the third world, the move of ecology and feminism out of their pigeonholes and onto the center stage of the revolutionary arena—were just as absent from the dominant discussion as any recognition of the basic changes that have gone on in the world at large, from industrial restructuring of the periphery and the qualitatively new level of commodification of information, to the sociopolitical implications of the looming ecocatastrophe. These were "children (or relics?) of the 1960s," but they had seemingly forgotten their roots.

Leaving aside the handful of die-hard Stalinists, the view among U.S. socialists seems to be that the socialist project "took a wrong turn" somewhere, that the "prophets" of the early days had predicted something very different from what has since happened. Faithless disciples (Stalin or whoever) led the believers down a false path, consciously away from the correct one that the prophets had discovered. But that path is still there to be taken—otherwise the prophets wouldn't have been prophets.

The implication is that Marxism is a universe more or less independent of profane reality, immune from the sharp knife of its own materialist analysis. That analysis demands that the past and present be tested by the future. They are not assumed to be correct and hence able to foretell the future, and that holds true for the analyst as well. There is no returning to the beginning of a historical process and trying again. Too much has happened, and too much more is about to happen, for us to waste time delving into the wisdom of the ancients. They passed on to us a method, dialectical materialism, that is heritage enough, and that in any case forbids such theological exercises.

At the conference, as at other places where radicals have gathered in recent years to discuss or act, there was also a significant minority oriented toward a new alternative that has often been identified as "Green." The label may be misleading—first, because it implies single-issue environmentalism to many people, and second, because it evokes a sometimes exclusive association with the prestigious Green parties of the German republics. Both these associations are important, but they do not entirely describe the growing alternative movement, especially since the key element of feminism is thereby often forgotten.

With this reminder of feminism's central importance, I will use the term "Green alternative" to describe this new challenge to the capitalist order. It is, I believe, the direction radicals will have to go in as we emerge from the era during which socialism was *the* unquestioned alternative. This is not the call to join a new party or sect, but an appeal to socialists to involve themselves in a process that has begun, and needs their experience and commitment. Nor is it a call to abandon our socialist heritage—quite the opposite. It is now time to decide how much of that heritage was specific to the era that has ended and how much is for the ages, or at least for the duration of the battle against capitalism.

A New Left

The radicalism of the 1960s and 1970s evolved within the context of a major social transformation, and was centered on the emerging intellectual class. While it certainly did not dominate this new stratum, the New Left provided it with a politico-cultural construct that was uniquely its own. There were, of course, differences between the various advanced-capitalist countries: the United States stands out as the country in which the left was most isolated, even within the new class. In north-central Europe, on the other hand, its political and ideological influence was pervasive throughout the middle class and into the working class. It was in this social context that the Green and alternative parties emerged in West Germany and neighboring countries.

But what did "left" mean, divorced from the traditional capital-vs.-labor dichotomy? For one thing, the divorce was not complete: there was still capital and labor, even if society had not remained clearly divided into "bourgeois" and "proletarian" segments. The masses might have changed, but the rulers had not, and "left" still meant opposition to them and solidarity with the oppressed.

Beyond that, the answer lay in the practice of the radicals of that period, which was grounded in their social experience. The political leaderships of the underclass third world communities tended to be part of the new intellectual stratum themselves. Their critique of the fundamentally racist nature of societies founded on the exploitation of the non-European world by Europeans entered into the common political consciousness of the New Left. At the same time, young women entering the new social structure began to see that it reproduced the male-domination of bourgeois society. They rebelled against both. Their awareness included a recognition that the increasing disintegration of the marginal realms of modern society affected women and children with special ferocity. Women in the new intellectual class, in its radical minority, and in the underclass thus had a potential for political unity that increased their power at all these levels.

The decades since have seen numerous struggles centered around such "women's issues" as abortion rights or (in the United States), the Equal Rights Amendment, as well as a new awareness of the ways in which the oppression of women is a special part of other struggles.

Finally, the social and political emergence of the postwar generation coincided with a global awareness that was to have the most profound economic impact. It became clear that capitalism was completing what previous systems had only begun: its breakdown of the complex web of nature had finally reached the point where life itself was threatened. The new information-oriented generation, unlike others standing on the threshold of a new age, was presented not with a "new world to conquer" but with the problem of saving one from being ravaged.

The Greens Emerge

By the late 1970s, the political and social forces engendered during the previous decade ran into a head-on conflict with the corporate-state establishment over a matter of policy that had not previously upset the left at all, and which brought it too into conflict with the main institutional carriers of the traditional socialist movement, the trade unions and the socialist-bloc states. The issue was nuclear power, and it was to bring the new alternative movement to maturity while demonstrating its greater willingness for radical confrontation with the system than that of the traditional socialists.

Nuclear power had been planned during the 1950s and tested during the 1960s, with hardly anyone questioning its promise of cheap and abundant energy for all. To most socialists, this was part of the technological progress that would one day make capitalism obsolete: it was in effect celebrated as such in the 1962 Port Huron Statement, the manifesto of the U.S. New Left.

But the left was not only mired in obsolete ideas, it had not even done its homework. Also celebrating the new toys were the advocates of a different kind of new society, including such ideologized scientists as Edward Teller in the United States. In defeated and supposedly demilitarized West Germany and Japan, nuclear ministries were established while defense ministries were still taboo. They were headed by two young ultra-rightists burning to restore the greatness of their humbled lands, future Bavarian Premier Franz-Josef Strauss and future Prime Minister Yasuhiro Nakasone.

By the 1970s, the power plants were being built, and only a few critical scientists (such as Ernest Sternglass) were warning citizens that the blithe assurances of government and industry officials concealed a grave danger. By the mid-1970s, opposition was mounting in a number of countries, and by 1980 it had spread throughout the advanced capitalist world. A number of smaller countries— Austria, Luxemburg, Denmark, Norway—had scrapped their plans to enter the "nuclear age." Others—particularly the United States, Japan, and France—suppressed the opposition, which had few successes. Nevertheless, the movement had, on the basis of the "single-issue struggle" of its members, developed an analysis of the nuclear economy and its military ramifications that gave the lie to establishment charges that they were ignorant Luddites. They had called the bluff of the military-industrial complex and its pseudoscientists, and were being proven right. And they had done so largely without the help of the traditional left.

If Three Mile Island and Chernobyl provided the turning points, it was because they were preceded by protracted struggle. The major crunch came in 1976 and 1977 on the north German plain, where pitched battles were fought between well-organized demonstrators and massively mobilized police. The demonstrators ran the gamut from outraged local citizens who had never before protested anything to anarchists out to smash the state. In between were the relatively undogmatic leftists, including the Hamburg-based Communist League (KB), which adopted a position of rejecting nuclear power on principle.

The movement won victories and suffered defeats. In retrospect it can be said that it slowed the nuclear machine enough so that it lost its momentum, never to recover fully. But by 1978 the movement was facing a crisis of its own. The politicized environmentalists wanted to solidify their gains by forming an electoral party. To the anarchists, this was a sell-out to the capitalist state. The KB, in the middle, decided that if there were to be elections, they might as well lead them. Thus in June 1978 the environmentalists ran a Green slate in state elections in Lower Saxony, while a KB-led "Rainbow" slate (*Bunte Liste*) was on the ballot in the neighboring state of Hamburg on the same day. Each made a significant first-time showing.

For the next two years, the environmentalist Green and leftist Rainbow (or alternative) electoral movements grew, sometimes competing, sometimes cooperating, but both spreading throughout the country. By 1979, however, the Greens were attracting a number of leftists who were rejecting the KB and other leftist groups because of their "Leninist" organization and, more importantly, their inability to understand the new ecologist perspective. Most notably, Rudi Dutschke, a leader of the 1967–68 student uprising, called for leftists to vote Green in the Bremen state elections in August.[1] The Greens entered a state legislature for the first time, and the rush was on: the alternative movement soon lost its base, as its members flocked to the Greens. The KB itself split, as the majority tried to continue to rally the alternatives, while a minority joined the Greens. In January 1980, the Greens formally founded a national party, which included a considerable number of leftists.

The party was a synthesis of the issue-engendered citizens' opposition and left anticapitalism. The NATO rearmament proposal (passed a month prior to the Greens' founding) provided the Greens with a second major nuclear-related issue and the momentum to win them victories in five more state elections, followed, in 1983, by entry into the Bundestag in Bonn. Their prestige spread, sparking Green movements throughout the advanced capitalist world and in Latin America. The Greens had arrived.

But it was not so much their electoral success as the sociopolitical ramifications of their emergence that constituted the permanent gain. The ability of the West German left, by way of the Greens, to break out of its ghetto on the margins of society had by 1980 resulted in an *Umbruch* (breakdown and reconstitution) of all its structures that completely changed the parameters of left debate. The feminist, ecological, and anti-imperialist/antiracist themes that had emerged in the movement since 1968 were of course already present, but received new emphasis as the Greens developed.

The Greens were at least subjectively starting afresh, which meant that they were satisfied with a few basic philosophical guidelines that all could share. What appeared as simple political underdevelopment from the point of view of the leftists who joined their ranks—and the perception was often accurate at the level of individual Greens from grass-roots organizations—was in fact, at the level of the emerging body as a whole, a valuable freedom of movement, unencumbered by obsolete baggage. The principles—the famous four pillars, to which feminism would be added as Green women stormed the patriarchal walls at mid-decade—succeeded in providing a lasting framework within which Green ideas could develop.

Ecology

The first of these is ecology. In the Green view, the environment sets the parameters for the functioning of the human economy, which cannot long violate these parameters without destroying itself.

Hence maintaining the viability of the natural web of life is the precondition for any functioning economy. The most radical critique of the present economy—one that does not obviate, but rather deepens, other critiques—is that it is destroying the very foundation for continued human existence.

Environmentalism is a practice of crisis-management within capitalism. An ecological program, on the other hand, is an alternative to capitalism. Environmentalists recycle what can be recycled. They are now, for example, running up against a market-determined "glut" in recycled paper, in both Europe and North America. The need to produce, and the parallel ability of society to consume, do not "permit" a glut of new paper, which represents dead trees (and therefore dead habitats for numerous species), erosion, and monoculture. Instead, even recycled paper winds up in the incinerator—which also has to be built in order to fill out a capitalist bottom line. If we were to recycle everything that could be recycled, and ban the production of the poisons that cannot be, then the remainder would not catch fire. The ecologist makes these connections. There are Greens who understand these connections, but fail to identify capitalism as the problem. There is no easy explanation for this. Even more difficult to understand, however, is the Marxist who sees the connections and does not ask what the alternative to such an absurd system could be.

Green discussions of the economy deal with small-scale alternatives to capitalism, in terms of work organization (egalitarian collectives), of the nature of production (making useful things), and of environmental compatibility (recycling, nonpolluting production, renewable energy). Political and economic decentralization are considered necessary components for real, base-oriented democratization. Existing processes are subjected to a deeper and deeper critique that asks not only what is the mechanism of human exploitation, but what logic underlies that mechanism. The answer may show that an ecologically unsound practice is based on the logic and psychology of exploitation rooted in male domination, or in Western culture. Natural processes are being studied to shed light on human social processes, overcoming a taboo against mixing biology and politics that arose in reaction to the Nazis.

Grass-Roots Democracy

The traditional left had always tended to a top-down view of democracy which found its most elitist form in the "democratic-centralist" concept of the Leninist party. The result was that the quintessential institutional heirs to the socialist tradition, the Stalinist state and the social-democratic-run trade union, were both epitomes of bureaucracy.

In West Germany, as in other countries, during the 1970s the non-Leninist radical left evolved participatory-democratic alternatives to Leninism, including such organizations as affinity groups and economic-alternative collectives. The non-leftist component of the Greens also criticized the manipulatory nature of bourgeois democracy, without having any tradition—or inclination—to embrace Leninism as an alternative. Such alternative views dominated the movement during the 1980s, their only challenge coming from the growing right wing of the Greens, the "Realos," who advocated compromise with bourgeois society. But even for them, Leninism was dead. With the rise of the East German Greens and their allies during the anti-Stalinist revolution of 1989, new democratic forms—local citizens' committees and the radical-democratic para-parliament (the Round Table)—developed and became part of the Green-alternative heritage.

Such anarchist thinkers as Murray Bookchin in Vermont and Dimitri Roussopoulos in Montreal have strongly influenced Green concepts of grass-roots democracy.[2] Their ideas of radical municipalism identify the individually accessible local area as the context for developing political society, for mobilizing people to take charge of their own affairs. At the same time, the Greens experience in West Germany, where they are now represented on virtually every city and county council, shows that local politics is conducted within very narrow limits, due both to the regulations imposed at the state and federal levels, and, more importantly, to the realities imposed by global capitalist structures.

The "movement vs. party" debate is also a continuous one among the Greens. Parties, experience has shown, by definition accept the view that the electoral arena is *the* locus of multi-issue change. That implies a level of acceptance of the legitimacy of the parliamentary forum that tends to undermine the radical nature of the Green critique of capitalism. Parliamentary representation has had a tendency to replace grass-roots activism, not least because winning such representation has become a kind of goal that has to be won. In West Germany, the result has been that the more radical movements have distanced themselves from the Green Party, even if they remain sympathetic to it. Structures that tie the party to the grassroots movements have not yet been developed, although it must be remembered that the socialist movement was unable to find a successful formula for linking party and unions.[3]

The East German anti-Stalinist revolution, which generated six recognized mass movements in addition to the Green Party, is bringing these questions to a head. As Germany unites, the Greens face the problem of having to form a nationwide Green Party, and they need their friends in these grassroots groups. However, neither these groups, nor the Greens, want the radical-democratic potential of these organizations to be subsumed in an electoral party. The problem is a hot issue at the moment.

Social Solidarity

The atomized society of individual citizens brings forth a countervailing demand for the development of a universal solidarity. A specific social solidarity—the need to provide for the victimized—is also a central Green tenet, with roots in socialism. In addition to a heritage from the new social movements, the Greens have adopted the core of the solidarity philosophy of the New Left: labor unions and third world struggles have to prove themselves *unworthy* of support, not the opposite. But the Greens have put forward demands that tend to move away from the negative aspects of the socialist past (the famous demand, for instance, for "more") and toward their own view of the future. The battle for the thirty-five-hour work week, on the verge of being won in West Germany, was supported only by the Greens, not by the SPD. It was argued that socially necessary labor time had been reduced, and that this should be passed on to workers as freely disposable time. Even those elements of the SPD that supported the proposal—other than the trade union bureaucracy itself—wanted to link it to wage cuts, with the overall effect of fostering of labor-saving, capital-intensive production. The Greens wanted cuts in useless production as well as in the correspondingly useless labor time.

Another example of solidarity is the expansion of the Green movement to the third world, particularly Brazil. Here the local Greens, with support from their friends around the world, are aiding the struggle of the Amazonian Indians and rubber workers to block the encroachment of the multinationals (including McDonald's, which has turned huge tracts of forest into cattle ranches). This support for ecologically benign, small-scale, and labor-intensive forms of production is a departure from traditional socialist concepts of the "progressive" nature of capital-intensive technological development. The Greens have forged an alliance with the powerful Workers' Party (PT), one of the most important proletarian parties in the industrializing third world. Clearly, there is convergence in their demands. In other parts of the world, Greens are supporting the kind of small-scale development projects that leftists dealing with the third world increasingly favor over the disruptive, capital-intensive projects that the World Bank and the capitalist nations' "foreign aid" programs support.

The Green anti-growth philosophy is often seen as insensitive to the needs of third world people, both in the poor countries and in communities within the metropolis, such as blacks in the United States. These people need necessities, the argument goes, while nature is a luxury, and the necessities can only be provided through growth. In fact, of course, non-European peoples had built viable societies in harmony with the environment before being overrun by Europeans. It is the cancerous pace of growth of capitalist society that has so dramatically polarized wealth and poverty worldwide, and third world people have been concentrated at the poverty end of the scale. Their prospects for ending that condition by attempting one more effort in the same direction are not good.

Nonviolence

I prefer the term "antiviolence"—opposition to the structure of violence that determines human interaction. Antiviolence within the Greens ranges from a deep-seated moral pacifism to a critique of the structurally inherent violence of oppressive and exploitative society. It too can be an element of a comprehensive alternative to—rather than simply a change in—the existing system.

A thorny issue for Greens is the question of defensive violence by the oppressed. In West Germany, Greens have not considered the use of violence as a reason for withdrawing solidarity, and have been consistent in their anti-imperialist stance. In the United States, the nascent Green movement is still struggling with this question.

In the analysis of structurally inherent violence, Green-alternative politics has the potential for elaborating the Marxist heritage. Greens are part of an intellectual tendency that is examining the pre-class neolithic period in search of the roots of historical society. The ecological, and particularly the feminist, approach to this history raise issues about the connection between class-, gender-, and ethnic-based violence, and the connection of all of these to the assault on the natural world. Marxist historical materialism is essential to this discussion.

Feminism

As an outgrowth of the New Left, the Green-alternative movement has inherited an innate bond with the post-1968 women's movement. That has not, of course, meant that it has not also inherited the huge load of sexist thought and practice that society at large has created and continually reproduces. Greens have had no problem supporting women's social issues, including the important demand for abortion, although there has always been a minority which, in addition to women's right to choose, has also wanted to respect the life of the fetus. This has resulted in moralistic constructions, but has not substantially affected support for this key demand.

Greens in many countries have also carried quota-equality into their party, so that, for instance, the West German Greens elected twenty-five women and nineteen men to the Bundestag in 1987. The East Germans, in spite of a formally equal slate, managed, through the vagueries of the election law, to send a delegation of six men and two women to the People's Chamber in 1990—all the more scandalous because neither of the women was a member of the Independent Women's Association, which had supported the Greens and been promised one-third of the seats.[4] And nowhere—the only exception is the Icelandic Women's Party, which bars men from all positions of power—has formal, quota-based parity changed the fact that the men dominate the party and the movement.

Nonetheless, the Green-alternative movement has certainly incorporated the gains that women have forced on the movement since 1968, and is thus an improvement over the older left. In the area of theory, too, Greens are open to new departures on the part of the women's movement. The witch tradition, for instance, has won a strong place in the German movement: one of the first major women's actions after the fall of the Stalinist regime was a demonstration on the Blocksberg, a mythical witches' gathering place.

Theory and Changed Reality

In terms of its theoretical development, Green-alternative thinking—let's call it ecologism, again remembering its feminist component—is not necessarily a "separate trend" from Marxism. Rather, it is an emerging mixture of trends, partially synthetic, partially eclectic, a major part of which is intimately interwoven with the more imaginative independent Marxist thinking of our time.

State-oriented Marxism has for decades been characterized by a theory of almost clinical sterility. The important radical theoretical work of recent decades has investigated changes in social structure and relations, the labor process, the "post"-industrial revolution (high tech-cum-dependent industrialization), the techno-authoritarian state, cultural aspects of race and ethnicity, female approaches to social issues, social aspects of medicine and psychology, the reorientation of physical structures to human needs, the raising of children to be self-conscious and independent, and the connections between humans and the environment at numerous levels. In effect, these are the heritage of the political upsurge that began during the 1960s. Recent Western Marxism and Green-alternative leftism thus have grown up together, intertwined, overlapped, not easily separated. And they need not be, for socialism is not a tribal religion, but an attempt to replace capitalism. If the replacement turns out to be green as well as red, there is no reason to mourn—so let's organize.

Notes

1. Dutschke had been shot and seriously wounded by a fascist in 1968 and had been absent from politics for some years. His prestige survived, however, so that his appeal was effective. It was his last vital gift to the movement. He died that Christmas from the aftereffects of his injury.
2. Bookchin's huge body of work is probably the most influential single source of Green political ideas, at least in English. *Ecology of Freedom* is probably the most significant.
3. The link between the British Labour Party and the Trades Union Council is the exception that proves the rule. It has never given the workers control of their "own" party, only enthroned union bosses as party bosses. British proletarians are no less likely than those elsewhere to vote for the "class enemy."
4. The divergences in these lists—both of which were formally 50-50—is due to the fact that under the German system of proportional representation, there are parallel lists in each state. In the West, women headed almost all the slates. In the East, there were two competing alternative parties and a larger number of separate lists, mostly headed by men.

PAT DEVINE

SELF-GOVERNING SOCIALISM

The Present Crisis of Credibility

The traditional Marxist socialist project, which has been the predominant influence on all socialist (as opposed to social democratic) projects, can be summed up as the abolition of private ownership of the means of production and its replacement by social or common ownership. The emphasis has been on social ownership as a necessary condition for the abolition of exploitation and the anarchy of production, through the replacement of production for sale in the market in pursuit of profit by planned production for use. This project, in varying forms, has been the bedrock of traditional socialist belief, rarely challenged until recently.

In the past decade or so however, as a result of over half a century's historical experience of what has been taken to be socialism in practice and an even longer period of critical theoretical work, a crisis of credibility has arisen. Three interrelated areas of reassessment can be identified: the relationship between legal ownership, actual control, and exploitation; between planning and the market; and between individual freedom, planning, and the market.

First, the Marxist concept of exploitation is concerned with the extraction of a surplus product from the direct producers by an exploiting class. The traditional socialist assumption is that with the abolition of private ownership exploitation is also abolished. Although not explicit in the classical analysis, it is surely implicit that the abolition of exploitation cannot mean just that the surplus

187

product is no longer privately appropriated. It must also mean that the direct producers have some control over the production process and the use of the social surplus. It is now evident beyond doubt that workers in the statist countries of Eastern Europe and the Soviet Union have had control in neither of these senses.

For exploitation to be unambiguously abolished requires some form of worker self-management, together with democratic control over the state and the other institutions through which decisions over the use of productive capacity and the social surplus are made. The question then arises of how the output decisions of production units and the demand for their output are to be linked together, or coordinated.

This, then, connects with the second area in which a crisis of credibility has arisen, the relationship between planning and the market. Are the two antithetical, as in classical Marxism, or are they complementary, as argued by reformers in the East and market socialists in the West, with a regulated market mechanism constituting an essential instrument of planning. The replacement of production for profit by production for use presupposes some way of determining what production is socially useful, some way for that information to be communicated to production units, and reasonable confidence that they will respond to it.

For a small number of strategic objectives, given overriding priority, a centralized planning system in which the center communicates its requirements directly to the production units has been shown to be effective, at least for a limited period, both in capitalist countries in wartime and in the Soviet Union. Increasingly, however, experience in the Soviet Union, Eastern Europe, and China has forced recognition of the need for reform. While this was initially couched primarily in terms of eradicating inefficiency and corruption, within a basically unchanged system, the balance has now shifted decisively toward the need for systemic reform—the creation of some form of "market economy."

Simultaneously, theoretical work has increasingly stressed that the decentralized decision-making needed for efficient resource allocation in a complex modern economy can only be coordinated through the market mechanism. There are two interrelated strands to the argument. First, precisely because it does not involve a detailed blueprint being worked out in advance, it is claimed that only the market mechanism can convey sufficiently detailed information, in the form of market-determined prices, for individual production units to know what to do. Second, it is asserted that only through the market mechanism can a system of incentives be operated such that individual production units respond to the information, or signals, available to them by producing what society individually and collectively wishes to use.

Profit, resulting from the relationship between the supply of and demand for a product, between the costs and revenues of production units, acts as a signal that more, less, or the same quantity of a product is socially useful. At the same time, since the incomes of those working in the production units are related to profitability, there is an incentive for the production units to respond to the signal. Of course, most socialist advocates of the market mechanism, unlike the new right, are aware of the theoretical, not to mention empirical, shortcomings of the market: uncertainty, long gestation periods, indivisibilities, complementarities, externalities, monopoly power, injustice, insecurity, inequality. They take it for granted that the market would need to be regulated.

In a regulated market socialist economy, the market mechanism is used as a tool of planning. The pattern of prices and profit rates which makes up the economic environment to which production units respond is shaped by the use of economic regulators, by fiscal and monetary policy. The idea is that the market environment should reflect collectively determined as well as individual priorities, plus any other information that would not otherwise be felt at the level of the individual production unit.

The issues raised in the discussion of plan and market are real and important. Any convincing model of planning must deal with them. Soviet and East European experience has almost universally been accepted as having demonstrated the need for movement in the direction of greater and more explicit decentralization. The reason why market socialism has increasingly come to dominate serious theoretical work on socialist planning is that the market has appeared to be the only means for achieving this. However, another reason for market socialism's attractive power has been the belief that it provides an alternative to the threat to individual freedom that is increasingly seen as inherent in highly centralized command planning and monolithic statist societies.

This, then, is the third area contributing to the crisis of credibility of the traditional socialist program. Can a system of planning be devised that is not based on hierarchy and personal dependence? Is the market mechanism the only way in which the power of the state can be kept within bounds and individual freedom safeguarded? Few would argue that a market based economic system is in itself enough to guarantee individual freedom but, while it may not be sufficient, is it necessary?

A democratic political system is clearly a necessary condition for freedom. However, the argument that economic independence, in the sense of an absence of economic dependence on the state, is also a necessary foundation for political freedom has become increasingly convincing in the light of historical experience. Within socialist discussion, this has been taken to mean the creation of various forms of social ownership, such as workers' cooperatives or local community enterprises, with specified ownership rights, that is, rights of decision-making over the use to be made of the means of production involved. At the same time, some socialists continue to believe in the need for planning.

The Case for Planning

A democratically planned socialist economy has three essential advantages over the unplanned capitalist economy. First, the broad structure of resource utilization and the general direction of development of the economy can be planned in accordance with social priorities as determined through the democratic political process. At the most general level, of course, only very broad priorities concerning economic development and social welfare can be decided, setting the framework for the more detailed decision-making by decentralized self-governing bodies that is characteristic of a self-governing society.

In modern capitalism many issues arising at the level of society as a whole are not left solely to the spontaneous workings of the invisible hand. They are settled by the interaction of state policies, decisions of large corporations, and the struggles of the labor movement and other organized interest groups. Within this interaction, however, the private sector is favorably placed to dominate the outcome because of what Lindblom has called "the privileged position of business."[1] This privilege arises primarily from the need for governments to create an environment that will induce the private sector to perform satisfactorily. In addition, the economic power of business gives it preferential access to the decision-making institutions and processes of society.

For social priorities to be determined democratically requires a fundamental redistribution of economic and political power. That is why socialists have historically sought the abolition of exploitation and private ownership and the abolition or democratization of the state. A redistribution of economic power is also a precondition for a more equal distribution of income, since investment would then no longer be motivated by the pursuit of unearned income accruing to private capital ownership.

The second argument for planning—indeed, its principal technical advantage as a coordinating mechanism—arises from the fact that it enables the uncertainty associated with atomized decision-making to be overcome. Maurice Dobb, the most insistent and persuasive advocate of planning to date, has consistently stressed the significance for planning of the distinction between what he calls objective and subjective uncertainty. The former arises from our inability fully to know the future, the latter from the necessary lack of knowledge on the part of atomized decision-makers of their rivals' intended actions.[2]

The third essential advantage of planning as an economic mechanism is that it makes possible the coordination of interrelated decisions before they are implemented. It substitutes the conscious, planned coordination of decisions *ex ante* for the blind, anarchic coordination of market forces *ex post,* operating through the changing reactions of atomistic decision-makers to continuously changing market prices. In a sense this is the essence of economic planning and constitutes the fundamental difference between a planned and an unplanned economy.[3] It is this *ex ante* coordination that accounts for the potential superiority of estimates of the future in a planned economy. Those involved in carrying out particular investment projects know, rather than guess, hope, or even expect, that projects being undertaken simultaneously are complementary to their own rather than in competition with them.

The coordination of investment in advance not only enables rational decision-making, in the sense that decisions can be related to the future pattern of relative costs; it also economises in the use of resources by reducing waste. Investment embodies resources in fixed capital equipment which cannot normally be dismantled and then reconstituted in a new form. Most capital equipment is fairly specific, with a limited range of uses. Thus, if more investment in a particular branch of production is undertaken than is needed, some of the productive capacity installed will be underused and the resources embodied in it will be wasted.

Planning is necessary if people are to be able to shape their own lives, if they are to exercise self-government. Most major and many minor decisions have consequences for others. Interdependence is the defining feature of social existence, not in the sense of atoms bouncing off one another, but in the sense that our relationships with others shape both us and them. If we are to act rationally, in the fullest possible awareness of all the factors relevant to our actions, we must place our interdependence with others at the center of our considerations. In the economic sphere, this means that major decisions whose outcomes are interdependent should be coordinated in advance by those affected by them. Conscious, planned, *ex ante* coordination needs to replace the unconscious, blind, *ex post* coordination of the unregulated market mechanism.

Information, Motivation, and Local Knowledge

What are the systemic problems inherent in Soviet-style centralized administrative command planning that have fatally undermined it as a model for a socialist economy? They can be discussed under two interrelated headings: information and motivation. A modern economy consists of production units whose activities are coordinated in such a way that, as far as possible, together they produce efficiently the goods and services that people individually and collectively want, in the proportions in which they want them. For production to be socially valuable, as defined by the society in question, it has to be informed by two types of information: first, the detailed local information that is known only to the person or small group of people on the spot; second, information about how each local act of production fits into the activities required from the economy as a whole. People also have to be motivated to supply and act upon available information in a way that contributes to the social as well as to their private interest.

In relation to both information and motivation, the systemic problems that have been identified in the centralized command model stem from overcentralization. The center suffers from information overload and the enterprises from lack of sufficient autonomy. Since the information supplied by enterprises is used not only to coordinate production decisions, but also as the data on which the incentive system is based, enterprises have an incentive to supply biased information, and the center lacks access to the local knowledge needed to correct for this. Thus, the problem of adequate information arises not only from the necessary loss of local knowledge as aggregation proceeds; it is also inseparably associated with the bias imparted to the information flow arising from the self-interest of those supplying the information.

The conclusion to be drawn is that an effective planning system has to incorporate an appropriate balance between centralization and decentralization. The center can only carry out effectively its role of taking the decisions that affect the economy as a whole, thereby setting the framework within which local decisions are made, if it is not overwhelmed by responsibilities it cannot fulfill and swamped by biased information it cannot use. Enterprises can only make proper use of local knowledge if they are able to act reasonably rapidly in response to changes in their circumstances, which means that they must be relatively autonomous. The command planning system incorporates the wrong balance between centralization and decentralization and needs to be decentralized.

This, however, is where the real difficulties start. If enterprises are autonomous, and people are assumed to be narrowly self-interested, then there has to be an incentive system that will constrain the narrowly self-interested use of local knowledge in such a way that it nevertheless contributes to the social interest. It is claimed that the market mechanism achieves this, is incentive compatible, because the local knowledge of producers is used by them to further their narrow self-interest within the constraints set by market prices, and the market prices, although not consciously determined, are assumed to reflect relative scarcity and consumer preferences.

However, what if "free," or *laissez-faire,* market prices do not adequately reflect the social interest? Then regulation is needed, and for effective regulation the regulator has to have access to accurate local knowledge. Thus, the problem of devising an effective regulated market mechanism is analogous to that involved in creating an effective incentive system for command planning. In both cases, the challenge is consciously to create an environment within which people use their local knowledge to pursue their narrow self-interest, yet in doing so contribute to the general interest. In both cases, the creation of such an environment requires access to local knowledge that those at the center do not and cannot have. The "regulator game" and "regulation illusion" are the regulated market economy's equivalent to the command economy's plan bargaining.[4] In both types of economy, the problems of information and motivation are, in practice, inseparable.

What, then is the relationship between decentralization and motivation? In the standard analysis, decentralization is necessary so that responsibility for the use of local knowledge rests clearly with the narrowly self-interested people who possess it. They are then rewarded or penalized according to the use they make of it. An alternative view, which I hold, is that fully developed participatory democracy, and the non-narrowly self-interested motivation associated with it, require as much decentralization as is consistent with the involvement in decision-making at each level of all those affected by the decisions taken at that level. This is because people are more likely to be committed to decisions when they have participated in making them and, although there will always be decisions in which people can be only indirectly involved through the process of representative democracy, self-activation is most readily developed through direct involvement in decision-making.

Is Market Socialism the Answer?

In my view, the current vogue for market socialism on the nondogmatic left in the West reflects the ideological hegemony of the new right, the fact that the left has not gone beyond a legitimate rejection of statism and, in the absence of any alternative, has fallen for the market. Similarly, most democratic reformers in or from the East have seen the market as the only alternative to state domination and personal dependence. They have drawn the wrong conclusion from the fact that, historically, direct interpersonal relationships, between people as state functionaries and people as workers or citizens, have involved personal dominance and domination. The reaction has been to seek to depersonalize interdependence through recourse to the impersonal market mechanism. The alternative I advocate is to democratize interdependence, through a process of negotiated coordination between equals.

Perhaps the best-known model of market socialism is Alec Nove's "feasible socialism."[5] Nove's model, like all such models of which I am aware, does no more than nod toward some of the problems that would be likely to occur. The key issue of *ex ante* coordination is not *seriously* considered. The possibility of effective regulation is asserted but not discussed. Procedures for rewarding and penalizing differential success are considered, but not the underlying reasons for differential performance. Apart, that is, from a celebration of what Nove takes to be realism: "An imperfect world cannot be rendered perfect because we wish it so, and the assumption of original sin is (alas) a more realistic basis for organizing society than the assumption of a noble savage deformed by the institutions of capitalism and the state."[6]

It is a sad end to a fascinating, if infuriating, book. Nove gives the impression of having been taunted beyond endurance by fundamentalists, dogmatists, and utopians. Desperate to insist on realism, and fully justified in doing so, he has mistaken conservatism for realism. It is realistic to start from where people are. It is not realistic to deny them the possibility of changing. The basic problem with Nove's model, and with market socialist models generally, is their lack of any transformatory perspective, their lack of vision.

My reasons for believing that market socialism is not likely to be the way forward can be summarized as follows. First, the concept of market socialism, so far at least, is utopian in the bad sense. It assumes that it would be possible to plan and regulate, primarily by remote control, an economy in which private ownership of the means of production has been abolished. Yet why should state-run or worker-managed enterprises, pursuing their narrow self-interest within a regulated socialist market, aggregate to a system with fundamentally different characteristics from those of a capitalist system, in which privately owned enterprises pursue their narrow self-interest within a regulated capitalist market? Such a system would presumably be more just, since there would be no unearned income, but why should it be more stable and more subject to overall social control?

Second, the logic of market socialism is for there to be nondiscriminatory, or parametric, regulation—regulation that treats enterprises in the same category, say industry and/or region, in the same way. The reason for this is that the center cannot in principle have access to local knowledge, unless the locals choose to provide it. Since the locals are assumed to be narrowly self-interested, they will always use their local knowledge to bend the center's regulated environment to their own ends. The performance of individual enterprises may be due to factors about which they can do something, or to factors beyond their control, but the center is in general unable to distinguish between the two situations. To avoid regulation bargaining and the regulator game, which the center cannot win, the best it can do is to engage in parametric regulation.

However, while parametric regulation may be the best that the center can do, its outcome will inevitably appear arbitrary to some enterprises. People never accept the adverse outcome of impersonal market forces, if they can do anything about it, unless they are convinced that it is just, and sometimes not even then. They are no more likely to accept the outcome of impersonal parametric regulation. Instead, what is needed is a cooperative system in which information is provided in good faith as a basis for participatory decision-making.

Third, for all that is said about harmonizing social and self-interest through a regulated market environment, with the regulators reflecting democratically agreed national priorities and values, the underlying structure of market socialism is necessarily nontransformatory. No less than the direct instructions of command economies, the coercion of market forces reinforces and reproduces alienation. In both cases, workers in enterprises experience powerlessness and noninvolvement in relation to decisions that have major effects on them. In both systems, people are treated instrumentally, as objects to be manipulated by carrot and stick incentive systems that reinforce their narrowly self-interested consciousness, rather than being encouraged to transform themselves in the direction of self-activating subjects.

Democratic Planning Through Negotiated Coordination

In my view, the most urgent need for socialists today is to develop a convincing model of self-governing socialism. To be convincing, a model has to go beyond general principles and give at least an outline, however provisional, of the institutions and social processes envisaged. My project is to develop a model of democratic planning based not on market forces but on what I have called negotiated coordination. Given political and economic democracy, I believe the problems of information and motivation can be resolved.

I start from three assumptions: first, that neither capitalism nor statism is the way forward and a third way is needed; second, that people have the capacity for self-transformation; and, third, that planning is necessary for self-determination and self-government. If, as I have argued, market socialism is neither feasible nor desirable as a third way, what might the economic organization of a self-governing socialist society look like?

Self-government in the economic sphere, or economic democracy, has two aspects. It requires social control over the broad disposition of the means of production at the level of the society as a whole, and social control over the detailed use of the means of production at the local, or subsystem level. Political democracy is necessary to determine overall social priorities, and system-wide planning is necessary to give them effect. Within the overall framework set by this process, however, the detailed use of the means of production then needs to be decided at each level by those most directly affected by that use. I shall illustrate this initially at the level of the production unit (enterprise) and the branch of production (industry or sector).

At the level of the production unit, those who work in it are clearly affected by its activities. However, other categories of people also have an interest, including users of what is produced, the community in which the workplace is located, the society as a whole (in the case of large-scale enterprises), groupings concerned with equal opportunities and environmental effects, and possibly other interest groups. A way has to be found to enable all with an interest in how particular means of production are used to be involved in the decision-making process. Thus, in relation to the individual production unit, I distinguish between self-government, to be exercised by a governing body made up of representatives of all social groups with a significant interest in its activities, and self-management, to be undertaken by the production unit's workers within policy guidelines set by its governing body.

The same general principle of self-government would apply at the level of the branch of production—decisions would be made by those affected by them. The most novel institutional feature of my model of democratic planning is the negotiated coordination body. This is the place where all those with an interest in the performance of a particular branch of production come together to negotiate over decisions that affect its performance and the long-term future of its production units. The production units are obviously affected by such decisions, as are the communities and regions in which they are located, the principal customers and suppliers of inputs, the planning commission on behalf of society as a whole, and any other groups able to establish a legitimate interest. All would be represented on the negotiated coordination body for that branch of production.

Given this institutional setting, what can be said about the related issues of information and motivation? How would the governing bodies of production units and the negotiated coordination bodies of branches of production know what they should do to further the social interest? What reason is there to suppose that they would act in the social interest if such action conflicted with their own narrow self-interest? When addressing these questions, it is necessary to bear in mind the crucial distinction between market exchange and market forces.

The model assumes a democratic society, in which people participate through a variety of self-governing and representative bodies, with decision-making decentralized as much as possible, both functionally and vertically. At each level, representative assemblies, democratically elected in a context of political party pluralism, are vested with ultimate political power. Civil society is populated with autonomous, self-governing interest groups, coming together in chambers of interests to advise the representative assemblies. Collectively provided services are organized by functional social bodies, as vertically decentralized as possible, which coordinate their activities through negotiation.

Broad social priorities and changes in strategic direction are decided on through the democratic political process. These priorities and strategic decisions determine the planned overall allocation of available resources between different uses, and hence the planned distribution of purchasing power in the economy. They are also the basis for the determination of the primary input prices that are used by production units in setting their prices equal to long-run costs. The planning commission is responsible for decisions on major investment, sectoral coordination, and regional distribution. A similar process occurs at the regional and local levels.

Production units meet demand from customers who in general have a choice of supplier. Given that the distribution of purchasing power reflects socially determined values and priorities, meeting demand is a first approximation to furthering the social interest. Provided that there are alternative sources of supply, the extent to which a production unit is making good use of its existing capacity in the general interest will be indicated by the extent to which customers wish to buy from it. This information is generated by market exchange. The governing body of the production unit considers this information, representing the general interest, together with information supplied by those represented on it about their particular interests. It then embarks on a process of negotiation to arrive at a second approximation to the social interest, incorporating both general and particular interests. Thus, what is to count as the social interest would be determined by those whose interest it is.

It is at this stage above all that the model of negotiated coordination differs from coordination through the atomistic responses of autarchic production units to market forces, whether regulated or not. A distinction is drawn in the model between the use of existing capacity, involving market exchange, and changes in capacity, which are brought about not through the operation of market forces but through negotiation. The use of existing capacity is decided on by production units, as outlined in the previous paragraph. Changes in capacity are decided on by negotiated coordination bodies representing all those affected by the changes.

Negotiated coordination bodies would seek to arrive at an agreed set of investment decisions for their branch of production. They would take into account both the changing pattern of demand, including the impact of any major investment decisions decided on by the planning commission, and the particular circumstances and interests of the production units, communities and other groups involved. Their activities would therefore be a central part of the social construction by those affected of what is to count as socially useful productive activity. Thus, the model incorporates market exchange, which generates relevant information about desirable changes in capacity, but not market forces, which are replaced by the process of negotiated coordination.

The pattern of cross-cutting representation that lies at the heart of the system of negotiated coordination is the principal means for containing the antisocial impact of narrow self-interest. It is also the means for promoting transformation, by enabling people's initial perceptions to be modified in the light of those of others. First, it provides a safeguard against information bias. The records and accounts of all economic organizations—the self-managing sections of production units, production units as a whole, negotiated coordination bodies, the planning commission—would be open, subject to regular audit and available for public scrutiny by any organization, groups, or individual. It is unlikely that distorted information would long survive in such an environment, particularly if it was being used to justify exceptional treatment. Since the governing bodies of production units and the negotiated coordination bodies would contain representatives of other production units and negotiated coordination bodies, as well as of customers, other interested groups, and the planning commission, the possibilities for systematic distortion of information would be remote.

Second, openness of information would provide the basis for any incentives and sanctions that might be considered necessary. Within the self-managing sections of production units, decisions about individual incentives and discipline would be taken by the peer group, subject to the right of trade union representation. Production units themselves would have governing bodies representative of all affected groups, so no one group could insist on its sectional interest predominating.

Above all, the model's dynamic is transformatory. It cannot legislate narrow self-interest away, but neither does it reward it. Instead, it institutionalizes the requirement that particular interests are made explicit; brought up against one another so that their interdependence is recognized, confronted with representatives of more general interests, and encouraged to arrive at an integrated view through conscious interaction and negotiation. Negotiated coordination is a process in the course of which learning occurs, perceptions change, consciousness may be transformed, and the social interest is constructed.

At this point, I should like to emphasize three general conclusions that may be drawn from the discussion so far. The first is that the long overdue attention to the centrality of democratization in the process of socialization should not cause us to lose sight of the importance of the public or common aspect of social ownership. It is this aspect of social ownership that makes society-wide planning and conscious decisions about the overall use of resources possible. Interestingly, it tends to be an older generation of socialists who are most acutely aware of the danger of throwing the baby out with the bathwater. Perhaps this is because of the continuous and at times painful process they experienced of actively and creatively reworking a classical Marxist theoretical formation, acquired in the first half of the twentieth century, in the light of the changing reality of the second half.

The second conclusion is related to the first. There is a real danger that the chilling experience of Stalinism and the sobering experience of social democracy is producing a lowering of sights, a loss of focus on the priorities and values that make the socialist/communist project revolutionary and worthwhile. Ironically, a pessimism not only of the intellect but also of the will seems to have taken hold. It is as if the reactionary argument that you can't change human nature has triumphed after all, this time round in the guise of a hard-headed, postfundamentalist, postutopian realism. I continue to believe that a society in which "the antithesis between intellectual and physical labor" has disappeared is possible.

Thirdly, however, it is essential to be realistic. Yet the appeal to realism can be either conservative or revolutionary. Conservative realism starts from the way people are at any particular time and assumes that that is how they always will be.

The task of the present generation is to refuse the temptation of cozy incorporation in new rightist realism and assert an autonomous, historically situated revolutionary realism. Realism, to be revolutionary—in fact, to be realism—must be transformatory. The challenge for the present generation remains whether "enough of us can reasonably believe that a new human order is seriously possible."[7]

Notes

1. C. Lindblom, *Politics and Markets* (New York: Basic Books, 1977), chap. 13.
2. M. Dobb, *On Economic Theory and Socialism* (London: Routledge and Kegan Paul, 1955), p. 77; *An Essay on Economic Growth and Planning* (London: Routledge and Kegan Paul, 1960), pp. 7–8; *Welfare Economics and the Economics of Socialism* (Cambridge: Cambridge University Press, 1970), p. 148.
3. Dobb, *On Economic Theory and Socialism*, p. 76; *An Essay on Economic Growth and Planning*, p. 5.
4. J. Kornai, *Contradictions and Dilemmas* (Cambridge, MA: MIT Press, 1985), p. 89.
5. Alec Nove, *The Economics of Feasible Socialism* (London: Allen and Unwin, 1983).
6. Ibid., p. 229.
7. R. Williams, "Beyond Actually Existing Socialism," *New Left Review* (1980).

RESPONSES FROM THE THIRD WORLD

CARLOS M. VILAS

IS SOCIALISM STILL AN ALTERNATIVE FOR THE THIRD WORLD?

Very broadly speaking, socialism in the Soviet Union and Eastern Europe, and to a lesser extent elsewhere, has been successful in three main economic tasks: (1) superseding precapitalist remnants in the rural world; (2) promoting rapid industrialization and in so doing introducing greater complexity, diversification, and integration into the socioeconomic structure; and (3) satisfying the basic needs of the masses for nutrition, health care, education, stable employment, and (to a modest extent) housing. But socialism has experienced enormous difficulty in moving toward more advanced stages: from extensive to intensive development, from the satisfaction of basic needs to the satisfaction of more advanced and sophisticated ones. Moreover, insistence on a type of development that has already been exhausted and on the institutional network associated with it has tended to translate into stagnation, a general deterioration of conditions and standards of living, dissatisfaction of the people, and political tensions.

At bottom these are consequences of the very development of centrally planned economies and of success in the achievement of goals in previous stages. Improvements in education, advances in industrialization, urbanization, and the like transform the demands of younger generations and define sharp contradictions with political institutions and ruling groups. The achievement of full employment, high participation of women in the labor force, decreasing population growth, and modernization of the means of production exhaust the

205

possibilities of extensive development, and force a move toward technology-intensive development.

After thirty or forty years of state socialism in the East, the banner of free education and health care for all is no longer an exciting one, and official reminders of the evils of capitalism are no longer an effective tool for mobilization. No one worries about the evils of capitalism; on the contrary, the things people know about capitalism are usually its flashiest aspects. Moreover, free education and health care belong to the natural order of life for generations of people who have grown up in the socialist world. The children and grandchildren of state socialism, who have more education and higher aspirations than their forebears, who have not had to undergo war, famine, and reconstruction to get what they have, are now demanding other kinds of achievements. They want broad and free political participation, cultural alternatives, differentiated consumption, access to information—in brief, their right to be different and to have a say in the design of a different and better socialist world. The refusal of the ruling groups, entrenched in their privileges, to accept these demands for participation and for the right to be socialist in a different way diverts the new generation, first towards cynicism, depoliticization, and apathy, then towards the search for non-socialist alternatives.

The demands stemming from this new situation, the collisions with the highly centralized and bureaucratized state institutions and political systems, with the perennial and aged leaderships that cannot keep pace with the new social, economic, and political developments, give birth to the now-familiar features of protest movements and upheavals in the East: young people versus their elders, workers and consumers versus the managers, social movements versus the party, civil society versus the state.

In the early stages of nearly all socialist societies, the new governments have had to face backwardness, widespread destruction, and counterrevolutionary wars by the former ruling classes and their allies. External pressures, backwardness, lack of infrastructure, inadequately-trained personnel, concentration of developed resources in a small portion of the country, and the urgency of socioeconomic transformation and political consolidation all conspire to drive the new regime to build highly centralized administrative institutions and pervasive bureaucracies, to decrease the dispersion of political participation in the name of "efficiency," and to substitute "government on behalf of the interests of the workers" for government by the workers themselves.

The concentration of social and economic power in the hands of the socialist state has shown particular strength in societies where state building and tight control over the territory and the people had reached relatively high levels in prerevolutionary times—as in the autocratic empires of Russia and China, and their surrounding regions. After the revolutionary seizure of state power in these countries, the centralization and bureaucratization of administrative power structures in some cases have contributed to advances on the road to development and economic modernization. The industrialization of the USSR and the development of agriculture in China are outstanding cases in point. At the very beginning restrictions on mass participation were presented as temporary compromises necessitated by the lack of alternatives. Discipline, not democracy, was the name of the game. But with time and inertia, the lack of direct participation hardened into an integral part of the new system. The state/party displaced and then subordinated the masses, and turned their unions, cooperatives, and other organizations into apparatuses. It transformed itself into the official emblem of the revolution and of socialism; government on behalf of the workers' interests turned into the regime of officials; the primacy of the plan became the primacy of the planners; and the defense of the revolution became the rule of the state security apparatuses.

These authoritarian regimes survived the objective conditions that made them possible, and not only sacrificed democracy but inhibited subsequent economic development. Overcentralization and bureaucratization, and the ineluctable effects of time upon the ruling groups, brought an accumulation of tensions and contradictions that first exploded in the economic realm and then expanded over the entire social and political system.

The industrial economy piled one inefficiency upon another and lost any chance to be competitive in external markets. Bureaucracies are always very sensitive on this issue, and their sensitivity explains the economic reforms from above to modernize and make production more efficient—including an expansion of trade with capitalist countries and an increasing demand for Western technologies and equipment. On the domestic side, reforms consisted of the introduction and delegation of autonomy to enterprises and managers, price reforms and reducing or eliminating subsidies, and the implementation of many other features of the market economy: greater social inequality, frustration of popular expectations, heavier pressure on labor, unemployment, inflationary tensions, cuts in basic consumption, and the like.

People's responses to these reforms followed two main paths. On the one hand, they demanded that reforms not be confined to the economic field, but rather that they be expanded into the political realm: participation, leadership, renewal, political competition— that is, to extend the market principle from economics to politics. Such demands have come mostly from what in our societies are called the "middle classes": technicians, intellectuals, skilled labor, students, artists, and the like. Their material position in socialist society was not unsatisfactory relative to that of other classes, except with respect to housing, but they resented restrictions on access to information, freedom of opinion, and creativity, despised bureaucratization, and most of all complained about their living standards relative to those of their western counterparts. But politics and ideology, more than economics, made them angry with state socialism. On the other hand, they demanded moderation of the economic reforms that cause unemployment and depress the living standards of workers.

The questions of political pluralism, of effective observance of human rights, of freedom of expression and access to information, of national identity and autonomy, and the frustrations of the younger generations interact with one another and explode at the very moment when economic reversals take a heavy toll on people's living and working conditions, increasing political instability and social insecurity.

The prospects for socialism in the third world[1] are shaped by the crises of state socialism in the Soviet Union and Eastern Europe in three main ways: (1) Since the Russian Revolution, the chances of socialist transformation in the periphery of capitalism have always been linked to the availability of resources, cooperation, and assistance from more developed socialist countries; (2) the Soviet and East

European models of socialism have been extremely influential in shaping the way peripheral societies have envisioned their own socialism; (3) the pressures from former colonial and anti-socialist powers—which include funding and covert management of counter-revolution—are particularly severe in the absence of help from the socialist world.

But before we proceed, an insistent question must be addressed: except for China and Cuba, to what extent, or in what sense, may we call any of the third world countries socialist? Peripheral societies are by definition backward, with an incipient, distorted capitalism strongly tied to domestic forms of production and distribution that are non-capitalist but intimately linked to the international capitalist system. Such societies cannot be well characterized in the language of capitalist class conflict. The class that works under capitalist relations of productions is usually very small and unorganized, and so is the capitalist class itself.

These considerations sharply differentiate revolutionary transitions in such societies from any that might take place in more advanced countries. According to Marx, the transition process should lead from capitalism to communism; what Marx termed transition was in fact socialism, a phase that intervened between capitalism and communism, not between capitalism and socialism. The question of "socialist transition" has been posed by social revolutions in backward societies and has fundamentally to do with building up the socioeconomic and political preconditions for socialism—a transition to transition, as it is frequently and ironically called. The problem, in its specific aspects, was first posed by the Russian Revolution when faced with the defeat of revolution in Germany and the resulting isolation of the backward Soviet state.

Socialism has a different meaning for different people in different times. Economic and social transformations, democratization, and national liberation are usually closely interrelated in third world social revolutions,[2] but in most cases the question of backwardness and development has tended to dominate over other dimensions of transition, or to become a relatively autonomous issue. To a certain extent, therefore, Marxism as a theory of transition has become a species of left-wing developmentalism, a method for accelerating modernization.[3] The establishment of new relations of production, direct and effective workers' and peasants' participation, democratization of political institutions and relations, development of new attitudes and motivations, and fighting against gender and ethnic discrimination have not often kept pace with efforts to accumulate the means of production. In not a few cases there has also been a certain tendency to underestimate the contribution of higher levels of popular participation to economic development.

Social revolutions in peripheral economies confront transition under the most precarious conditions. Backwardness is the starting point, and an obstacle to transition. External vulnerability is increased by pressures from the "center"; class struggle becomes more acute as it mixes with ethnic confrontations and clashes among kinship structures; former colonial and imperialist states foment destabilization and counterrevolutionary wars.

Is socialism possible under these conditions? To begin transition from such a shaky starting point introduces new and specific issues, dimensions, and objectives, or superimposes on them an emphasis that would not exist when transition starts from higher levels of development and economic integration: the particular class structures of backward, nonindustrial societies; the need to build a state apparatus and an economic infrastructure at the national level; the question of the articulation of ethnic differentiation and kinship loyalties to incipient class contradictions; the quest for different external linkages; the need for foreign cooperation and solidarity; the search for specific and effective development strategies; and so on. These new dimensions impose on the transition from backwardness and underdevelopment a prolonged and relatively slow pace.

In some of these cases, complexities in the process of development, the very depth of backwardness, the destructive impact of the war of liberation or of counterrevolutionary war, the extreme insufficiency of natural resources, etc., have led to the assertion that transition must be approached in two stages. The first is reconstruction and development to bring about the conditions for the second, which is the socialist transition itself. But it has also been argued, in rejoinder, that reconstruction and development cannot be carried out without regard for the social relations in which it is embedded, if the end result is to be socialism. In addition, whatever the dimensions and extent of backwardness, there is a range of relative autonomy to the political leadership of the revolutionary process. Objective conditions themselves do not suffice to determine whether a transition will develop. The combination of these elements—weak material base, small working class, petty bourgeois leadership—usually introduces strong tensions between the democratic dimension of the revolutionary process and the urgent need for efficacy and control, usually aggravated by economic and military pressures from former colonial and imperialist powers.

These issues did not appear on the socialist agenda four decades ago. Their appearance and relevance to contemporary discussions of transition give to such discussions a revisionist aspect, and their absence from earlier Marxist thought has made it very difficult to use classical Marxism to gain an understanding of what is going on in the third world. Indeed, the outpouring of questions brought about by the problem of third world transition took Marxism by surprise.

One of the central features of the noncapitalist, socialist-oriented road is the establishment of economic relations with the USSR and the Council for Mutual Economic Assistance (COMECON). Foreign economic, technical, and military cooperation has been one of the most strategic resources for the socioeconomic transformation of third world countries and the establishment of these relations has turned out to be the central element in the conceptualization of these regimes as "socialist," in an epoch in which the USSR was waging an aggressive political competition with U.S. expansion in the third world. From this point onward, the socialist-oriented, or at least noncapitalist, road that these countries were walking was more a function of the friends they could gather abroad than of the policies they were pushing at home. Or to put it a different way, the political classification of third world regimes becomes more an issue of international politics than of political economy. Not infrequently, such "socialist-oriented" regimes were highly authoritarian, and their only connection to socialism was their orientation toward the foreign policies of the Soviet Union—two examples are Sri Lanka and Uganda under Idi Amin.

Be that as it may, the socialist transformation of peripheral societies calls for massive cooperation from abroad for a long time and under extremely generous conditions. This is not a new problem. Marx and Engels raised it when dealing with the possibility of a socialist revolution in Russia that would bypass capitalism almost entirely. They accepted this possibility with one important condition, that the revolution in Russia could count on the support and cooperation of the victorious Western working class. "Only when the capitalist economy has been overcome at home and in the countries of its prime, only when the retarded countries have seen 'how it's done,' how the productive forces of modern industry are made to work as social property for society as a whole—only then will the retarded countries be able to start on this abbreviated process of development."[4]

In addition to what a vast bibliography and long experience teach us about the need for Third World countries to appeal for external cooperation, progressive and revolutionary regimes call for such assistance because the rhythms and conditions for building the new political and economic orders are out of phase, and because the old social and economic orders break down faster than the new orders can be made to work. Gaps always exist between removing old elites from political power and building new institutions and political processes, and there are inevitably lags in achieving socioeconomic changes. The latter are dimensions of the deep transformation that bears its fruits only in the long run, but the aggressive reactions of the former ruling classes and colonial powers are felt in the very short run.

This is not the place to discuss the extent, conditions, and shortcomings of external technical and economic support from COMECON countries to revolutionary and progressive governments in the third world. For our purposes, only two important points must be brought out.

One point is the fact that this cooperation was vital for these regimes to survive and to implement some important social and economic reforms, to confront counterrevolutionary wars, to train workers, and so on. Perhaps the most outstanding case in point is Cuba. Socialism in Cuba is, above all, a result of the Cubans' own determination—both of the leaders and of the masses—to face down U.S. hostility and aggression. But this determination has been fed for three decades by the support of the USSR and COMECON. Cuba's recognition of the vital character of this support is stated at the very beginning of her Constitution, and Fidel Castro has been particularly explicit on this matter:

> We, I repeat, have solved our problems, not just through social changes, but also because as a third world socialist country, as a developing socialist country, we have built in a certain way a new international economic order with the socialist international community. Without this foundation, our great social and economic successes, our extraordinary victories in the realms of public health, of education, of sports, in the uprooting of unemployment and malnutrition, in the raising of the material and cultural standards of living of our people, would not have been possible.[5]

To a lesser degree, the same might be said about other third world revolutions and processes of social reform in Central America, Asia, and Africa, a number of which received vital support from Cuba.

In some cases, this cooperation engendered the fantasy of something like an imported socialism, or a socialism "from outside": the conception that socialism can be imposed on a society as a technical procedure for development—as in some aspects was the case in a few Central European countries after World War II. The enthusiastic rhetoric of a number of third world governments and leaders obviously stemmed from some such fantasy, which was reinforced by the way the Soviet government conducted its relations with third world countries during the 1960s and 1970s, as a dimension of the USSR-U.S. conflict. But even without manipulation and exaggeration, the record points to the fact that only with abundant and cheap external support can small peripheral societies overcome imperialist domination and develop their societies.

The second point to stress here is that because of the economic and political crises in the USSR and Eastern Europe, abundant and cheap socialist support for progressive governments overseas no longer exists. The very concept of a "socialist community of nations" is outdated.

From the mid-1980s, and in some cases dating even earlier,

centrally planned economies have increasingly turned to the inter-national, i.e., capitalist, market. This reorientation has lent the USSR and Eastern Europe's economic relations with the West a traditional third world profile: they mainly export primary goods to the West and import industrial goods. At the same time, they act toward the third world in a reverse way; they mainly export industrial goods and import primary commodities. The East German case has been par-ticularly striking: two-thirds of its exports to COMECON have been manufactured goods, whereas more than half of its exports to West Germany have been raw materials.

This opening to the West has exposed the socialist economies to ups and downs that they cannot control. Cuba's case has been particularly dramatic. Rising sugar and oil prices in the 1970s made it attractive to open the Cuban economy to some degree to the international market. Increasing export earnings in hard currencies allowed the Cubans to import equipment and technolo-gies from capitalist countries. But falling prices of sugar and oil at the beginning of the 1980s, and the sustained decline in the U.S. dollar, led in subsequent years to a crisis of foreign debt in hard currencies that coincided with the termination of the Cuban-Soviet agreement on economic cooperation and deferred debt repayment. After a failed attempt to build a united front of Latin American debtors, Cuba had no choice but to deal with the problem by itself. In 1988 and 1989, imports from capitalist countries were cut by half, forcing the government to tighten rationing of some basic products and to seek new sources of hard currency by increasing production for export and encouraging Western tourism.

In addition, changes in the USSR and Eastern Europe threaten Cuba with a reduction in foreign cooperation and rising import costs. Increasing problems with spare parts and other supplies, new shortages of foodstuffs, and other problems stemming from economic readjustment threaten the availability of social services and the high standard of living achieved in the years since the Cuban Revolution.

Contrary to widespread belief, the separation of the socialist or socialist-oriented countries from the international capitalist mar-ket is mostly a result of Western, U.S.-led, pressures and confrontations, and not a strategy deliberately adopted by those countries. Such deliberate strategy as has been adopted is mainly a reaction to an objectively negative situation, a search for an alternative. The alternative more often than not turns out to be more expensive than its predecessor, a misfortune that the peripheral revolutionary countries are not easily able to cope with by themselves.

The isolation of Cuba from the U.S. market and from much of Latin America was a decision made in the White House. The same must be said of the embargo of the Nicaraguan economy from 1985 to 1990 and the resulting reorientation of Nicaragua's foreign trade toward COMECON, and of the U.S. refusal to establish normal relations with Vietnam once the war was over, notwithstanding Vietnamese appeals on this point. Establishing or strengthening economic and trade ties with the Soviet Union and Eastern Europe enabled third world revolutionary regimes to adjust partially to the perverse impact of the rupture with the international capitalist market. This proved to be an expensive way out because of higher comparative costs and technological lags in the centrally planned economies and the costs of reorienting peripheral economies to different technologies. The generally favorable economic relations between the USSR and Cuba cannot be generalized to the rest of the third world, and recently the leadership of Cuba has become less enthusiastic about this relationship than it has been in the past:

> We have learned uneven exchange in our trade with the USSR. Year after year our sugar and nickel have been worthless.... I fly Soviet jets and they are very safe, but they need twice the gas. Soviet trucks are terrible, they only make seven kilometers per gallon and waste the oil the Soviets themselves send to us.... While we send them prime quality sugar and nickel, they sell us outdated technological stuff.[6]

> ... time has forced us to change the scheme of economic cooperation between the two countries, a scheme where financial management was frequently overruled for the sake of political concerns.... Soviet firms are not interested in supplying equipment to Cuba because they face obstacles buying commodities with the rubles transferred from Cuba, which have to be deposited in bank accounts. It is not even possible for

them to compensate the negative balance through direct exchange, because our Cuban partners' payments are made to the Soviet state considered as a whole, not to the specific dealer.[7]

Socialist cooperation with the third world, then, has been reduced as a result of economic hardship, crisis, and restructuring in recent years, and of the ongoing negotiations between the Soviet and U.S. governments. Trade increasingly replaces aid, under conditions that no longer resemble those of an earlier era.

It is true that there are no great differences among the ways the current economic crisis is being faced by the socialist, national liberation, and capitalist regimes in the third world or the governments of Eastern Europe. All of them pursue the "adjustment policies" favored by the International Monetary Fund (IMF) and the World Bank, move toward privatization and dismantling of government controls, emphasize market relations and incentives, promote exports to the detriment of domestic use, and cut subsidies for mass consumption. Nor are there large or relevant differences in the outcomes of these policies: rising unemployment, recession, a drastic fall in basic consumption, deterioration of education, health, and welfare, social unrest, and political instability.

Yet international comparisons still favor the third world socialist regimes relative to their capitalist neighbors. Standard indicators of poverty and underdevelopment are much higher in India than in China, despite the recent market-oriented reforms in the latter that have led to retreats from previous achievements. In any case, famine is a nightmare of the past for China, but an everyday occurrence for millions of Indians. Closer to home, during the so-called lost decade for Latin American development, the 1980s, the gross domestic product per capita in Cuba grew by about 33 percent, while it fell by about 8 percent in the rest of Latin America. Moreover, in Cuba the high rate of economic growth was accompanied by rising indicators of social development and welfare, and by a progressive trend in the distribution of income.[8] From this perspective, it may be said that although socialism is facing profound crisis, capitalism—whether flowering or in crisis—has been unable to handle the economic, social, and cultural problems of impoverishment, oppression, and marginalization of the rapidly growing populations of what were once called developing societies.

In spite of their ambiguities and contradictions, the attempts to construct socialism produced, in the third world as elsewhere, very important improvements in the living conditions of the masses. In many cases these achievements could not be sustained, much less increased, and in global terms the economic performance is far from satisfactory. But this disheartening conclusion is the result of a comparison between socialist goals and socialist achievements. A more promising balance is obtained when the comparison is made between socialist and capitalist achievements in the third world. From this second perspective, the condition of the countries that have attempted a socialist transformation is, in general, significantly better than that of their capitalist-oriented neighbors. And even where the gap between socialist goals and achievements is particularly deep, it has more to do with the extremely aggressive international environments created by U.S. imperialism than with the shortcomings of socialist or socialist-aligned strategies. This conclusion is valid not just with regard to economic performance, but with regard to access to social resources through direct participation, and to building an expanded consciousness of political effectiveness.

The international conditions that *enabled* some third world countries to choose a socialist strategy no longer exist, but those that *forced* them to do it are stronger than ever. The traditional socialist slogan that "the Soviet Union is the strategic ally of the third world" can no longer be repeated without hesitation. But at the same time, the failure of capitalism to solve *any* of the most urgent and appalling problems of vast and growing populations all over the third world is perfectly evident. De-accumulation and wretched poverty are the most salient traits of market economies in peripheral societies, in a pervasive environment of political instability and personal insecurity.

In spite of the enormous present difficulties, therefore, there can be only a positive answer to the question posed in the title of this essay. Socialism is still the only possible alternative for third

218   *The Future of Socialism*

world countries that are looking, not just for economic development, but for real and effective democracy as well.

Notes

1. This section and the two that follow contain a number of rather sweeping generalizations as well as various specific points about particular countries. Doubtless there is no one country in the third world to which all the generalizations apply, but there is likewise no country that is exempt from all of them.
2. Carlos M. Vilas, *The Sandinista Revolution* (New York: Monthly Review Press, 1986), Ch. 1.
3. Carlos M. Vilas, *Transición desde el subdesarrollo* (Caracas: Nueva Sociedad, 1989), Ch. 3.
4. Frederick Engels, "Afterword to On Social Relations in Russia," Karl Marx and Frederick Engels, *Selected Works*, vol. 2 (Moscow: Progress Publishers, 1969), pp. 403–4.
5. Fidel Castro, *La impagable deuda externa de América Latina y el Tercer Mundo, entrevistal al diaro Excélsior de México* (La Habana: Editora Politica, 1985), p. 35. Translation mine.
6. See, for example, the statements of Fidel Castro in *Excélsior* (Mexico), 23 March 1990, pp. 1, 10.
7. *Pravda,* cited in *Excélsior* (Mexico), 10 April 1990.
8. Figures form CEPAL, *Balance preliminar de la economía del América Latina y el Caribe,* 1989 (Table 3). See also Claes Brundenius, *Revolutionary Cuba: The Challenge of Economic Growth with Equity* (Boulder: Westview Press, 1984).

PABLO GONZALEZ CASANOVA

THE THIRD WORLD AND
THE SOCIALIST PROJECT TODAY

For Milos Nikolic

In order to analyze the struggles of workers and peoples, it is not enough to analyze capitalist states; the forms of domination of socialist states must inevitably be taken into account. Thus the struggle may be that of capitalist states against socialist states, that of workers and peoples against bourgeois states or against their "own" states, as well as against the "bureaucratic deformations" that affect them (which already existed even in 1920, as Lenin himself said). Today the question of revolution and the state needs to be posed with regard to existing and former socialist states.[1]

Among socialist states, it seems useful to distinguish between those comprising the USSR and its neighbors in Eastern Europe and those that arose out of the colonial system of the modern age and belong to the so-called third world. In struggles between socialist states it is essential to single out those of the hegemonic or imperial type, such as those of the USSR and China, when they try to subordinate "liberation movements" in colonies or among oppressed peoples; those which both kinds of states wage over the ethnic groups or "nationalities" that form part of their territory; and those that the USSR and China have waged in order to control the less powerful "socialist states."

The restructuring of the USSR and the movements that have taken place among its European neighbors clearly show a struggle for world hegemony of nation-states and of nations that combines with

219

class struggle and a struggle over systems. Given the difficulties involved in categorizing the contending states, classes, and systems, it is ever more obvious that the advanced capitalist countries—from Europe to Japan, with the United States in the center—have scored an obvious political, military, and ideological victory with the crisis of so-called real socialism. It is also clear that on the basis of this victory the great capitalist powers are preparing to play an ever greater role, not only containing "Soviet expansionism," which means any victorious revolution, but strengthening in the so-called socialist world the movement toward "market socialism," and from there toward a restoration of capitalism of the neoliberal variety. From this angle, the problem of states and revolutions is that there are postcapitalist states, and that although the revolution in those countries may not have been socialist, today's struggles may head them in the direction of a neoliberal and neocapitalist counterrevolution.

Socialist states and socialist-tending states in the third world feel very much threatened by the restructuring of the Soviet Union and Eastern Europe. Many of them have lost a significant portion of the aid they were receiving from the advanced socialist countries. For their part, after the initial victories over authoritarian socialism, the workers are being affected or threatened by being inserted into capitalism, not always a "central" capitalism. Those most threatened and most affected are undoubtedly third world states and workers.

The trilateral offensive of the United States, Japan, and Europe against the third world and its socialist experiments is taking place directly through a reactivation of the battle lines, from Cuba and Central America to Vietnam, by way of southern Africa, the edge of Palestine, and Afghanistan. It is also taking place indirectly, through attacks on the USSR and the advanced Eastern countries.

Following, or accompanying, the struggles of nations or workers against authoritarianism socialism is the struggle of nations and workers against an imperialism and a capitalism that have become reenergized and increasingly aggressive. What is clear about revolution and the state is that they encompass at least two struggles, one against the bureaucratic-authoritarian socialist state and the other more traditional struggle against the neocapitalist and neocolonial state. It is also obvious that after the Reaganite decade of the 1980s, the capitalist states have not only managed to hold back the struggles of peoples and workers against imperialism, but they have proven their ability to take advantage of, and redirect, the struggle of peoples and workers against authoritarian, populist, and socialist states.

The interpretation of these facts is very much bound up in an intense ideological struggle. Those leading the charge in Washington see not only a chance to open socialist markets and connect them to the capitalist world market, but they also anticipate the possibility of gaining decisive control over third world countries through the weakening or subjection of the USSR to the advanced capitalist countries, or conceivably through a U.S.-USSR alliance that would begin a stage of joint government and world stability by means of a shared global colonialism. Besides the USSR, some advanced countries, such as Czechoslovakia and the German Democratic Republic, once they have been integrated into Europe, would fit into this global colonialist alliance. The world would be divided into "spheres of influence" with interconnected fortresses. The USSR would get to control its own nationalities, Japan would get China, and South Africa, Israel, and Australia would get "subimperialist" control over their neighboring countries—and would in turn be dominated by the United States–Canada and by the new multinational European state envisioned for 1992. The United States—as a multiethnic state—would be enriched with the definitive integration of Puerto Rico and with the associated and subordinate integration of Mexico. The world would constitute a perfect "animal farm" with a human advantage over Orwell's: added to a "perfectly" functioning market with its "natural" inequalities would be a struggle for a particular kind of democracy, which while making allowances for its necessary limits and assuring its governability, would not only make the face of capitalism more human, but would absorb and blunt any revolutionary process against the neoliberal state: peoples everywhere, rather than taking the Winter Palace, would strive to take the supermarkets (as they did in Buenos Aires); and rather than struggle against capitalism, they would struggle, as was the case in Argentina, against militarism and for the various forms of civilian dictatorship.

Everything would take place within a global state which would constantly readjust the ascendant economic colonialism. Under normal conditions, citizens would settle their disputes in pluralistic political systems, which would be limited in terms of participants and classes. Workers in skilled trades or cutting-edge industries or white-collar workers—and their democratic unions—would negotiate better conditions and salaries, following a logic of managerial cooperation. Whenever possible there would be a combination of "Japanese management style with Mexican salaries." At the same time, workers in free zones and on plantations or in subcontracting companies in the informal sector would understand that in the world of supply and demand you cannot acquire more than what you have money to buy. Barefoot entrepreneurs and informal workers would struggle to attain the degree of competitiveness one needs so as not to drop "beneath the poverty level." Only "deviants" would fall into the crimes of the underground economy, especially shady drug trafficking or "terrorist" politics. Having no ideologies or utopias, these people would be pursued solely as delinquents. The forces pursuing them would serve to fortify centrist positions favoring governability. Extremist premodern positions would be eliminated among both the "poor masses" and among the associated and dependent governments, and whoever sought to maintain them would be pushed aside.

In Washington and the advanced capitalist countries as a whole there is a clear anticipation of achieving these objectives, with the help of the USSR and the Eastern countries. The overwhelming victories they have scored in subjecting or bringing into line first world social democracies, third world populisms, and now second world socialisms bolster their amply evidenced confidence. Their reading of the Twenty-Seventh Congress of the Communist Party of the Soviet Union, in which there is reference to the use of armed force in third world conflicts and to the dangers of a growing "global" escalation, leads them to conclude that the Russians are not going to use their arms even if the West advances, and they see this confirmed in the USSR's restrained approach to conflicts such as the Iran-Iraq war, Lebanon, Libya, and others. They read Gorbachev's statement to the effect that "crises and conflicts are fertile soil for international terrorism" as a criticism of what they call "intellectual Communism," and as a chance for Soviet-Western cooperation—à la James Bond—in a "struggle against terrorism," which they regard as a reflection of ideological retardation, universally rejected in a "post-ideological" modern world. From this standpoint they think the USSR itself will abandon the "revolutionary Marxism" and "orthodox Communism" that have caused so many serious problems and that entail so many dangers for the Russians themselves, as they are finally admitting. They see the withdrawal from Afghanistan—at least for a time—as a decision to leave this zone to the overt influence of the United States. In the break in solidarity between East European countries and governments like that of the Sandinistas, they see another U.S. victory in the monopoly over its "backyard," and likewise sense that a similar policy of abandoning Cuba is being announced. These interpretations are put forth as the hope of those analysts or politicians who make them, or as propaganda for readers and citizens in the Western world, or as an invitation to "modern" and "progressive" leaders in the East to pursue the restoration of capitalism within the process of democratization itself or as a threat to the "conservatives" who resist giving up their authoritarianism, their hegemony, or any system other than that of neoliberal capitalism.

With reasoning that is both triumphalistic and intended to exert pressure, they assert that in the case of Cuba the Soviet Union is well aware of U.S. military superiority in the Caribbean. Or they point out that "anti-Soviet insurgencies" have been extraordinarily successful in economically and socially destabilizing governments such as those of Ethiopia and Mozambique, Angola and Nicaragua, Kampuchea and Afghanistan, not to mention tiny Grenada—where the leadership split—or in the earlier case of democratic socialism in Chile, where after a calculated process of destabilization with hyperinflation, shortages, withholding of goods, unrest, and psychological warfare against the people, the treason of the army headed by Pinochet served their purposes.

The seriousness and thrust of the crisis derive from the unavoidable necessity of struggling on two fronts: against authoritarian socialism and against domination by private monopolies. In that struggle more advanced capitalism seems to be triumphing over a socialism that can no longer deal with its authoritarianism, inefficiency, and corruption. But the objective process indicates that the democratic revolution is as important for the masses as the social revolution: unable to carry out both, many peoples have decided to confront dictatorships like those of Eastern Europe which had nullified socialism's general logic. Soon enough they will confront a system like the capitalist system which leads to the impoverishment and exploitation of the bulk of humankind. Some hope to enjoy its benefits, but there is no question that the majority will not be able to do so. Thus the overall question of the struggle for democracy and also for socialism will be raised once more: the struggle against bureaucrats and also against capital. Today both struggles seem to be a necessary condition for victory, although sometimes one takes priority over the other.

The complexity of what is happening can be seen in the political categories commonly used to describe events: those who strive to maintain the system are called "conservatives," independent of whether what they seek to defend is authoritarian socialism as a source of personal privilege—as did Honecker—or socialism as a revolutionary project—as does Fidel Castro.

The confusion is not easily clarified when one moves to the level of class analysis. In socialist countries there is something like a bourgeoisie made up of state officials, middle classes, and a petty bourgeoisie. But this class is divided into supporters of authoritarian socialism, democratic socialism, and the restoration of capitalism. Corrupt bureaucrats split into those who stubbornly hold onto hereditary neo-Stalinism and those who have received some benefits or who, in order to obtain further benefits, defend the restoration of the market economy in order to continue and extend their businesses with companies and banks, through new concessions, permissions, credits, investments, and so forth. Finally, there are honest state officials and middle classes or members of the petty bourgeoisie who are in favor of both socialism and democracy: whether they will win is questionable, as is their strength.

The working class, which now has behind it a half century or more of questionable socialism, in a variety of ways experiences forms of oppression that make it something quite remote from being a class *in itself* or *for itself* (as the expression used to go). In the Soviet Union itself many workers are anti-Soviet. Ignorant of Marxism, they do not want to hear about "socialism," since their rulers have told them over and over (in a monotonous discourse that in no way resembles the art of thinking of Marx or Lenin) that *this* is socialism. And as for what they think about Communism: in the USSR of *perestroika,* in order to win elections, Communists often request that they not be listed as Communists.

When workers, reduced to their economic anguish and want, surrounded by ignorance, political and philosophical disenchantment, and a high level of alcohol consumption, engage in petty struggles or even stealing from factories, that is simply a matter of their daily experience; sometimes they do so with the complicity of the police, who also have to steal and then sell in the black market to make ends meet. By many indicators, the working class does not even exist. From a subjective standpoint, it lacks class consciousness vis-à-vis an exploiting class; from an objective standpoint, the aggression and exploitation it undergoes for the sake of an authoritarian and corrupt socialism does not pit it against the "bourgeoisie" as a clear class but rather against something that looks like a corrupt bureaucracy. In the struggle against state officials who have gotten criminally rich and who resist any change, the transnational bourgeoisie jumps in and when necessary professes piety, as in Poland.

In any case, *objectively* speaking, in many "socialist" countries, the main struggle tends to be democratic even if that means it is capitalist. "Revolution in the revolution" is unavoidable, and many are not concerned at all that it may very quickly turn into counterrevolution.

In modern history corruption is one of the most important categories for understanding the politics of ideals, especially in states where egalitarian or libertarian programs are the moving force. Authoritarian socialism in the hands of corrupt bureaucracies causes socialism to lose the logic of the common interest and its power of persuasion among the masses. Succeeding the classic bourgeoisie of private business people, a kind of bourgeoisie of public officials who call themselves Marxist-Leninists takes over the state, with the accompanying privileges. The costs of the enormous investments in war industry and in military spending falls on the middle classes, the workers, and the peasants, with cutbacks in great social programs and secondary effects on the overall plan and the economy. This is made all the more dramatic by the way *overall* authoritarianism and corruption undermine *efficiency* throughout the whole fabric of society, culture, science, administration, and politics. The beneficiaries of the system accentuate their class composition, in a variety of ways becoming like capitalist business people, opening accounts

226 The Future of Socialism

outside the country or engaging in business: some end up opting for an overall restoration of capitalism; others retrench and try to halt the process so as not to lose the power they say they are defending in the name of Marxism-Leninism (in which no one believes any more and which they were the first to ignore as both method and philosophy).

When we analyze the process of reconversion of third world countries with a "socialist orientation," it is clear that most of them are changing the central objectives of development. Of the victories scored by workers and peoples in these countries in the struggle for social justice and economic decolonization, there is no doubt that the most profound of these victories are those of "really existing socialism." With all the limitations and contradictions, it is there that the processes of social justice and economic decolonization have reached their highest level of expression. Populism or third world democracy never achieved a success as widespread as that of state socialism or of the nation-state tending toward socialism. Hence, the crisis of socialism is severely affecting those political approaches to development with social justice and commercial or financial sovereignty that led to income distribution, degrees of stratification, and social development considerably more equitable than in any other kind of victory by labor or popular forces.

In countries that arose out of colonialism, restoration is far advanced. The central objective of an "egalitarian society to come," called a "Communist" society, and of liberation itself is changing, as development plans and the market fall under the control of monopolies which again become the beneficiaries of accumulation. Moreover, the social relations of production and domination are reestablished with a new kind of colonial authority or supranational state, embodied in the IMF. This is hardly rare. While in Cuba the foreign debt is equal to only 20 percent of national output, in Angola it is 55 percent, in Mozambique it is 67 percent, in Nicaragua 165 percent and in Vietnam, although comparable data do not exist, the debt is $5.5 billion. The situation is similar in sixteen underdeveloped socialist-tending countries. With varying kinds of resistance or acceptance, through direct pressure from the IMF and the World Bank, or from the bureaucracies and internal "bourgeoisies" themselves, and even through pressures or hints from the USSR, "socialist-tending" countries have applied a kind of policy which throughout the third world has entailed a return to dependence and social inequality. While in populist states this kind of policy is a matter of giving up an overall thrust toward "independent national development" and ceding the processes of accumulation to the transnational and associated bourgeoisie, in "socialist-tending" countries it means in effect giving up socialist accumulation and *changing the dominant class or dominant bloc;* instead of the working people, the axis becomes the body of state officials and local bourgeoisies, in partnership with transnational bourgeoisies.

While state socialism is primarily devoted to raising of living standards, policies of structural adjustment make the payment of debt service the tactical objective and the restoration of capitalism and colonialism the strategic objective. The depth of the change is evident in the reorientation of all economic measures toward the accumulation of associated and transnational private capital, reducing the weight and function of public and social property for the benefit of capital, and in the *transformation of work into a commodity* of the owners of the means of production, that is, into a commodity of "organized capital," which is also monopoly and colonialist capital.

While not all socialist-tending countries are at the end of this dramatic process, all those that are negotiating with the IMF receive and accept, willingly or begrudgingly, the well-known pressures toward its policies of structural readjustment through which the "foreigner" or the "capitalist" reassumes basic control over the economy. In Mozambique, denationalization began in 1979; in 1984 private companies benefited when the state monopoly of foreign trade was ended; in 1986 legislation on foreign investment was liberalized, while a very severe program was imposed on the population, with a currency devaluation of 420 percent, new indirect taxes, price hikes of 200 to 400 percent (although wages rose only from 50 to 100 percent), and reductions in social spending by the state. Similar policies can be observed in other countries, from Nicaragua—even before the electoral defeat—to Vietnam. All these countries seem destined to lose the economic and social war after winning the war of the battlefield. "We are very good generals of the people," Nicaraguan Comandante Tomas Borge said bitterly, "and very bad economists."

In Vietnam the "readjustment policy" is leading to the creation of private companies, the spread of private agricultural companies, the "free market," suppression of subsidies for consumption, the reduction of the public sector, and a very liberal set of laws for foreign investment. Only Cuba has set up an "austerity policy" which is not changing, and does not hint of changing, the class basis of accumulation, and is not changing labor into a commodity subjected, or ready to be subjected, to the laws of supply and demand of capital. Perhaps this is what makes its defiance most odious to an empire that regards it as part of its zone of influence, both geographically and in terms of its system.

If the phenomenon of foreign indebtedness does not mean that socialist states, as a whole or those in the third world in particular, have ceased to be socialist, it does mean that in many of them the socialist project has lost, or is about to lose, whatever has made it a victory of the workers and the people. Neoliberal arrogance has objective foundations: what remains to be determined is whether all the socialist states or all the forces still present in such states have been defeated. Nor does this mean that the victory of capitalism is universal or will last a millenium. But it is disturbing to discuss the future.

The policy of restoring capitalism in "socialist" countries affects all liberation projects; it threatens nationalist and populist projects of the past along with those that are still tending to strengthen their coalitions with working class and popular bases. For now, the success scored against developed and authoritarian socialism weakens third world movements and states that have received support from the USSR and other countries that have passed to capitalism or are shaky in their economy, technology, politics, and thinking. Many states and movements in the third world feel more and more exposed as they confront their fate in a way they had not foreseen. Many are experiencing their own contradictions, having decided to cede more and more or—as is the case of Cuba—to wage a heroic struggle that even the most hearty are not sure will be victorious.

The neoliberal offensive takes advantage of the various contradictions in which third world countries and popular movements are entangled and further fuels them. These contradictions are the same as those of "developed socialism": the absence of a democratic organization to guard against the authoritarianism and corruption of the bureaucracies, without limiting the discipline necessary for struggling against the former owning classes and against imperialism; and the enormous failings of the productive apparatus, which is also a victim of the authoritarianism and corruption that thwart any "plan" (if indeed there is one worthy of the name) and economic development for the majority. This serious situation is also reflected in the authoritarian ideas that pay obeissance to doctrinaire "Marxism-Leninism" and that are adapted to "realistic policies" with local color, mixing and jumping from "doctrine" to "reality" without the slightest moral, let alone epistemological, scruple. What sets them apart is perhaps their greater weakness vis-à-vis imperialism, the incipient nature of their economic and social development, and the colonial distortion of official thought.

The contradictions present in central socialist states appear in peripheral countries with much lower levels of economic and social development.[2] The masses are not seized with the hope of taking their place alongside the more developed capitalist countries, but many individuals and families in the middle sectors are tantalized by the consumer society they see elsewhere, and they would like to travel freely to other countries or express new ideas and feelings in ways that clash severely with the rulers, whether because of their authoritarianism or their corruption or both. Even in Cuba, where the honesty of the leaders is beyond doubt, where the people have the opportunity for extensive democratic participation, and where the official language still objectively represents the general interest, nevertheless there arise demands that the leadership finds hard to accept, either because of the danger they represent, given the encirclement and harassment under which the island lives, or because they are demanding a political pluralism and a replacement of cadres that would weaken the revolution when Fidel Castro leaves the scene, or because they demand a degree of information, a language, a freedom to criticize, and an independence of thought to which the bureaucratic circles are unaccustomed, and they cannot find a way to carry out such opening without being weakened—even though they will be weakened if they do not open up. Certainly the future of Cuba will depend upon the ability of the government to respond to such pressures for change, and certainly both the government and the people are aware of this need, but precisely for this reason and because they are not changing the class content of either the leadership or labor, the main force of the worldwide U.S. offensive is aimed at them, and that makes the needed democratic changes in the spirit of Martí even more difficult.

In other countries, from Angola to Vietnam, the contradictions of underdeveloped socialist states are much greater. There we cannot exclude the possibility that in those countries, rather than reform the state, the people will be forced to overthrow it, lest they pass through the bitter experience of a neocolonial restoration, no doubt at a very high cost, setting back even further the struggle for democratic socialism. The situation of socialist countries, or countries striving for socialism, seems to demand a struggle on three levels: first, the defense of third world socialist countries—from Cuba to Vietnam—vis-à-vis imperialism and capitalist restoration, letting them determine the characteristics of, and time frame for, the democratic revolution; second, support for movements struggling for a democratic socialism in the USSR, Eastern Europe, and "socialist-tending countries"; third, the *essential* struggle against the exploitation of workers *and* for democracy, with the participation of people against the domination *and* exploitation of nations, both ethnic groups and nation-states. These three points seem to constitute a coherent strategy for defending today's socialism in power and for promoting democratic socialism as a political direction.

The threat against peoples and workers falls back against nation-states. In governing circles in China, Vietnam, and Cuba, there is already a growing awareness of the very serious dangers entailed in returning to the market economy and democracy when these are dominated by private monopolies. China's reentrenchment in so-called "market Stalinism" after the grave threats to the leadership, embodied in the Tiananmen Square uprising, of an "ungovernable democratization taken advantage of by imperialism" does not necessarily lead to either Stalinism or the market. If the student demonstrations led to the hardening of a regime that stands in flagrant contradiction to the general interest, and if inflation, unemployment, speculation, and increasing national inequality are the consequence of a rising market that entails an ever greater domination by corrupt officials and private monopolies, we cannot discount the possibility that a movement against corruption, the private market, and authoritarianism might win out. In Vietnam, foreign indebtedness and ever sharper economic and social contradictions will not necessarily lead to the reinstatement of the Saigon government and capitalism or to a civil war: they may lead toward the restructuring of the state so as to overcome these problems without restoring capitalism. Something similar is the case with Cuba: although it is much further ahead in both its moral level and the integration of power, Cuba has pioneered the revision of its systems of popular participation in decisionmaking, in watching over bureaucracies in charge of production and services. It is true that "rectification" has to go further and take in areas so far untouched.

Although Cuba has been abandoned by Czechoslovakia, Poland, Hungary, and Bulgaria, the fact that the USSR has renewed its economic aid agreement strengthens not only Cuba's position but that of the USSR itself vis-à-vis the U.S. offensive. Countries like Cuba are unlikely to fall into the maelstrom being experienced in the socialist states today.

Keeping power, and democratizing it, will represent an essential challenge for all concerned. In some cases it will be resolved by accentuating the general character of the state as instrument of the organized people, and in others by enriching the mediations of an ideological and religious pluralism, which in its more advanced manifestations will also be expressed in pluralistic political systems. To the ideal balance between people's power and democratic politics will be added a balance between plan and market, in which the large enterprises in the public and social sector direct the free play of the market without authoritarian subordination to bureaucratic party power. To the culture of class contradictions, and to the analysis of the contradictions proper to capitalism, will be added the culture of the contradictions of socialism itself, the most prominent of which will be those proper to the politics of ideals, as politics of clienteles or of groups or micropolitics in which the ideal is lived as a daily reality. Moreover, development of direct dialectical analysis of social relations will be especially encouraged, without using the thought of the classics or leaders as proof, along with the empirical analysis of socialism or the analysis of systems that can improve operations and organizations. All this will have to be carried on in the midst of a struggle on two fronts, against imperialism and within socialist forces which take a position in critical cases to retain power, as a general logic, or to democratize power, as a necessary mediation. It seems that this contradiction is going to be part of both the struggles of states, or within states, as well as those struggles waged from within civil society. While everyone's ideal will remain democratic socialism, some will emphasize socialism as majority power and others as majority pluralism.

—*Translated by Phil Berryman*

Notes

1. I am using the term "socialist" to designate states generally run by Communist parties; this fits the terminology many of them use (or formerly used) to identify themselves. We are also using the expression "state with a socialist orientation or vocation" to distinguish those states that consider themselves or are considered to be in transition to socialism. Marxist critical terminology, or terminology close to it, uses the expressions "deformed workers' state," "postcapitalist state," "state social- ism," or "authoritarian socialism." Liberal writers generally use the expression "Communist states." The new philosophers speak of "real socialism." To think that all those who call themselves socialists are (or that none are) is itself part of an ideological struggle that can be taken up more precisely by understanding "social- ism as project" (Ernesto Laclau) and seeing the way those who take up the banner of this project struggle against the neoliberal project, the supreme ideological expression of capitalism.
2. The undeniable advances in industrialization, education, health, and nutrition do not do away with underdevelopment and do not, with the possible exception of Cuba, make these countries equal to "developed" countries.

MARIA HELENA MOREIRA ALVES

THE WORKERS' PARTY OF BRAZIL: BUILDING STRUGGLE FROM THE GRASSROOTS

Events in Eastern Europe in 1989 call attention to the failure of one understanding of the socialist project. Events in Brazil in 1989—the near election of a socialist steelworker as the candidate of a very different kind of workers' party—betoken another. It is this Brazilian socialist movement that is the subject of this essay.

The desire to build a "party of the workers" which led to the founding of the Partido dos Trabalhadores, or PT, in 1979 was deeply embedded in the shared aspirations of Brazilian workers to move onto the center stage of politics as actors and not as backstage organizers. Many workers were newly empowered by their participation in the new trade unions, grassroots neighborhood associations, and peasant associations. They were frustrated by traditional left parties, whose rigid disciplinary regulations left little room for internal debate. They insisted on participation in political platform decisions and were blocked by established party bureaucrats. Having learned through their involvement in grassroots social movements to coordinate political action collectively, to make decisions collectively, to organize in a decentralized manner, and to rotate leadership, they now regarded the limitations of traditional left parties as a straitjacket that curbed their potential participation. The new "Party of the Workers" therefore had to channel—in the political sphere—all of the experience gained during the years of organization of grassroots social resistance to military government. The PT would have to be a mass organization, flexible, dynamic, shifting, dialectically related to the grassroots

233

movements, capable of changing without losing that crucial connection. The PT would have to be born from the workers' movements; to be deeply embedded in them; to interconnect levels of organization so it was always strongly *rooted* there, never losing touch with its base. Yet the PT would also have to maintain a *separateness* from the social movements so that the autonomy of the grassroots could be preserved. One of the lessons learned from the populist period was that grassroots movements die when they become purely a base of support for politicians, easily manipulated through the cooptation of the leadership: it was time for the people to learn where and how to swim by themselves. The workers had to learn how to swim, to follow along with the currents of history, to ride the waves, to dive through them, to build bridges or float to the other side. This is what the PT was meant to be from its founding days, as indicated by its Political Declaration of 1979:

> The idea of the Partido dos Trabalhadores arose with the advance and reinforcement of this new and broad-based social movement which now extends from the factories to the neighborhoods, from the unions to the Basic Christian Communities, from the Cost of Living Movements to the Dwellers' Associations, from the student movement to the professional associations, from the movement of black people to the women's movement, as well as others, like those who struggle for the rights of indigenous peoples.

The "Newness" of the PT

The "newness" of the PT lay in the nature of its relationship to grassroots social movements. Born from these movements, the PT connects with all types of organization: in the urban areas, the PT organizes in the trade unions, and in the neighborhood and *favela* associations. The PT is present in the struggles of the homeless for housing, of street children for recognition of their rights, and in the mobilization for better health and education. In the rural areas, the PT is the moving force behind the rural unions of agricultural laborers, workers, and marginalized *bolas frias** of the coffee and sugar plantations. The PT has also backed the struggle of landless peasants for land and of the rubber-tree trappers of the Amazon to preserve the forest. Although the PT is not the only party on the Brazilian left that supports the struggles of working people for better living conditions, it has become the political party most represented in the social movements. The PT is, in addition, active in the women's movement, the black consciousness movement, and in indigenous people's organizations.

What is of particular interest, however, is the way in which the PT relates to working class and other social movements. The PT does not have the traditional "departments" or "party committees" of women, blacks, rural workers, rubber tappers, trade unionists, etc. Activists and militants are members of these social movements and organizations *as well as* of the PT. This is different from the way in which left parties have traditionally been organized in Brazil. The PT cannot decide on a "party line" that will be imposed, say, on a particular trade union or defended in the women's movement. The militants are not "party delegates" to social movements. They have a double militancy and are encouraged to keep the two as separate as possible. Although a member's connection to a grassroots *base* is important for his or her standing in the party (in fact, you must be active in a grassroots movement to become a member of the PT), the opposite is not true. There are no formal mechanisms for molding a particular member's militancy in the social movement to the positions of the party. The influence is *from the grassroots to the PT* and not the other way around. For example, militants in the black movement have been extremely important in shaping the PT's platform, in electing black people to public office, in education, and in coordinating concrete programs. Similarly, women do not have a "women's committee" but permeate the PT, shape the platform on women's issues, exert consider-

---

*The term *bola fria* refers to an agricultural laborer who lives on the periphery of a city and is employed by the day. These workers number about 16 million throughout Brazil; they have no work contracts, no fixed wages, no guaranteed employment, benefits or social security of any kind. They are in many ways akin to illegal immigrants in the United States. The term means "cold lunch," a reference to the food they must bring with them to the plantations.

able influence on the party, and have been elected to a variety of public offices throughout the country. The PT has already, in the brief period of its existence, elected three women as mayors of major cities (Fortaleza, Santos, and São Paulo), a black woman from a *favela* organization as Brazil's first elected black congresswoman, and a number of other members of the black consciousness movement to state and municipal bodies. They represent their *social movements* within the PT but do not have disciplinary mechanisms built into their militancy at the grassroots. In congresses and meetings, PT members do not have to vote in a formal manner according to predetermined party directives, although they naturally tend to reflect the PT's platforms in their work at the grassroots level.

The autonomy of social movements is felt to be too important to be eliminated through regulation on the part of a political party. In the past, the experience that the grassroots movements in Brazil have had with political parties has been largely negative: when parties worked in an organized manner within social movements, these tended to become divided and weakened. Party members would meet before regular meetings to decide on key issues, who to elect, etc. This encouraged bitter political/ideological divisions and led to rigid positions that were often non-negotiable within the movement organization because decisions came from outside. In addition, because key decisions were often made by political leaders or party bureaucrats outside of the social movement itself, the decisions sometimes became profoundly disconnected from the rank and file and the real needs of the organization. This blocked growth and effectiveness. At worst, it crushed the organization entirely. In Latin America, the work of political parties in trade unions, peasant movements, and social movements in city and countryside has at times made cohesion and effectiveness very difficult. The imposition of party lines has divided and destroyed many an important movement in our history. The PT thus consciously attempts to avoid this by encouraging the autonomy of social movements vis-à-vis the political party.

This concern for the autonomy of social movements is also intended to avoid a second problem: the cooptation of rank-and-file leadership into political posts in order to tie the organization to the government. During the populist period this was the most frequent relationship between reformist governments and social movements. The dangers of such a policy are shown by the control that the PRI has exerted over grassroots movements in Mexico. The cooptation increases the likelihood of clientelism and of developing dependent relationships that incorporate the workers' organization into the corporatist state. Since the PT was born from a social movement deeply influenced by resistance to both corporatism and clientelism, there is widespread concern within the party about the possibility of cooptation. In fact, the PT has often erred in the opposite direction: in virtually *all* city governments with a PT mayor, the social movements quickly became active critics, not even hesitating, as was recently the case, to call a strike against the mayor.

The PT is very concerned with preserving the role that organizations of civil society play in "keeping the government on its toes." One of the most dearly held PT concepts is that power often turns an oppressed person into an oppressor. Therefore those who vote people into power should not simply relinquish power to them, but should remain constantly watchful, suspicious, and critical. This is the role that organized groups in civil society must play, and it is most important that a revolutionary government not coopt them in such a manner that they lose their watchdog function. In *The Pedagogy of the Oppressed* Paulo Freire, one of the most influential PT thinkers, analyzed the manner in which the oppressed carry the oppressor within themselves and may, when put in a position of power, reproduce the relationships of domination, becoming themselves tyrants. In the PT's experiences in local government, we have watched this happen in a variety of ways.

The question that is difficult to resolve, however, is how to institutionalize mechanisms to prevent the installation of patron-client relationships, nepotism, and other forms of public misconduct. Because so many members of the PT were wary of "democratic centralism," concerned about guaranteeing internal debate, and anxious to avoid the dangers of "purge committees," procedures to institutionalize mechanisms to punish members are regarded with enormous suspicion. This contradiction has resulted in a high degree of inefficiency for all the "ethics committees" within the PT. Only a very few PT representatives have actually been expelled for unethical behavior or to enforce party discipline, and in each case it was a traumatic experience for the party as a whole. It is still a problematic area. The question of how to enforce party discipline and keep the PT's representatives faithful to the program remains one of the most unresolved aspects of the PT experience.

The "Different" Nature of the PT

The decision to build a democratic and socialist mass party carried with it certain consequences. First of all, it meant the abandonment of revolutionary theories of *focismo* and of all strategies of armed struggle. Second, the PT was designed to be a legal party, organized on a mass scale and capable of competing with bourgeois parties for electoral office. This required meeting certain legal requirements and a day-to-day existence above ground. The decision to form a legal party meant the need to conform to an established party structure and to electoral laws that were enacted by a military government. The difficulty lay in trying to build a party that was both within the system and in opposition to it.

The PT is organized on the basis of units known as *nucleos* (nuclei), that are organized by neighborhood or workplace. People organize wherever they work, much in the same manner as the factory committees described by Gramsci in his *Ordine Nuovo* articles. People also organize *nucleos* in their neighborhoods. As a *militante* of the PT, for example, I belong both to the *nucleo* of the University of the State of Rio de Janeiro, where I teach, and to the *nucleo* of Laranjeiras, where I live. In turn, the neighborhood *nucleo* of Laranjeiras is a part of the larger unit of the Sixteenth Electoral Zone, which also includes people who live in Santa Tereza, Flamengo, and Cosme Velho. All of the *nucleos* in the Sixteenth Electoral Zone meet together once a month. At the neighborhood level and at the workplace, some groups meet once a week, some twice a month, and some only once a month. To belong to the PT, you must be accepted by at least one of the *nucleos,* although it is not necessary to be a part of both a workplace and a neighborhood organization. This is meant to ensure that only those who are in fact embedded in social movements become members of the PT. People who apply for membership must have the support of their workmates or immediate neighbors, who know their past militancy well. Once approved by the *nucleo,* the candidate must still be approved by the *zonal* (district) and the Executiva Municipal (Municipal Executive Committee). Those who are accepted locally usually have no trouble being approved by the higher level committees, who respect the decisions made by the rank and file.

The PT voting system is also different from that of traditional political parties in Brazil. Internal democracy is exercised through a complex system of proportional voting at all the pre-conventions. The PT includes people who come from the progressive Protestant and Catholic churches, members of Marxist-Leninist groups, former members of armed struggle organizations, former members of the Brazilian Communist Party, independent socialists, Trotskyists, and militants from a variety of social movements who hold no particular religious or political position. In order that their ideas may be properly debated and their positions reflected in both party posts and party platforms, the PT has created a mechanism whereby each group can form an organized sector in the party (known as a *tendencia*) and propose platform points as well as candidates for party posts or electoral office. Those documents presented by such organized groups that receive a majority vote at the pre-conventions are approved. For party posts, the *tendencias* may organize a slate and can win seats in proportion to their voting strength.

The proportional system of voting encourages internal party debate and maximizes the representation of rank-and-file members of all different positions. It also allows for a high degree of control by the rank and file in choosing candidates for political office. There is enormous rivalry among the *tendencias* and an unwary visitor to a PT convention might be surprised by the degree of activity, off-the-record negotiations between groups, shouted debates in plenary sessions, and even organized cheering at the time of voting. Once it is all over, however, once the votes are counted and the posts distributed (sometimes with loud disputes over fractional proportionate rights), rivalries are set aside and *militantes* cheer and wave the PT flag. At campaign time, everyone works together—"taking to the streets," in the PT's terminology. This aspect of campaign militancy is what makes political analysts agree that the PT is a "party on the move"—meaning that the PT has won surprising victories at the last minute as millions of eager *militantes* flood the streets and talk to each and every voter.

Socialism, for the PT, must be understood in the context of Brazil's historical experiences and society. For many decades Brazil had one of the highest growth rates in the world, and it remains a country with immense potential. In 1955, the Brazilian economy ranked forty-ninth in the world; in 1988 it ranked ninth. Brazil is enormously rich in material and mineral resources and has the largest industrial park in the third world. It is the fourth largest food producer and its climate makes the production of all kinds of crops possible, from the temperate south, to the semi-tropical center, to the tropical Amazon. Larger than the continental United States yet with less than half the population, Brazil has room to grow. Nevertheless, the land is divided unequally: only 1 percent of rural owners control over 45 percent of the total land area. And income distribution is among the most skewed in the world: the richest 1 percent of the population has as much of the national wealth as the poorest 50 percent.

According to the World Health Organization, approximately 40 million Brazilians receive less than the daily minimum nutritional requirements for survival, and Brazil ranks lower in nutrition standards than India or Pakistan. Government statistics show that there are 32 million children living in absolute poverty and more than 7 million abandoned in the streets of the cities. Child labor is rampant and unregulated: according to the Instituto Brasileiro de Geografia e Estatistica, in 1980 30 percent of children between the ages of 10 and 17—almost 15 million—worked full time and 90 percent of these received less than the minimum wage.

Women are poorer than men. Thirty-four percent of men and 58 percent of women earn less than $30 dollars a month. The death rate for women from childbirth and abortion is also one of the highest in the world. The situation of black people is also worth discussion. Blacks make up 45 percent of the population and approximately 40.2 percent of the labor force, but only receive 25 percent of total wage income.

Under the circumstances, the socialism that the PT defends, rooted as it is in the *actual reality* of the population, is based on the immediate reversal of economic and social injustice. Together with the social movements, the PT has developed a series of concrete proposals for agrarian reform, to guarantee urban land and housing, to redistribute income and wealth, to provide guarantees for women workers, to fight racial inequality, to improve public education and health, to protect working children, and provide for abandoned children.

The PT program also defends national sovereignty with a program to control multinational investment according to guidelines aimed at limiting the repatriation of profits, ending tax subsidies, and imposing strict regulations on labor conditions, health standards, occupational safety standards, wage levels, and job security. Because Brazil is immersed in the international capitalist economy, the PT *must* deal with the problems presented by multinational corporate investment, taking into account the different incomes and benefits received by workers in rich nations and third world nations. The program therefore seeks to ensure that similar benefits will be provided to workers in the Brazilian affiliates of the multinationals.

Workers' control is also on the program, in the form of factory committees with the power to negotiate workplace conditions, and eventually comanagement and profit-sharing.

Because the Brazilian economy is approximately 40 percent state-owned, the PT has a detailed program for the rehabilitation of state companies and the democratization of the decision-making process within them. Comanagement and workers' control also is at the heart of the PT's program for the state sector.

The defense of national sovereignty also involves the suspension of interest payments on the foreign debt. The PT defends an immediate suspension of such payments, coupled with an auditing of the debt itself to determine its makeup. That part of the debt that has already been paid—especially the part paid as a result of increased (and floating) interest rates—will be deducted from the principal, for the PT considers floating interest rate clauses illegitimate. In conjunction with its defense of national sovereignty, the PT also proposes an active foreign policy among third world nations.

In the long run, the PT strives to build socialism from the day-to-day struggles of working people in Brazil. Democratic socialism, in the PT's conception, must necessarily be historically rooted and dialectically related to the on-going requirements of social movements. The incorporation of workers into the decision-making apparatus of the state—at all levels—must be coupled with the institutionalization of mechanisms for worker participation at the workplace. Democratic socialism involves the democratizing of political *and* economic life—not simply in the distribution of production but also in the redistribution of political, social, and economic power. With the understanding that "we plant the seeds of socialism in the day-to-day struggles of the workers," the PT organizes factory committees, workers' councils, neighborhood committees, health, education, and transportation committees and other citizen committees to develop programs and find solutions to common problems.

In the political sphere, the PT has been the backbone of the Movimento para Emendas Populares (Movement for Popular Amendments), which has organized group discussions to present formal amendments to the Constituent Assembly. Some of these "popular amendments," such as the one dealing with agrarian reform, had over 6 million signatures. As with other social and economic reform programs, the agrarian reform proposal was drafted with the participation of representatives from social movements in the countryside and the Amazon region. The proposal therefore reflects the priorities of those most directly concerned. For example, the PT defends different types of agrarian reform to take into account regional diversity. A rural property of over 500 hectares that is left largely idle in the south and southeast (Minas Gerais, Rio de Janeiro, Espirito Santo, São Paulo, Parana, Santa Catarina, and Rio Grande do Sul) would be considered unproductive and available for redistribution. However, a rural property of up to 1,500 hectares in the Amazon region that is left idle would not: the People of the Forest Movement, the rubber tapper unions, and other peasant movements of the Amazon believe that idleness should be encouraged in the forest. Productivity of land would also vary, with very specific regulations for the preservation of the Amazon forests of the central and northern states. The northeast, made up of small states hurt by periodic drought, would be subject to reforms that take into account the climate and soil. All of these detailed economic and social proposals have been drafted in a similar manner and reflect the day-to-day participation of those directly concerned with the issues addressed.

The Popular Administrations of the PT

Democratization of decision-making at the state level is a primary concern of the PT, which organizes *conselhos populares* (popular councils) with actual budgetary power to work with the municipal administrations that the PT controls. The concept of "building socialism in the day-to-day struggle" is put into practice in the *administraçoes populares,* or popular administrations, where the PT has won local elections for mayor. Democratizing the state means institutionalizing mechanisms of popular participation for drafting and implementing public policy. One such mechanism is the popular council, which is organized by neighborhood and issue. The urban areas are divided into districts, or *bairros.* These are equivalent to the boroughs of large U.S. cities, such as Brooklyn, Queens, Manhattan, etc. The residents of each *bairro* organize into a committee, usually with one representative for each street, to discuss and draft proposals for issues of immediate importance to them: street paving, lighting, running water, and sewage systems, the building of schools, daycare centers, playgrounds, health clinics, etc. The members of the *bairro* committees elect people to a conselho popular, or popular council, whose size varies according to the number of people in the *bairro.* The popular councils draft their own statutes, and some have incorporated a recall vote to increase their accountability to their constituency. The councils meet regularly with members of the municipal government to discuss budgetary issues, to establish priorities, and to work out difficulties of implementing programs. For the first time in Brazilian history citizens, particularly poor citizens, participate directly in budgetary decisions and policymaking on a regular basis. This process of direct participation results in distinctly different programs to deal with social problems.

With the encouragement of the PT and the municipal administration, the citizens of the *favelas* organize *conselhos da favela* (shantytown councils). These are composed of elected members of the community and also have their own statutes. They are responsible for much of the work involved in planning and implementing programs. The local *favela* councils are only accountable to their specific units and work in a limited area. High-level representatives of the municipal government and PT officials are present only when invited.

The municipal governments under PT control hire engineers, urban planners, geologists, architects, sociologists, and other technicians to work on urban revitalization projects. They liaison with the *conselhos de favelas* and provide them with technical assistance. They meet together, draft plans together, and work collectively to implement programs.

The experience of Mayor Luiza Erundina of São Paulo, elected by the PT in November 1988, is an example of the process of building democratic socialism. São Paulo, with approximately 13 million people, is the world's third largest city and the most advanced industrial park in the third world. Every year an estimated 500,000 migrants move into the city looking for work, greatly increasing the social and housing problems in the *favelas*. Programs for better health and education, and self-development projects, are urgent priorities. First of all, however, the popular administration is placing enormous emphasis on modifying the administrative patterns that have created a huge state bureaucracy. The need for democratization and decentralization was clear after an evaluation carried out during the first year, when it became clear that the implementation of programs that encourage direct participation in policymaking was being hampered by the resistance of tenured government employees who had been hired largely on the basis of patronage. This problem was particularly evident in education, where teachers resisted the innovative ideas of Secretary of Education Paulo Freire, and went so far as to organize a large strike against the PT government. The response of the Secretary of Education was not less but *more* democracy. Freire called on teachers to elect a committee to work with him and his staff. All of the administration's records were opened to the public and the budget made available for examination by the teachers' representatives, as well as by members of the Citizen's Education Committee. A tripartite group of government representatives, parents, and teachers began to work on solutions. In the end, the teachers voted overwhelmingly to end the strike and to institutionalize a program to educate teachers, school employees, and parents in the new philosophy of education for liberation.

It seems clear that the new popular democratic governments will have to engage in large-scale education to raise the level of the political organization of the population if it is to be successful in the endeavor to democratize public policy. At the same time, the PT's experience shows that developmental projects can have a profound impact on how people view government and develop an understanding that participatory democracy depends upon people's involvement, as critics as well as co-decisionmakers.

The process of building democratic socialism on the basis of day-to-day struggles includes the courage to face criticism and dissent. It is the PT's position that legitimate protest is an inherent, even primordial, aspect of democracy. The response of a popular democratic government must therefore be to increase efforts to broaden direct democracy through the institutionalization of mechanisms that allow participation in government policymaking. Bridges must be built between organizations in civil society and the state through the implementation of programs in the historic experience of popular governments. These bridges must be continuously redesigned and rebuilt as the result of an on-going evaluation of their effectiveness in broadening the scope of democratic institutions.

It can certainly be said that the PT and its allied social movements are "socialist" as the term is understood by most readers, but as this description of the PT has hopefully made clear, it is a socialism rooted in the Brazilian working people's experience and felt needs. It is a socialism that springs from the people.

THE UNITED STATES AND THE FUTURE OF SOCIALISM

ERIC FONER

WHY IS THERE NO SOCIALISM
IN THE UNITED STATES?

It is now nearly eighty years since the German sociologist Werner Sombart raised the question, "Why is there no socialism in the United States?" In the ensuing decades, the problem has been a source of apparently endless debate among historians examining the distinctive qualities of the American experience, American radicals seeking an explanation for their political weakness, and Europeans alternately fascinated and repelled by the capitalist colossus to their west. Indeed, long before Sombart, the exceptional economic and political history of the United States commanded attention on both sides of the Atlantic.

Marx and Engels themselves occasionally sought to solve the riddle of America, the land where, as Marx once put it, capitalism had developed more "shamelessly" than in any other country. They could never quite decide, however, whether the unique qualities of nineteenth-century American life boded well or ill for the future development of socialism. Would the early achievement of political democracy prove an impediment to class consciousness in the United States or encourage it by making economic inequalities appear all the more illegitimate? Was the absence of a feudal tradition a barrier to the development of class ideologies, or did it make possible the early emergence of a modern, socialist political culture? If America was, in so many ways, the most capitalist nation on earth, should it not also become the most socialist? Marx and Engels could never quite answer such questions to their own satisfaction, and subsequent writers who have entered in the "why is there no socialism" quagmire have rarely been more successful.[1]

In the end, Marx and Engels remained optimistic about prospects for socialism in the United States (Engels even advising the "backward" workers of Britain to learn from the example of the Knights of Labor). Other observers, however, believed that the nature of American society precluded the emergence of class-based political ideologies on the European model. In 1867, E. L. Godkin, the Irish-born editor of *The Nation,* sought to explain why, despite the wave of strikes in the United States, the "intense class feeling" so evident in Great Britain could not exist in America:

> There [in Europe] the workingman on a strike is not simply a laborer who wants more wages: he is a member of a distinct order in society, engaged in a sort of legal war with the other order. . . . His employer is not simply a capitalist in whose profits he is seeking a larger share: he is a member of a hostile class, which . . . it is considered mean or traitorous for him to hope to enter. This feeling, we need hardly say, does not exist in America. The social line between the laborer and the capitalist here is very faintly drawn. Most successful employers of labor have begun by being laborers themselves; most laborers hope . . . to become employers. Moreover, there are . . . few barriers of habit, manners or traditions between the artisan and those for whom he works, so that he does not consider himself the member of an "order." Strikes, therefore, are in the United States more a matter of business, and less a matter of sentiment, than in Europe. . . . Should the worst come to the worst [the American worker] has the prairies behind him, a fact which . . . diffuses through every workshop an independence of feeling, a confidence in the future, of which the European knows nothing. Besides this, the American working class are in the enjoyment of political power.[2]

I have quoted Godkin at some length because the "why is there no socialism" debate has not advanced very far beyond the answers he proposed over a century ago. Godkin touched upon nearly all the elements from which modern responses to the question are generally forged: American ideology, social mobility, the nature of the union movement, the political structure. In this essay, I propose to examine the most recent trends in this seemingly timeless debate. The essay is not meant as a history of socialism in the United States, or as an exhaustive survey of the immense body of literature that now exists on the subject (since nearly every work on American radicalism and labor explicitly or implicitly propose an answer to the question, "why is there no socialism"). It will not examine expressions of American radicalism, such as abolitionism and feminism, whose impact upon American life has been far more profound than socialism. I hope, however, both to draw attention to the most recent contributions to this debate, and to raise questions about both the adequacy of specific explanations, and the underlying premises upon which the entire discussion appears to rest. It might well be worth raising at the outset the question whether the experience of socialism in the United States is, in reality, exceptional, or whether it represents an extreme example of the dilemma of socialism throughout western society.

To some extent, the "why is there no socialism" debate remains inconclusive because the participants define socialism in diverse, sometimes contradictory ways. It is often unclear precisely what it is whose absence is to be explained. When Sombart wrote, in the period before World War I, there existed a reasonably unified body of socialist theory and political practice. But since the shattering of the international labor and socialist movements by World War I, the Russian Revolution, the rise of socialist and communist parties and, indeed, governments hostile to one another but all claiming the mantle of "socialism," and the emergence of new forms of socialism in the third world, it is impossible to contend that "socialism" retains a coherent meaning. Socialism itself possesses a history, but too often contributors to the debate treat it as an ahistorical abstraction.

Nevertheless, by common consent, the extremely imprecise problem, "why is there no socialism in the United States" has been reduced to a discrete set of questions. It does not mean, "why has the United States not become a socialist nation?" or even, "why is there no revolutionary labor or political movement?" Rather, the problem is generally defined as the absence in the United States of a large avowedly social democratic political party like the Labour Party of Britain, the French Socialist Party, and the Communist Party of Italy. From the strength of such parties, moreover, American writers generally infer a mass socialist consciousness among the working classes of these countries. Thus, "why is there no socialism?" really means, why is the United States the only advanced capitalist nation whose political system lacks a social democratic presence and whose working class lacks socialist class consciousness?

Posed this way, the question does not seem to have a prima facie plausibility, although, as I will suggest, it may well rest on assumptions about Western European politics and class relations that are out of date today and may never have been fully accurate. One must, in other words, be wary of explanations for American exceptionalism based upon trends and phenomena equally evident in other countries. But this is only one of the pitfalls that characterize many analyses of the problem. Too often, it is assumed that a fairly simple, direct connection ought to exist between the social structure, class ideologies, and political parties. Many explanations of the connection exist, some, it is true, mutually exclusive. Poverty is sometimes seen as a barrier to radicalism, sometimes as its most powerful spur; social mobility sometimes is said to increase, sometimes to decrease class awareness; ethnic cohesiveness is seen as an impediment to class solidarity, or as the springboard from which it emerges. But whatever the specific argument, disproportionate influence is too often assigned to a single element of the social structure, and politics and ideology are too often viewed as simple reflections of economic relationships.

Particularly in the case of the United States, the conflation of class, society, and politics has unfortunate consequences. One cannot assume that the absence of a powerful social democratic party implies that American workers fully accept the status quo (although, as we shall see, such an assumption is often made). Actually, what needs to be explained is the coexistence in American history of workplace militancy and a politics organized around nonideological parties appealing to broad coalitions, rather than the interests of a particular class. David Montgomery has expressed the problem succinctly: "American workers in the nineteenth century engaged in economic conflicts with their employers as fierce as any known to the industrial world; yet in their political behavior they consistently failed to exhibit a class consciousness." Why was militancy in the factory so rarely translated into the politics of class? Labor and socialist parties have emerged in the United States (indeed, Americans, in the late 1820s, created the first "Workingmen's parties" in the world), but they have tended to be locally oriented and short-lived. As Montgomery observes, the American form of socialism has centered on control of the workplace, rather than creating a working-class presence in politics.[3] "Why is there no socialism" thus becomes a problem of explaining the *disjuncture* of industrial relations and political practice in the United States.

Finally, there is the problem of proposed answers that simply explain too much. Descriptions of an unchanging American ideology, or timeless aspects of the American social order such as mobility, leave little room for understanding the powerful American radical tradition based upon cross-class movements and appeals to moral sentiment rather than economic interest. Nor can they explain those periods when socialist politics did attract widespread support. It is too little noted that at the time Sombart wrote there *was*, in fact, socialism in the United States. In the first fifteen years of this century, the American Socialist Party appeared to rival those in Europe, except the German, in mass support and prospects for future growth. Around 1910, the American Socialist Party had elected more officials than its English counterpart; certainly, Sombart's question might as readily have been asked about Britain as the United States before World War I. Thus, what must be explained is not simply why socialism is today absent from American politics, but why it once rose and fell. Such a definition of the question, I will argue, requires that we "historicize" the problem of American socialism. Rather than assuming an unchanging pattern of American exceptionalism, we need to examine the key periods when American development diverged most markedly from that of Europe.

With these admonitions in mind, let us review some of the most prominent explanations for the weakness of socialism in the United States. Probably the most straightforward approach is the contention that the failure of socialism results from the success of American capitalism. Various aspects of the American social order, according to this argument, have led workers to identify their interests with the socioeconomic status quo. This, indeed, was the burden of Sombart's own analysis. The economic condition of workers in the United States, he insisted, was far better than that of Europeans in terms of wages, housing, and diet. Socially, moreover, they were far less sharply distinguished from the middle class than their European counterparts. And finally, they were conscious of being able to move west if dissatisfied with their present conditions. The success of capitalism, Sombart believed, made the American worker "a sober, calculating businessman, without ideals." "On the reefs of roast beef and apple pie," he added, "socialistic utopias of every sort are sent to their doom."[4]

From Frederick Jackson Turner's "frontier thesis," which saw in the westward movement the key to American distinctiveness, to more recent studies attributing the failure of socialism to high rates of geographical and social mobility and the ability of the American workers to acquire property, the success of capitalism has been seen as making the American working class complacent and rendering socialism irrelevant to American politics. As anyone who has lived in both America and Western Europe can testify, extremely high rates of geographical mobility are a distinctive feature of American life. In the nineteenth century, each decade witnessed a wholesale turnover of population in working-class neighborhoods, presumably with adverse effects on the possibility of creating permanent class institutions. Even today, the lure of the Sunbelt draws workers from the depressed industrial heartland, an example of the individual "safety-valve" that Turner identified as the alternative to class conflict in the United States. A recent variant on the theme was the contention, popular during the 1960s, that the white working class had exchanged material security and a privileged status in relation to minorities at home and workers abroad for a renunciation of economic and political radicalism. Socialism, according to this view, could come to the United States only as the indirect result of revolutions in the third world, or the activity of marginal social groups like migrant workers and welfare mothers, not yet absorbed into the American mainstream.

Plausible as they appear, the "success of capitalism" and "mobility" approaches raise as many questions as they answer. First, they rest on assumptions about the standard of living of American workers that are rarely subjected to empirical verification. Have the wage levels and rates of social mobility of American workers always been significantly higher than in Western Europe? Vague references to the "scarcity of labor" in the United States do not suffice to answer the question. Many immigrants complained that certain aspects of their lives—the length of the work day, the pace of factory labor—compared unfavorably with conditions at home.

More importantly, the precise implications of the ability to acquire property for class consciousness and socialism are far more problematic than is often assumed. A venerable tradition of analysis, dating back at least as far as Alexis de Tocqueville, insists that far from promoting political stability, social mobility is a destabilizing force, raising expectations faster than they can be satisfied and thus encouraging demands for further change. Certainly, recent American and European studies of labor history suggest that the better-off workers—artisans in the nineteenth century, skilled factory workers in the twentieth—were most likely to take the lead in union organizing and radical politics. As for geographical mobility, until historians are able to generalize about the success or failure of those millions who have, over the decades, left American farms and cities in search of economic opportunity, the implications of the extraordinary turbulence of the American population must remain an open question. But in any case, the historian must beware of the temptation simply to deduce political ideology from social statistics or to assign disproportionate influence to a single aspect of the social structure. And finally, the "success of capitalism" formula can hardly explain the relative weakness of socialism during the Great Depression, which failed to produce a mass-based socialist movement, or the radicalism of the 1960s, which arose in a period of unparalleled affluence.

Even more popular than the "social mobility" thesis is the contention that the very ethos of American life is inherently hostile to class consciousness, socialism, and radicalism of any kind. Probably the best-known expression of this point of view is Louis Hartz's *The Liberal Tradition in America*. To summarize Hartz's argument very briefly, Americans were "born equal," never having had to launch a revolution to obtain political democracy or social equality, with the result that American ideology has been dominated by a Lockean, individualistic outlook against which neither socialism on the left nor serious conservatism on the right can make any headway. A thoroughly bourgeois "fragment" spun off by Europe, America possessed only one part of the European social order. Lacking a hereditary aristocracy and a dispossessed working class, it had no need for class ideologies and politics.

No feudalism, no socialism. This oft-repeated aphorism sums up Hartz's contention that socialism arises from a vision, inherited from the feudal past, of a society based upon a structure of fixed orders and classes. Without a feudal tradition, and a sense of class oppression in the present, Americans are simply unable to think in class terms. Indeed, in its ideals of social mobility, individual fulfilment, and material acquisitiveness, American ideology produced a utopia more compelling than anything socialism could offer. Socialists called for a classless society; Americans, according to Hartz, were convinced they already lived in one.[5]

Dominant in the 1950s, the "consensus" school of American historiography exemplified by Hartz has lately been supplanted by an interpretation of the American past marked less by ideological agreement than by persistent conflict among various racial and ethnic groups and classes. The rise of the new social and labor history, and a new sensitivity to the historical experience of blacks, women, and others ignored in Hartz's formulation, have made historians extremely wary of broad generalizations about a unitary "American ideology." The work of Hartz, Richard Hofstadter, and others appears to a generation of historians who came of age in the turmoil of the 1960s as excessively celebratory of the American experience.

Actually, like Hofstadter's *The American Political Tradition*, the first major expression of the consensus interpretation, *The Liberal Tradition* was not a celebration of American distinctiveness at all, but a devastating critique of a political culture incapable of producing anything approaching an original idea. There was a right-wing bias in much consensus writing (represented, for example, by Daniel Boorstin, who gloried in the native pragmatism that, he contended, enabled Americans to escape the disruptive political ideologies of Europe). But Hartz and Hofstadter, who shared Marxist backgrounds, believed America's imprisonment within the confines of liberal ideology rendered it incapable of understanding the social realities of the modern world. They were concerned less with socialism and its failure than with affirming the underlying unities on which the American experience was girded, and with supplying a corrective to older interpretations that had mistaken the family quarrels of American political parties for ideological struggles over the nature of American society.[6]

The work of the new labor and social history, as I have indicated, has battered the consensus interpretation. In contrast to the universal diffusion of liberal values, students of working-class culture have stressed the development of semi-autonomous working-class and ethnic cultures resting on an ethic of community and mutuality, rather than individualism and competition. The idea of an unchallenged bourgeois hegemony is also weakened when one considers that until the Civil War, the most powerful political class in the United States was composed of southern slaveholding planters, a group bourgeois in neither its relationship to labor nor its social ideology. Although the Old South was hardly "feudal" (a term Hartz invokes without providing any precise definition), it was certainly pre-bourgeois in many respects. One might almost suggest that with its aristocratic social order and disfranchised laboring class, the South should, if Hartz is correct, have provided fertile soil for socialism.

Hartz's thesis has also been weakened from an entirely different direction: intellectual history. Recent writing on eighteenth-century American ideology has not simply dethroned Locke from the pivotal ideological role accorded him by Hartz, but has virtually expelled him from the pantheon of early American thought. The political rhetoric of the American Revolution, according to recent studies, owed less to Lockean liberalism than to classical republicanism, an ideology that defined the pursuit of individual self-interest as a repudiation of that "virtue" (devotion to the public good) indispensable in a republican citizenry. Eventually, liberalism triumphed as the dominant rhetoric of American political culture, but not until well into the nineteenth century, and as the result of a historical process whose outlines remain unclear. But if Hartz's liberal consensus did not characterize all of American history, then other elements of his argument, such as the absence of a feudal past, lose much of their explanatory power. The notion of an overarching liberal consensus went far toward understanding the context within which Hartz wrote—America of the 1950s— but has proved of little value in explaining the strength of challenges to the capitalist order ranging from the class violence of 1877 to the Knights of Labor, Populism, and the old Socialist Party.

Nonetheless, Hartz's contention that even American radicals have been trapped within a liberal ideology devoted to the defense of individualism and private property is not entirely incompatible with recent studies of the radical tradition. From Tom Paine's studied distinction between society and government (the former an unmixed blessing, the latter a necessary evil) to the abolitionists' critique of all social and political relationships embodying coercion, to the American anarchists whose individualist outlook differed so markedly from the class-oriented anarchist movements of Europe, a potent strand of the American radical tradition has rested upon hostility to the state and defense of the free individual. The ideologies of the nineteenth-century labor and farmers' movements, and even of early twentieth-century socialism itself, owed more to traditional republican notions of the equal citizen and the independent small producer than to the coherent analysis of class-divided society.

Precapitalist culture, it appears, was the incubator of resistance to capitalist development in the United States. The world of the artisan and small farmer persisted in some parts of the United States into the twentieth century, and powerfully influenced American radical movements. The hallmarks of labor and Populist rhetoric were demands for "equal rights," antimonopoly, land reform, and an end to the exploitation of producers by nonproducers. These movements inherited an older republican tradition hostile to large accumulations of property, but viewing small property as the foundation of economic and civic autonomy. Perhaps we ought to stand Hartz on his head. Not the *absence* of non-liberal ideas, but the *persistence* of a radical vision resting on small property inhibited the rise of socialist ideologies. Recent studies of American socialism itself, indeed, stress the contrast between native-born socialists, whose outlook relied heavily on the older republican tradition, and more class-conscious immigrant socialists.

According to Nick Salvatore, American socialists like Eugene V. Debs viewed corporate capitalism, not socialism, as the revolutionary force in American life, disrupting local communities, undermining the ideal of the independent citizen, and introducing class divisions into a previously homogenous social order.

Salvatore and other recent writers are not reverting to a consensus view of American history, though their work explores the values native-born socialists shared with other Americans. But ironically, at the same time that one group of historians strongly influenced by the radicalism of the 1960s was dismantling the consensus view of the American past, another was resurrecting it, as a theory of the "hegemony" of middle-class or capitalist values in the United States. In one version of the consensus/hegemony approach, labor and capital were seen as united by an ideology of "corporate liberalism" that, beneath an antibusiness veneer, served the interests of the existing order. Government regulation of the economy, hailed by American reformers as a means of blunting capitalist rapaciousness, and seen by many radicals as a stepping stone to a fully planned economy and perhaps even socialism itself, was now interpreted as the vehicle through which capitalists were able to control the political economy without appearing to do so. Because of the resiliency of corporate liberalism, virtually all popular protest movements had been incorporated within the expanding capitalist order.

A somewhat different version of the "hegemony" argument emphasizes culture rather than political ideology. The rise of mass culture, the mass media, and mass consumption in twentieth-century America, according to this view, not only rendered obsolete the socialist goal of building an alternative culture within capitalist society, but shaped the aspirations of workers, making leisure and consumption, rather than work or politics, the yardsticks of personal fulfillment. Recent studies of nineteenth- and early twentieth-century American radical movements have focused not on such traditional concerns as political ideology and organizational history, but on the creation of "counter cultures" within the larger society. Obviously influenced by the theory of hegemony (and in some cases, by a perhaps idealized understanding of the much-publicized cultural activities of the modern Italian Communist Party), these works have implied that the seedbed of socialist politics is a counterhegemonic set of cultural institutions, rather than the polity or the workplace. But studies of the modern working class have emphasized the disintegration of "working-class culture." "Social life," contends one such analysis, "is no longer organized around the common relation to the production of both culture and commodities. The working-class public sphere is dead."

Unfortunately, the consensus interpretation in its radical "hegemony" variants still suffers from the problem of homogenizing the American past and present. Indeed, in adopting the notion of hegemony from Gramsci, American historians have often transformed it from a subtle mode of exploring the ways class struggle is muted and channeled in modern society into a substitute for it. The sophisticated analysis of a writer like Raymond Williams, who observes how diverse ideologies can survive even in the face of apparent "hegemony," is conspicuously absent from American writing.[7] The notion that mass culture and mass society render any kind of resistance impossible, moreover, can hardly explain the dissatisfactions reflected in the radicalism of the 1960s. In the end, the "hegemony" argument too often ends up being circular. Rather than being demonstrated, the "hegemony" of mass culture and liberal values is inferred from the "absence" of protest, and then this absence is attributed to the self-same "hegemony."

An entirely different set of answers to the "why is there no socialism" question derives from the sociology of the working class itself, and examines aspects of the American social order that make it difficult for workers to organize successfully. The assumption is that socialist politics is unlikely to emerge in the face of an internally divided working class. The traditional assumption that capitalist development must produce an increasingly homogenous proletariat with a single set of interests, represented by unions and a political party, has given way before a recognition of the many kinds of divisions and stratifications built into the capitalist labor process itself. Divisions between the skilled and unskilled, craft and industrial workers, often reinforced by divisions along lines of race, ethnicity, and gender, belie the notion of a unified working class. It is doubtful, however, that such divisions are very useful in explaining the unique features of American labor history, for it appears that similar segmentation exists in other advanced capitalist societies. The United States is hardly the only country where capitalist development has failed to produce a homogenous working class.

Even more common than labor market segmentation as an explanation for the distinctive history of the American working class is its racial and ethnic heterogeneity. The complex web of backgrounds from which the American proletariat emerged is often seen as rendering unity along class lines all but impossible. Although apparently straightforward, the notion that the exceptional diversity of the American working class has inhibited both class consciousness and socialist politics actually encompasses a number of distinct approaches to American labor history.

On the simplest level, it is easy to point to the critical role racism and ethnic prejudices have played in shaping the history of American labor. For most of American history, black workers were systematically excluded by most unions. On the West Coast, prejudice against the Chinese shaped the labor movement, helping to solidify the domination of conservative skilled craft workers over a less-skilled majority. The racism of many labor organizations in turn fostered prejudice against unions among minority workers. And even in the case of white ethnic groups, differences of language, culture, and tradition clearly made organization difficult early in this century, when massive immigration from southern and eastern Europe coincided with the rapid expansion and consolidation of monopoly capitalism. The constant redefinition and recreation of American labor (a process that continues today with new waves of immigration), also meant that working-class institutions and traditions had to be rebuilt and battles refought over and over again. "The making of the American working class" (a subject yet to find its historian) was a process that occurred many times, rather than once.

The diverse backgrounds from which the American working class was forged is sometimes seen as affecting class consciousness in other ways as well. Racial and ethnic loyalties often drew men and women into cross-class alliances, while racism, nativism, and ethnic hostilities inherited from Europe all inhibited the development of a consciousness of workers' collective interests. Immigrant groups created a complex network of ethnic social, religious, and political institutions, diverting working-class energies from institutions like unions and radical political parties that explicitly sought to unite men and women across ethnic lines. Others contend that the cultural heritage of Catholic immigrants, who comprised so large a portion of the industrial working class, made them unreceptive to any form of political radicalism. In his pioneering study of Irish immigrants in nineteenth-century Boston, Oscar Handlin portrayed a religious community that saw efforts to change the world as at best futile and at worst sacreligious. Handlin's argument has sometimes been generalized to the proposition that ex-peasant immigrants are inherently indifferent or hostile to radical movements. (This contention begs the question of why, for instance, groups like Italian immigrants played so prominent a role in the creation of the labor and socialist movements in Argentina, while allegedly eschewing radicalism in the United States.) Another line of argument derives from the large numbers of early twentieth-century "new immigrants" (Italians, Poles, Greeks, etc.) who were actually migrant laborers, planning only a brief stay in the United States. In 1910, for example, three-quarters as many Italians left for home as entered the United States. Not intending to make the United States a permanent haven, Gerald Rosenblum argues, these new immigrants reinforced the narrow "business" orientation of American labor organizations: higher wages, not efforts at social change, were what attracted them to unions.[8]

Despite the popularity of what might be called the "ethnic" interpretation of the weakness of American socialism, it is by no means clear that cultural divisions were an insuperable barrier to class consciousness or political socialism. Racism and ethnic prejudice are not, as they are sometimes treated, "transhistorical" phenomena that exist independent of historical time and place. What needs to be studied is what kind of organizing and what conditions have allowed unions to overcome pre-existing prejudices. Unions organized on an industrial basis have under certain circumstances been able to bring black and white workers together. The Industrial Workers of the World (IWW) managed to lead successful, militant strikes early in this century by recognizing that ethnicity can, under certain circumstances, generate distinctive forms of radical protest. This is especially true where class and ethnic lines coincide, as in turn-of-the-century American industrial communities. Ethnic group solidarity, Victor Greene has argued, actually increased militancy during strikes by immigrant workers in the Pennsylvania coal fields, and the IWW's tactic of establishing strike committees composed of democratically elected representatives from each ethnic group brought to its strikes all the strength of the pre-existing network of immigrant institutions. So long as each group believed no one group was receiving favored treatment, the bonds of ethnicity in no way contradicted a willingness to work with others. Like many "global" explanations of the failure of socialism, in other words, the ethnic approach proves too much: rather than investigating the specific circumstances under which radical and ethnic divisions inhibit class solidarity, it assumes that a diverse working class can never achieve unity in economic or political action.

From the recent emphasis upon the resiliency of immigrant subcultures has emerged the latest explanation for the failure of American socialism. In *The Radical Persuasion*, Aileen Kraditor, a former radical historian who has repudiated her earlier writings and taken a prominent role in a new conservative historians' organization, argues that the very strength of ethnic cultures rendered political radicalism irrelevant to the immigrant proletariat. In early twentieth-century America, according to Kraditor, workers were able to create cultural enclaves so self-sufficient that they saw no need for far-reaching political change: all they wanted was to be left alone, enjoying relative local autonomy. Those radicals who did try to organize in lower class communities were perceived either as misfits who had rejected their cultural inheritance or as representatives of a hostile outside environment. In a sense, Kraditor's book represents a rightward, but in some ways logical, extension of the new social and labor history. Her emphasis upon the cultural resiliency of immigrant workers' ethnic communities reflects a major preoccupation of recent historical writing, as does her subordination of political and ideological considerations to ones of culture. Correctly criticizing an older stereotype of the unified class-conscious proletariat, Kraditor substitutes another equally ahistorical construct, the self-satisfied, community-oriented worker, for whom the private sphere is sufficient unto itself and who is therefore uninterested in radical ideologies or political change.[9]

Related to the composition of the American working class, of course, is the distinctive character of American trade unionism itself. Why, despite a history of labor violence unparalleled in Europe, does organized labor in the United States appear so much more conservative and apolitical than its European counterparts? Sometimes attention is drawn to the exclusionary policies of American Federation of Labor unions, whose craft basis of organization reinforced pre-existing divisions between skilled and unskilled workers, and excluded large numbers of workers—blacks, women, new immigrants, etc., from the labor movement. Indeed, it has been argued by James O'Connor that, in a nation in which no more than a quarter of the workforce has ever belonged to trade unions, the higher wages of unionized workers are, in effect, subsidized by lower paid nonunion workers via inflation. Other writers contend that the problem is not the nature and role of unions per se, but the fact that labor leaders have constantly sought to undercut the militancy of the rank and file, preferring accommodations with capital to prolonged class struggle. Whether this is a question of the perfidy of individual "misleaders" or the growth of bureaucratic structures isolating officials from their membership, the result has been a union movement uninterested in posing a political challenge to capital.

No one, however, has satisfactorily explained how and why a presumably militant rank and file constantly chooses moderate "misleaders" to represent it. And it should be noted that the implicit portrait of class-conscious workers betrayed again and again by a corrupt or moderate leadership assumes a unity and militancy among American workers that other approaches to the "failure of socialism" question have discounted. One might, in fact, argue that at a number of points in American history, the image of a moderate leadership curbing a radical rank and file ought to be reversed. In the 1930s, for example, it is now clear that socialist and communist organizers played a pivotal role in galvanizing working-class protest and creating the CIO industrial unions.

Thus far we have considered approaches to the question of socialism that focus on the society or the workplace. An alternative point of view looks to the nature of the American political system, since it is a political party whose absence is to be explained. Various aspects of American politics, it is argued, have made it difficult for labor or socialist parties to establish themselves effectively. First, there is the early achievement of political democracy in the United States, the "free gift of the ballot" as Selig Perlman has termed it. Unlike the situation in Europe, the vast majority of male American workers enjoyed the suffrage well before the advent of the Industrial Revolution. In England, class consciousness was galvanized, at least in part, by the struggle for the vote, and the exclusion of workers from the suffrage paralleled and reinforced the sense of a class-divided society learned at the workplace. In the United States, however, the "lessons" of the polity were the opposite of those of the economy. In the latter, the worker often perceived himself as a member of a distinct class; in the former, he thought of himself as an equal citizen of the republic. Alan Dawley, indeed, writes that "the ballot box was the coffin of class consciousness" in nineteenth-century America. Not only were the major parties remarkably adept at absorbing labor leaders into political office, but the early achievement of political democracy gave workers a vested interest in the existing political order. American workers, according to this argument, developed a strong sense of their "rights" in both polity and workplace, but were not convinced of the necessity of launching a direct national political challenge to capital. Perhaps labor parties never advanced beyond the local level in the United States because workers did not see the national state as being under the control of a hostile class. And even on the local level, Ira Katznelson argues, workers traditionally allocated economic issues to unions, while politics revolved not around questions of class, but rather the distribution of patronage among competing ethnic groups by urban political machines.[10]

The unusual structure of American politics has also affected the possibilities for socialist parties. The electoral college method of choosing the president helps entrench the two-party system (since votes cast for a third candidate who cannot achieve a majority are "wasted"). The size and regional diversity of the country has made it difficult to translate local labor strength into national power. American political parties have proven remarkably adept at absorbing protest, adopting the demands of reformers in watered-down form, and forcing radicals to choose in elections between the lesser of two evils. The contrast between the American 1930s, when Franklin D. Roosevelt's New Deal made broad concessions to labor and thereby cemented an alliance with the union movement, and the conservative policies of Depression-era British governments, is only one example of the remarkable flexibility of American parties. To liberal historians, such actions vindicate the receptivity of the American political order to demands for reform; to radicals, they often appear as frustrating barriers to truly radical change.

Other political factors have also inhibited the rise of labor and socialist politics. American historians have yet to assess the full implications of the disfranchisement of Southern blacks from the late nineteenth century until the 1960s. Here was a group comprising a significant portion of the American working class that, when given the opportunity, proved receptive to parties like the Populists which sought far-reaching changes in American life. Their exclusion from political participation shifted American politics to the right while entrenching within the Democratic Party a powerful bloc of Southern reactionaries. At various times, immigrants and most migrant laborers have also been barred from voting. Industrial workers, moreover, have never formed anything approaching a majority of the American electorate. In a vast nation, predominantly rural until well into this century, parties resting exclusively upon labor could not hope to win national powers. In 1900, the United States was already the world's foremost industrial power, yet a majority of the population still lived in places with fewer than 2,500 residents.

A final "political" consideration often stressed by historians sympathetic to American socialism but minimized by those who are not, is outright repression. The Populists were deprived of electoral victories throughout the South by blatant fraud in the 1890s. Violence by federal and state troops and private police forces suppressed strikes on many occasions, and court injunctions defeated many others. The first Red Scare of 1919–1920, which jailed and deported radical leaders, devastated both the Socialist Party and IWW. The second, after World War II, effectively destroyed the Communist Party.

Each of these "political" approaches contains an element of plausibility, but many suffer from a shortcoming shared by other explanations for the failure of socialism: they invoke aspects of American politics common to other countries to explain American exceptionalism. To take one example, virtually every European socialist movement suffered governmental repression at one time or another in its history, sometimes far more severe repression than anything experienced in the United States (very few American radicals, after all, were ever executed by the state). The Spanish labor and communist movements suffered under Franco, the Italian under Mussolini; German socialists faced Bismark's antisocialist laws. Yet all managed to survive, and some emerged stronger than ever. The 1919 and post-World War II Red Scares were not confined to the United States. Why, one may ask, has repression proved more effective against radicals in the United States than elsewhere? Of course, one might argue that the very openness of American politics, the normality of democratic procedures, makes it difficult for radical movements to deal with repression when it does appear. American radicals, because of the democratic political culture from which they have emerged, have lacked the tradition of underground organization that might have enabled them to survive repressive governments. Of course, one might also ask why, if the state has been unusually repressive in the United States, American workers have persisted in viewing the national government as somehow being above class politics.

Other political explanations also leave important questions unanswered. The electoral college system biases American politics toward a two-party system, but does not explain why socialists have been unable to replace the Republicans or Democrats with a socialist or labor party (as the Republicans replaced the Whigs in the 1850s). The fact that industrial workers form a minority of the total population is hardly unique to the United States. Socialist and labor parties everywhere have come to power by appealing to middle-class and rural voters as well as industrial laborers. In every industrial country, moreover, a considerable minority of workers has always voted for nonsocialist parties. The implicit comparison between a class-conscious European working class and the politically fragmented American proletariat may not stand up to a careful scrutiny of European political history.

Thus far, the answers to the socialist problem have been largely "external"—they have focused upon aspects of American society and politics that have inhibited the growth of socialist politics and working-class consciousness. There are also explanations that might be described as "internal"—those that focus on the nature and presumed errors of the radical movements themselves. Such an approach has an obvious appeal for more optimistic left-oriented historians. For if essentially unchanging aspects of American society—social mobility, the "American ideology," the nature of the political system—are responsible for the failure of socialism, there appears to be little reason to hope for a future revival of socialist fortunes. If, however, tactical, strategic, or ideological errors sabotaged previous socialist movements, then perhaps future radicals can learn from past mistakes, avoid repeating them, and rebuild American socialism.

The "internal" approach also has the virtue of directing attention to the actual histories of past socialist movements and the specific circumstances that contributed to their rise and fall. After all, if one accepts as sufficient an "external" explanation, one need not study in any detail the history of particular attempts to create a socialist politics in the United States. The "internal" approach, in other words, tends to "historicize" the socialism question, forcing the historian to examine the specific contingencies that affected the failure of socialist parties, rather than focusing on generalizations about American society so sweeping as almost to stand outside history itself. Not surprisingly, the two periods of American history that have attracted most attention from those interested in tracing the history of past socialisms are the first two decades of this century, and the 1930s and 1940s. Both stand out as eras when the trajectory of socialist movements in the United States diverged most markedly from that of their European counterparts. Why did the Socialist and Communist parties fail to build upon their undoubted successes and establish themselves as permanent parts of the American body politic?

One kind of internal approach, associated most prominently with Daniel Bell, argues that American Socialists and Communists failed to attract broad support because of their sectarian orientation and concern with ideological purity rather than the give and take essential to success in American politics. "In the world but not of it," they eschewed reforms in favor of a preoccupation with socialist revolution, thereby isolating themselves more or less by choice. A somewhat analogous argument is that of James Weinstein, who begins by challenging Bell's portrait of the Socialist Party, insisting that between 1900 and 1919 it acted as a traditional reformist party, taking ideology less seriously than the winning of votes. In the end, however, according to Weinstein, the party succumbed to the kind of ideological rigidity described by Bell, the attempt of one faction, allied with the Comintern, to impose the Soviet model of a highly disciplined, ideologically correct party upon what had been a broad coalition in the mainstream of American politics.[11]

Despite its success in winning local elections (the Socialist Party by 1912 had elected some 1,200 local officials and 33 state legislators, and controlled municipal governments in such cities as Schenectady, Milwaukee, and Berkeley) and attracting a respectable vote for Eugene V. Debs for president in 1912 (900,000 ballots, or 6 percent of the electorate), the Socialist Party suffered from a number of internal weaknesses. Paul Buhle stresses the nativism of many Socialist Party leaders and their unwillingness to reach out to the new immigrant proletariat. The party's electoral obsession, which led it to measure the advance of socialism almost solely in terms of the ballot box, led it to neglect organizing when votes were not at stake. Preoccupied with electoral strategies, the party failed to respond to the massive upheaval of the unskilled immigrant factory workers between 1909 and 1919. Where was the Socialist Party at McKee's Rocks, Lawrence, or the great steel strike of 1919? The Industrial Workers of the World demonstrated that it was possible to organize the new immigrant proletariat, but despite sympathy for the IWW on the part of Debs and other left-wing socialists, the two organizations went their separate ways.

Here, indeed, was the underlying tragedy of those years: the militancy expressed in the IWW was never channeled for political purposes while socialist politics ignored the immigrant workers. Indeed, the Socialist Party's strength lay not among factory workers but in an unusual amalgam of native-born small farmers, skilled workers in certain cities, ethnic groups from the Russian Empire like Finns and Jews, and professionals and intellectuals. Leon Trotsky was perhaps unkind when he remarked that the American Socialists were "a party of dentists." But its thinness among the industrial working class was certainly among the party's most debilitating weaknesses.

Another explanation for the decline of American socialism focuses on the crisis brought about by World War I. The Socialists' principled opposition to America's participation in the war fundamentally transformed the party, alienating many native-born members and intellectuals, while attracting a new constituency among immigrant workers. Ironically, at the moment of its final collapse, the Socialist Party for the first time accurately reflected the composition of the American proletariat.

Opposition to the war laid the party open to the massive repression that was, at least in part, responsible for its demise. One may speculate whether, had American Socialists, like their European counterparts, supported the war and perhaps even entered a coalition wartime government as junior partners, as the Labour Party in Britain did, they might have shielded themselves from repression and established their political legitimacy. (Of course, given the experience of our own times, one may well ask whether participation in governing an imperialist nation involves a socialist party in an inevitable sacrifice of principle, at least so far as foreign policy is concerned.) What is clear is an outcome fraught with irony, in view of the assumption that American socialism is so much weaker than that of Europe. Of the two great "isms" created by the nineteenth century—socialism and nationalism—the latter in Western Europe proved far the stronger in 1914. Socialist internationalism was crucified on the cross of socialist support for the war effort. Was the American party's opposition to the war a courageous act of suicide? At least, history ought to record that the American Socialist Party went to its death not because there was *less* socialism in the United States than in Europe, but because, apart from the Russian Bolsheviks, the American was the party that remained most true to socialist principles.

If the period before World War I represented one opportunity for the development of a mass socialist party in the United States, the 1930s appears to represent another. By the mid-1930s, the Communist Party had established itself as the major force on the socialist left. The achievements of the Communists, recent research has made clear, were indeed impressive. Moving far beyond the electoral emphasis of the old Socialist Party, they understood that struggle on a variety of fronts is the most effective means of mass mobilization and education. In contrast to the Socialists' isolation from the militant struggles of the pre-World War I years, the Communists took the lead in a remarkable array of activities— union-building, demonstrations of the unemployed, civil rights agitation, aid to Republican Spain, etc. Indeed, the wide variety of their activities becomes all the more amazing when it is remembered that the party at its prewar peak numbered well under 100,000 members.

Given the mass militancy of the CIO and the range of party concerns, why did a larger socialist or labor political presence not emerge from the Great Depression? Some accounts stress the resiliency of the political system itself, the way President Roosevelt managed to absorb labor militancy into a redefined Democratic Party coalition. Others point to the internecine warfare between AFL and CIO unions as sabotaging efforts toward the creation of an independent labor party. Still others blame the Communist Party's quest for legitimacy, especially in its Popular Front period. The party's determination for forge an alliance of all antifascist elements, including the Democratic Party, and its ideological emphasis upon American nationalism ("Communism is twentieth-century Americanism," as the mid-1930s slogan went), foreclosed the possibility of independent socialist politics. According to James Weinstein, here also lay a cardinal difference between the old Socialists, who at least had made socialism a part of American political discourse, and the 1930s Communists, who saw themselves as the left wing of the New Deal coalition.

But like the old Socialist Party, the Communists were unable to cut the gordian knot of the relationship between nationalism and socialism. On the one hand, the party achieved primacy on the left partially by virtue of its relationship with the USSR, the only existing socialist state. On the other, the Soviet connection proved a point of vulnerability, opening the party to repression as "un-American" after World War II, and leading to inevitable questions as to whether specific policies reflected American or Soviet interests and realities. It is not clear, however, how much emphasis ought to be put on the Soviet connection for the party's failure to grow in size. After all, every Communist Party in the world had to deal with the Comintern. What is certain is that the U.S. Communist Party was most successful precisely when it was most American. As Maurice Isserman's recent study demonstrates, the Popular Front, whatever its relationship to socialist ideology, was exactly the policy that most American Communists desired, and the party's membership was highest in the mid-1930s and again toward the end of World War II, precisely when socialism and nationalism coincided. Indeed, recent studies of the war years criticize the party for subordinating labor militancy to the war effort and a quest for nationalist legitimacy, via the no-strike pledge. (The implicit assumption that calls for greater efforts to win the war alienated American workers concerned only with their paychecks may, however, be open to question.)

Through the no-strike pledge, subordination of criticism of the Roosevelt administration, and the decision to transform itself from a party into a "political association," the Communist Party sought "legitimacy"—a permanent foothold in American politics—during World War II. The experience of war and the resistance movements did legitimize European Communist parties as defenders of their nations (no one, whatever his political outlook, could call the French or Italian Communist parties "un-French" or "un-Italian" after the experience of World War II). But American Communists ended up with the worst of both worlds. The no-strike pledge alienated shop-floor militants, without winning "legitimacy" from those with the power to dispense it—the price, perhaps, of trying to exist at all at the very focal point of world imperialism. The party remained vulnerable to the wave of repression that began with the onset of the Cold War. The base Commu-

nists had laboriously created in the labor movement was effectively destroyed, with disastrous consequences for the entire direction
of the postwar labor movement.

Let us return, in conclusion, to our original question. Why is
there no socialism in the United States? As we have seen, all the
explanations that have been proposed—the internal and the
external, the social, ideological, economic, and cultural—have a
certain merit, and all seem to have weaknesses as well. Nor can we
simply add them all together in a kind of mixed salad and feel
satisfied with the result. Perhaps the debate has gone on for so long
and so inconclusively because the question itself is fundamentally
flawed. Perhaps beginning our investigation with a negative question inevitably invites ahistorical answers.

Like a kindred question that has bedeviled the study of American slavery—"why were there no slave rebellions in the United
States?"—the socialism question rests on a number of assumptions that may not survive careful analysis. The rise of socialism, or
the outbreak of slave rebellions, are defined as normal occur-
rences, whose absence needs to be explained. In the case of
slavery, the question is premised upon the conviction that the
"normal" human response to severe repression is armed rebellion,
an assumption for which human history, unfortunately, does not
offer much support. In the case of socialism, the premise is that
under capitalism the working class will develop class consciousness, expressed in unions and a labor or socialist political party,
and that consequently the failure of either to emerge must be the
result of some outside interference. No one asks, for example,
"why is there no feminism in Europe?" (a legitimate question
when either independent feminist movements or the historical
participation of women in socialist parties in Europe and the
United States are compared) because socialism is held to be an
inevitable, universal development under capitalism while feminism is assumed to emerge from local contingencies that vary from
country to country.

In the end, of course "why is there no socialism" rests upon an
interpretation of history that accords socialism a privileged position among radical movements because it arises inexorably out of
the inner logic of capitalist development, and holds out the prom-

ise of a far-reaching social revolution. To the Marxist paradigm that underlies this vision, I have no objection. But it does seem to me that the empirical evidence that justifies the question—the existence of mass labor, Socialist, and Communist parties in Western Europe and not in the United States—fundamentally contradicts the Marxist foundation of the question. A Marxist question, in other words, arises from a non-Marxist outcome, for the "absence" to be explained is not socialism (a revolutionary transformation of society) but the existence of political parties of a decidedly social democratic bent that aim at no such transformation. The left parties of Western Europe have without doubt improved the conditions of life of their constituents, but they have proved incapable of using their impressive political strength to reshape fundamentally their societies. They have, one might say, promoted liberalism and egalitarianism more successfully than socialism, and presented themselves as the proponents of modernization and social rationalization rather than class rule, thus operating in ways more analogous to American political parties than either Americans or Europeans would care to admit. The issue for Western European socialist parties is not precisely socialism, but the equitable distribution of the products of capitalism. In other words, one might well ask not "why is there no socialism in the United States," but "why has there been no socialist transformation in any advanced capitalist society?"

To put the question this way challenges another underlying premise of the socialist question: American exceptionalism. Too often in American historical writing, "Europe" is posited as an unchanging class-conscious monolith in contrast to the liberal, bourgeois United States. In much American writing, "Europe" equals France, and "France" equals the French Revolution. The heroic struggles of European workers and socialists are highlighted and the more recent erosion of working-class consciousness and socialist ideology ignored. Too often, American historians equate the official doctrine of "revolutionary" labor movements, such as the French earlier in this century, or political platforms calling for collective ownership of the means of production, with a pervasive socialist consciousness among a majority of workers. They ignore the fact that large numbers of European workers have always voted for "bourgeois" parties. American commentators often cite the history of British labor as one example of class-conscious "European" working-class development, unaware of the debates among British writers about what some see as an exceptional *absence* of socialism compared with the continent. Certainly, recent events demonstrate that "the containment of . . . working-class movements within the limits of trade union economism and social democratic reformism" is hardly unique to the United States.

To abandon American exceptionalism as an organizing theme is not, of course, to assert that the history of every capitalist nation is identical. The history of the United States is, in important ways, unique, as is that of England, France, Germany, and every other country. But a preoccupation with the exceptional elements of the American experience obscures those common patterns and processes that transcend national boundaries, most notably the global expansion of capitalism in the nineteenth and twentieth centuries and its political and ideological ramifications. It also diverts attention from the "Americanizing" influences so prominent in Western Europe during the past generation. America, Sombart wrote, was "the land of our future." Are not the economies, and the working classes, of both America and Europe today being transformed by the decline of old basic industries, the backbone of traditional unionism and socialism? Is not European politics, like European popular culture, becoming more and more "American," with single-issue movements rising to prominence and political parties, even those calling themselves socialist, emphasizing the personalities of their leaders and their appeal to the entire electorate, rather than a carefully delineated ideology representing the interests of a particular social class? Western European Socialist and Communist parties today occupy points on the political spectrum ranging from distinctly moderate (the Italian, Danish, and Portuguese Socialist parties) to various shades of left and some, like the British Labour Party, are bitterly divided against themselves. In such a situation it is not at all clear that "socialism" retains any clearly defined political content.

Perhaps, because mass politics, mass culture, and mass consumption came to America before it did to Europe, American socialists were the first to face the dilemma of how to define socialist politics in a capitalist democracy. Perhaps, in the dissipation of class ideologies, Europe is now catching up with a historical process already experienced in the United States. Perhaps future expressions of radicalism in Europe will embody less a traditional socialist ideology than an "American" appeal to libertarian and moral values and resistance to disabilities based upon race and gender. Or perhaps a continuing world economic crisis will propel politics in both Western Europe and America down a more class-oriented path. Only time will tell whether the United States has been behind Europe in the development of socialism, or ahead of it, in socialism's decline.

Notes

The original published version of this article contained extensive bibliographical notes, which have been deleted here for reasons of space. They can be found in *History Workshop Journal* (Spring 1984): 76–80.

1. Among the many reviews of the "why is there no socialism?" debate, two of the better recent surveys are: Seymour Martin Lipset, "Why No Socialism in the United States?" in *Sources of Contemporary Radicalism,* Seweryn Bialer and Sophia Sluzer, eds. (New York, 1977), pp. 31–149, which contains an interesting section on how Marx, Engels, and other European socialists viewed the problem, and Jerome Karabel, "The Failure of American Socialism Reconsidered," *Socialist Register* (New York, 1979), pp. 204–27. See also R. Laurence Moore, *European Socialists and the American Promised Land* (New York, 1970). An excellent collection of discussions of the history of American socialism and introduction to the Sombart question is John H. M. Laslett and Seymour M. Lipset, eds. *Failure of a Dream? Essays in the History of American Socialism* (Garden City, NY, 1974). Still indispensable for the history of socialism in the United States is Donald D. Egbert and Stow Persons, eds. *Socialism and American Life,* 2 vols. (Princeton, 1952), the second volume of which consists of an exhaustive bibliography.
2. E. L. Godkin, "The Labor Crisis," *North American Review* (July 1867): 177–79.
3. David Montgomery, "The Shuttle and the Cross: Weavers and Artisans in the Kensington 'Riots' of 1844," *Journal of Social History* (Summer 1972).
4. Werner Sombart's original essay has recently been printed, for the first time in its entirety, in English translation: *Why Is There No Socialism in the United States?* (White Plains, NY, 1976).

5. Louis Hartz, *The Liberal Tradition in America* (New York, 1955). The "fragment" argument is expanded in Hartz's *The Founding of New Societies* (New York, 1964). One may wonder, however, why Australia, another "bourgeois fragment" society, did give rise to a powerful Labour Party.

6. Richard Hofstadter, *The American Political Tradition* (New York, 1948); Daniel Boorstin, *The Genius of American Politics* (Chicago, 1953).

7. Raymond Williams, "Base and Superstructure in Marxist Cultural Theory," *New Left Review* (November-December 1973): 3–16.

8. Oscar Handlin, *Boston's Immigrants* (Cambridge, 1941); Stanley Aronowitz, *False Promises: The Shaping of American Working Class Consciousness* (New York, 1973), whose third chapter, an excellent survey of the formation of the American working class, seems to accept the notion that Catholic immigrants of peasant background are inevitably conservative; Gerald Rosenblum, *Immigrant Workers: Their Impact on American Labor Radicalism* (New York, 1973).

9. Aileen Kraditor, *The Radical Persuasion, 1890–1917* (Baton Rouge, 1981). Kraditor's earlier work, which she now claims was written under the influence of "liberal ideology," includes *Means and Ends in American Abolitionism* (New York, 1969), and *The Ideas of the Women's Suffrage Movement* (New York, 1965). She is now a member of the editorial board of *Continuity*, a conservative historians' journal.

10. Selig Perlman, *A Theory of the Labor Movement* (New York, 1928), p. 167; Alan Dawley, *Class and Community: The Industrial Revolution in Lynn* (Cambridge, 1976), esp. ch. 8; Ira Katznelson, *City Trenches: Urban Politics and the Patterning of Class in America* (New York, 1981). David Montgomery, *Beyond Equality* (New York, 1967), also stresses how politics served as a "safety-valve" for labor discontent.

11. Daniel Bell, *Marxian Socialism in America* (Princeton, 1967); James Weinstein, *The Decline of Socialism in America, 1912–1925* (New York, 1967). Of course, every European Socialist Party experienced the same split between those adopting the Bolshevik model and those preferring traditional social democratic politics. See Albert S. Lindemann, *The "Red Years": European Socialism versus Bolshevism, 1919–21* (Berkeley, 1974).

PAUL BUHLE

WHY SOCIALISM IN THE UNITED STATES
WILL BE DIFFERENT

We are now at a distance—how near or far it would be foolish to speculate—from the reorganization of a socialist movement in the United States. The necessary conditions for that level of mobilization probably include a serious economic downturn, but an acceleration of class divisions (with its explosive results) and a growing public anxiety about the overwhelming damage to the ecosystem should be sufficient to prompt massive anticapitalist sentiment. Sooner or later that sentiment will coalesce into a movement.

We can say, however, that the movement to come will be quite different from its North American predecessors and from its opposite numbers around the world. This difference is due not to any peculiar national genius—far from it. But being the epicenter of capitalism's world empire, as well as of consumer spending and communications, guarantees a particular style of operation, whatever the immediate constituency and chosen agenda. Other long-standing particulars, such as the openly ideological and material struggle of women, the role of recent immigrants, and the millenarian-spiritual quality of radical idealism, will no doubt persist and find new forms.

Perhaps it is useful to begin at the point where the most dynamic prospects for a socialist movement will almost certainly *not* appear. The decline of the organized U.S. labor movement, now in an advanced state, offers one special dimension for international and historical comparison and contrast. No such movement as Solidarity in Poland, COSATU in South Africa, or the formations around the PT

278

(Workers' Párty) in Brazil exists or will be permitted to exist under current conditions. Neither can the indirect but important influence that the U.S. left exerted on the AFL before World War I, and on the CIO before 1946, be reconstituted without almost unthinkable changes. A leap out of present circumstances will require an entirely different kind of labor movement, and this can be accomplished only if the present leadership is pushed aside, their historical approaches abandoned, and their special claims on empire dissolved.

Political commitments and mobilizing strategies obviously differ considerably from union to union and region to region. Often admirable reform movements of various kinds, within and outside institutions, take on new forms. But in two regards no dramatic changes can be realistically predicted. At the policy level, the AFL-CIO has linked its international budget, prestige, and profile to the protection of U.S. hegemony worldwide and to the intelligence services which (along with economic and diplomatic arms) work to ensure that hegemony. Meanwhile, the very structure of the AFL-CIO, a carryover from the industrial union upsurge of the 1930s and 1940s (when not a carryover from the exclusivist craft unions of the turn of the century), is in no way suited to deal with the dramatic shift to a service economy and a correspondingly changed workforce.

The unions, now sinking steadily with the shrinkage of the industrial labor force, still tend to emphasize pro-business internationalism. The leadership—with a few important exceptions—coalesces around the preservation of its central authority at any cost. Worsening actual labor conditions (measured in terms of health, wages, and the rapid growth of the most exploited sectors of workers) amid vaunted prosperity are met with sweeping concessions, two-tier wage agreements, and other signs of outright surrender. Moments of militancy exist, in sectors as different as coal miners and teachers, but solidarity comes mostly from outside the labor mainstream. Dramatic new organizing campaigns (such as that at Harvard University) take place only when the accepted rules are broken, and enthusiastic local support substitutes for the ritual of staff operations. Individual union or extra-union solidarity campaigns, outside the structure of the internationals, have grown up around specific issues but are ferociously opposed as potential alternative centers of expression.

Scarcely anything *less* than a Polish Solidarity-type of movement can break through such layers of bureaucratic conservatism. Although such a massive and relatively cohesive phenomenon is rendered more difficult by ethnic, racial, and gender divisions (often corresponding to generational divisions) and by the small scale of many service industries, it cannot be precluded. But it is most likely to arise as a by-product of other movements. In the meantime, bitter opposition to democratic openings will help clarify the status of the radical movement, making up for long-lost ground: it will help those the AFL-CIO leaders scorn, and will renew the old cry of solidarity and generosity, hastening the abandonment of the racial, gender, and sexual preference politics of contemporary labor organizations.

With all that historical baggage unloaded, the labor movement (or *this* labor movement) may once again become what it was in its best days, the defender of the exploited. And more than that: the economic expression of the workaday community's aspirations for a better life. Until then, however, socialist work in this sector will remain what it has been for twenty years or more: support for democratic movements (or resistance against exceptionally reactionary leadership) within, and participation in worker-education opportunities outside. While helpful, this activity gives little concrete sense of what a different stage of struggle would bring.

At no point in U.S. history have unions fully represented the cultural aspirations of their radical constituency, and they have never been further from doing so than they are today. U.S. workers live in the most advanced mass culture in the world, and have for more than a century. Indeed, we may regard the United States as a laboratory for mass or popular culture's interpenetration with working class, ethnic, and racial cultures.

And it is here, more than likely, that the newest socialism will first indicate its nature, both its strengths and its weaknesses. From the 1960s to the 1980s, as has been widely noted, the New Left and its successors (movements of sexual and gender liberation, antinuclear, ecological, and third world support movements) all but formulated the verses of some of the most popular lyrics of the day. The inner resistance to the cash nexus, the striving for alternatives at every level, found their voice in Bob Dylan, Bruce Springsteen, Tracy Chapman, and so many others. Film and television drama, at its best moments (and they were many), articulated what two-party politics denied—the rottenness of the economic-social system and its crushing moral effect on the sense of public decency. To select but one metaphor, the bitterly antiwar film *M*A*S*H*, written by former blacklistee Ring Lardner, Jr., became through its small-screen adaptation and residualization the most watched television show of all time.

It is often forgotten how the rebellious signs sent outward from U.S. society have been as much cultural as political in character, the ways they have encompassed the racial diversity of U.S. working-class life, and how wide an impact they have had. Early Wobbly melodies defying bourgeois industrial morals and manners were sung throughout the English-speaking world. Their emphasis on the unskilled worker, the outcast, bespoke the pluralism of the emerging international workforce. Garveyism and the Harlem Renaissance turned Harlem into a world-center of black consciousness, placing cultural and political avantgarde side by side. The New Left's antiwar culture, Black Power, and feminism sent their messages far afield, with continuing echoes in revolts today.

In our own depoliticized age, we see only precious fragments. But from the bottom up, and drawing on the widest international currents, Afro-Pop, folky antiracist and anticapitalist lyrics, Rap music, Hip-Hop, and a dazzling variety of other forms offer social space for political statement. This unconquerable vitality, despite its internal contradictions, will doubtless provide a vital (if by no means the only) avenue for socialist ideas to reach the young, the minorities, and the politically detached. The socialist movement cannot simply "organize" these activities, but it will provide a faithful interacting audience, and its intellectual and cultural approaches will shape the understanding of many creative performers.

On just these cultural grounds, however, the urgent need for a socialist vision and a socialist movement in the imperial center remains what it has been for generations. As the Popular Front at its best sought to express, democratization must bring about more than a "melting pot" of formerly viable cultures. On the contrary, racial and ethnic groups with more or less optional identities apart from their wider membership in society, gain through a socialist presence the hope for collective cultural survival and an egalitarian sharing of expressions. In turn, the socialist movement defines itself by articulating this widespread hope, now so battered by orchestrated antagonisms and by the hypocritical assertions of money-is-king pluralism, with a choice portion of the underclass on display as commercial entertainment. How well a socialist movement solves this problem—organizing politically for cultural ends—will determine to a large degree its capacity to make itself known to ordinary people.

The deepening social crisis will finally add expressed political dimensions to this strategic cultural dilemma. And here the complexities of the rich cultural fabric become perplexing and even frightening contradictions. We cannot escape these contradictions, as the pre-1920 socialist movement sought to do through bland generalizations about a class interest that transcended racial, ethnic, and gender lines. Nor do we have a great "social experiment"—as many believed the Soviet Union, China, and Cuba to be—in which these questions are nearing solution. The problems must be addressed in their own right, weighing the prospects for group expression, subjectivity, and potential cooperation in a nonoppressive social order.

To take a specific case in point: black nationalism. The solidification of a black middle class and the emergence of a moderate-to-conservative black political leadership guarantees the massive return of black nationalism as a discourse of the dispossessed. This black nationalism will assume different forms, but one wing will surely be amenable to socialist ideas, broadly speaking, and to radical alliances. The hue and cry against *all* black nationalism will have long since filled the columns of most liberal newspapers and magazines, most especially those that have identified "tolerance" with the unquestioned acceptance of the sanctity of private property and view black nationalists as an extension of the dreaded third world.

The most that can be said at this juncture is that the dialogue will be difficult but inevitable and full of unanticipated points of reconciliation, most especially for the young. Those who have shared a sense of personal disillusionment with the American dream, and a generation or two of cultural enthusiasms, may still break apart at the cruel racist differentiations mandated by the surrounding society. But not entirely. As Stuart Hall has long been fond of saying,

"Hegemonizing is hard work," most especially in the delicate establishment dance of celebrating individual African-American achievement and denigrating the community life out of which that achievement arises. A more harsh, brutal, and reactionary racism will swell with the rising tide of political energy, but this source is less powerful, less calculating, less dangerous than the machinations of those who manipulate the great levers of society and its commercial media. The current attempts to refurbish and restore the Eurocentric "Western tradition" against cultural pluralism in the curriculum is only one, albeit extremely prominent, example of a racist campaign from on high.

Against elites, new truly *radical* Jewish American, Greek, Irish, Italian, and Puerto Rican movements will arise that will be able for the first time in many years to articulate left, antiracist positions within their communities. A socialist movement will immeasurably strengthen the hand of third generation radicals, graduates of the New Left and its successors, idealists who have seen their families and neighbors hoodwinked by racist sloganeering and by internalizing the self-hatred of the dominant society.

The recently arrived Caribbean, Latin American, and Asian people offer an especially dynamic, if also deeply contradictory, picture. In the present era, the most conservative emigrés from impoverished or politically transformed homelands—the Cuban-Americans and the erstwhile Asian-American clientele from the Vietnam war—dominate the politics of the new disadvantaged. But the hegemony of the right, save in exceptional circumstances, cannot be sustained in the face of an economic downturn. New cultural and political movements, tied alike to the fate of the homeland and to the immigrants themselves, will take on a left face, despite crime and terrorism. How well these forces integrate themselves into the wider rejuvenated left depends on the subtle understandings arrived at, and the capacity of U.S. radicals to offer a world-picture in which internationalism becomes more than an abstraction.

On another note, any substantial socialist movement will call back to the colors the feminist and gay activists who have been forced in recent years to act with few radical allies. It will recreate the space that opened in the mid-1970s and closed again a few years later, through which the critique of sexuality and of gender practices seemed to merge with the concept of a renewed socialism. It will then be seen how very much the left has always owed to its "invisible" constituencies, those willing to be on the margin in all walks of life.

Such a coalescence will revive a distinctive contribution of the historic, pre-Marxist U.S. left. From the 1848 Seneca Falls convention declaring the "Rights of Man" to belong to woman as well, feminists and proto-feminists have observed the "sex war" fought in U.S. private life (abundantly described in books, films, and television) and the various women's movements arising out of it. The politicization of the gay movement—not surprisingly, by the left-led Mattachine Society of the early 1950s—also added a dimension often missing in the efforts of homosexuals and heterosexuals elsewhere to organize for their rights. U.S. feminism's political presence, as well as its cultural aura, reached around the world and continues to have an astonishing ripple effect. The future holds more promise yet.

In particular, the emergence of feminist expressions (whether joined to a formal feminist organization and ideology or not) among minority and blue-collar women is certain to follow the trail of rising female employment. This broadening, so long awaited by the faithful, will in a sense complete the unfinished business of the women's liberation movement and prompt a fresh infusion of energy from new generations.

Homosexual organizations, fighting past the enormity of the AIDS tragedy but also gaining inner strength from the tasks at hand, will take a long-denied place at the forefront of a large left. As the importance of collective comradeship for gay movements can scarcely be overestimated, so its importance for the left can be easily envisioned. Here prognosis falls short, because so many assumptions will change with shifting political consequences.

The massing of a social movement among the unemployed (and, in existing society, unemployable), the homeless and the hapless will soon be a phenomenon such as has not been seen since the 1890s and 1930s. Not even the ominous presence of debilitating drugs and disease can in the long run halt the formation of a vast army of these discontented.

Looking to the past, the "industrial armies," "bonus marchers," and others set out across the country to attract attention and bring locals to their cause. Along the way they gained the amiable help of all types of radicals, who provided accommodation and political strategy. In Washington, they met with utter hostility and, in several cases, brutal repression.

Sooner or later, when the misery index rises to a particular height, new organizations of the unemployed will combine with rising public pressure for local, state, and federal relief. At that point, we can predict that the already smoldering hostility to the ultra-rich will become a political onslaught with threatening implications. The call for "reparations," aired repeatedly by black leaders, will resurface in some form of appeal for a drastic allocation of wealth across racial lines.

The consequences will be explosive. Whatever shifts the immediate future holds, Democratic Party politicians, save a few, will run for cover. The movement of the homeless and unemployed, like that of disillusioned Vietnam veterans (with whom, indeed, it shares a strong constituency) is likely to be chaotic, anarchistic, given to threats of violence and to police infiltration. And yet it will find its own voice.

The often expressed American (and human) wish to "live and let live" is increasingly reduced to a fight for survival. Clearly, the catastrophe of the inner cities, the spreading homelessness, drug addiction, and associated ills find no answers—scarcely even pretended ones—from capitalism. If a period of vast economic expansion cannot meet these elementary needs, what does a system in contraction portend? Socialists will find no easy route out of the dilemmas class society has created. But they must and will find new means to propose the transfer of wealth that has always been the touchstone of socialist economics.

One cannot easily point to socialist strategies at a moment when the sacredness of private property has become the ruling principle across much of the globe. Nor can the familiar forms of taxation (too easily avoided in an international economy) and nationalization (too easily turned into a bureaucratic apparatus at the command of class interests) be offered confidently. Socialists of the future will have to return to Marx's own suggested example—the Paris Commune—

and to those moments in modern history that threw up the Soviets, the Workers' Councils in Hungary in 1956, and Solidarity in Poland, among other models. The *replacement* of the state apparatus, the substitution of direct rule for bureaucratic rule of any and all kinds, becomes more than ever the necessary standard.

Socialists will have on their side in this struggle the much-abused concept of "community," the survival of the extended human family under the worst circumstances. Once again from a historic standpoint, the immigrant community, fundamentally working class in character, was the backbone of left organization for most of the period between 1870 and 1950. The African-American community has been at the center of resistance at many points of conflict, from the Populist era to the Civil Rights struggle to the Jesse Jackson campaign. While localism has often been made into an excuse to evade national issues, from civil liberties to environmental controls, the embryonic "bio-regionalism" now much on the Green agenda meets the problem of an all-powerful imperial nationalism with an appealing alternative.

Cooperationism draws upon many experiences, from religious volunteerism to a vague civic spirit, and places them in the necessary perspective: the replacement of harmful, inherently undemocratic business rule. Questions that can hardly be posed openly today, due to current confidence in business leadership (or trepidation about alternatives) will suddenly become open ones, especially as the environmental situation worsens. Painful polarization will no doubt be exacerbated by defenders of the absolute prerogatives of property. Socialists who find a means to place the imperative of community life and survival above parochial interests and short-run gains will have found a means for making socialism real.

At some times and places they will no doubt sweep into local office. And there they will find themselves (as did hundreds of socialist officials in the 1910s) made captive to the limitations on their power, hemmed in by business representatives, and advised to a numbing caution by political operatives. Only a national movement can provide a true escape from this dilemma. But the articulation of a firm ecological and antiracist (which is to say, anti-imperial) doctrine and the replacement of existing political power structures with community controls will take us considerably further than is now possible.

In the Utopian novel *News from Nowhere,* William Morris called his version of socialism an "epoch of rest." Ancient myths kept alive among indigenous peoples have frequently predicted catastrophe and the consequent need for sleep and dreaming as a means of revitalization. To no people on earth, perhaps, are these forgotten ideals likely to mean quite so much as to Americans of the next era. The furious acceleration in the need of skills, the lengthening of the work day through extended commuting and two-income families, the growing fears about career choices and financial security, and the increasing remoteness of any life outside the cities or the suburbs—all these have prompted a widespread exhaustion and a scarcely hidden clinical depression.

Two neglected and recently deceased radical thinkers, Lewis Mumford and William Appleman Williams, offered basic explanations for such ills and a larger view of a solution. Socialists will need to listen to their prescriptions. Both Mumford the critic-at-large and Williams the historian pointed to the "breakdown of the medieval synthesis" (Mumford's phrase) that lay at the heart of North American colonization. The prevailing Mercantilism, in Williams' analysis, sought to balance the welfare of the community with that of the individual but was overpowered by the project of Empire. The Founding Fathers—who regretted but took as inevitable the devastation of Native Americans and the enslavement of Africans—sought to fructify their concept of the Republic with the constant growth of the U.S. empire of the West.

In the end, Republic was lost to Empire, and in the process some fundamental building-blocks of socialism were scattered as well. As Mumford put it, even socialists or communists wrongly tended to assume that "modern society possessed all the material essential to a good social order [and] that all that was necessary was a change in power and control; the Social Commonwealth would simply diffuse and extend all the existing values." This was, in fact, anticipation of "a bourgeois order of society in which everyone would have the comfort and conveniences of the middle classes, without the suffering, toil, anxiety and frustration known to the unskilled worker."

How shallow we know that productivist vision to be today, more than sixty years after these words were written, wallowing as we are in the garbage of consumer society and gasping for air among our

super-plentitude of automobiles (the ultimate "convenience").
Mumford's probing "beneath the organized vivacity of our American
communities," where one finds "a blankness, a sterility, a boredom, a
despair," seems to predict the vaunted triumphs of Yuppiedom in
flashy urban settings, and the vacuous lives that tell a different story.

A socialist solution, as Williams outlined it, lay with the mature
acceptance of U.S. imperial history and the understanding and
courage to leave that history behind. Feminists have demonstrated
how much of the public striving for wealth and celebrity have been
an evasion of responsibility for a failure of personal life. Third world
critics have long pointed out that even escapism, in one form or
another, is taken largely at the expense of the world's victims—who
can never be more than"other," alternatively romanticized and
denigrated but never accepted as equal subjects of their own destiny.

The sins of the world are old, and the youthfulness of the United
States is in itself no vice. Yet socialism has surely come to demand
the long view, not only of civilization proper but of the species and
indeed of the planet. Socialists will have a final say on these subjects,
for no defender of class society can offer anything more for the future
of humanity than diminished life in a diminished ecosphere.

Note

The author would like to give special thanks to Stan Weir and to Scott McLemee for
comments and criticisms.

PAUL M. SWEEZY

POSTSCRIPT ON
POST-REVOLUTIONARY SOCIETY

Conventional wisdom in the capitalist world before 1985 held that the societies involved in these events—together with others produced by twentieth-century revolutions—were unchangeable totalitarian monoliths, and no amount of argumentation, however well reasoned or supported by historical evidence, could shake this belief. After 1985, however, the reality of change, far-reaching and internally generated, could no longer be denied. The accession to power of Mikhail Gorbachev in the Soviet Union, his launching of far-reaching reforms under the banner of *perestroika* and *glasnost*, the winding down of the Cold War in Europe, and the collapse of the Communist-Party-controlled regimes in Eastern Europe—have focused attention on the subject matter of this book in an entirely unprecedented way. Under the altered circumstances, the question of the nature of these societies has taken on a new interest and a new urgency.

Among the questions of greatest concern to people on the left after what has happened during the last few years are whether the crisis in the Soviet Union and collapse of the regimes in the Soviet-bloc countries of Eastern Europe means that socialism in practice has failed and, if so, what conclusions are to be drawn. While these questions obviously could not have been posed ten years ago, definite answers are nevertheless implied in the positions taken in my book, *Post-Revolutionary Societies*. I think the best use I can make of this space is to spell them out as clearly and concisely as possible.

A fairly common view on the left holds that the answer to these

289

questions is simple: the Soviet society that emerged from the October Revolution and all those that later followed in its footsteps, according to this view, had nothing to do with socialism (the reasons given are varied and need not concern us here), from which it follows that socialism has never been tried in practice and hence cannot have failed. The opposite view, also widely held on the left and almost unanimously on the right, is that the societies in question were socialist, as they claimed to be, and hence that their failure is indeed the failure of socialism.

My position is that neither of these views can be squared with the history of the more than seventy years that have elapsed since the Russian Revolution of 1917. The problem is much more complicated than they make it out to be.

I have no doubt whatever that the Russian Revolution and the ones that followed—with a few obvious exceptions like the Iranian revolution—were genuine socialist revolutions with deep roots in an international movement that traces its origin back to the first half of the nineteenth century. The parties and their leaders who headed the revolutionary struggles were for the most part seasoned Marxists whose mission in life was to overthrow an unjust and exploitative system and to replace it with one based on the principles of socialism as expounded by Marx and Engels and their followers in the late nineteenth and early twentieth centuries. Under these circumstances the revolutionary regimes that came to power were clearly socialist in character, and any attempt to deny or obscure this well established fact is a falsification of history.

After the revolutionary seizure of power comes the struggle to shape the post-revolutionary society, and it is with this that the present work is almost exclusively concerned. My central thesis, reduced to its barest essentials, is as follows: All the socialist revolutions of the twentieth century took place under extremely unfavorable conditions and against the fierce resistance of the leaders of the capitalist world from which they had broken away. The new revolutionary regimes were able to overthrow and expropriate the old rulers, and to this extent they succeeded in laying the foundation for a socialist society. But the life-and-death struggle to develop and protect the embryonic new society gave rise—whether inevitably or not remains a matter for debate—to a military-style cleavage between the leaders and the people which in time, and against the will and intentions of the original revolutionaries, hardened into a new self-reproducing system of antagonistic classes. This was obviously not a restoration of capitalism: that would have been the result of a victory of the counterrevolution, not of a development clearly internal to the revolutionary regime itself.

In the Soviet Union this process lasted roughly for a decade and a half, coming to a climax with Stalin's purges of the mid-1930s that wiped out what was left of the old Bolshevik Party. The character of the post-revolutionary society was now established—neither capitalist nor socialist, an authoritarian class society with state ownership of the main means of production and central planning. It has no generally agreed-upon name, and in this book is referred to simply as post-revolutionary society. A more convenient label might be "Soviet-type society" since on the whole the other twentieth-century revolutionary societies have conformed more or less closely to the Soviet model.

This new society gained legitimacy and prestige through the role played by the Soviet Union in the defeat of the Axis powers in World War II. And the system of central planning that enabled the Soviet Union to industrialize so rapidly in the late 1920s and 1930s proved equally effective for the postwar tasks of reconstruction and building up a nuclear-weapons and ballistic-missile capability sufficient to maintain a rough balance of power with that of the United States and its capitalist allies.

By the late 1960s and 1970s, the Soviet model had attained a large measure of legitimacy and stability, and its continuation into the indefinite future seemed assured. But by 1979, it was already clear that the surface calm was seriously misleading. I wrote at that time:

> [T]he performance of the Soviet economy, even in purely quantitative terms, has for some time now been lagging behind its leaders' ambitions and the potential of its human productive resources. . . . It would perhaps be too much to say that post-revolutionary society, as represented by its oldest and most advanced exemplar, has reached a dead end. But at least one can say that it seems to have entered a period of stagnation, different from the stagflation of the advanced capitalist world but showing no more visible signs of a way out.

Now, with the benefit of hindsight based on the flood of new information coming from the Soviet Union under Gorbachev, we know that things were much worse than they appeared in 1979. The system was not only at a dead end but had already entered a period of decline which was reversible, if at all, only by radical reforms reaching deep into its foundations.

These developments, I think it is fair to say, are entirely compatible with, and indeed foreshadowed by, the analysis of post-revolutionary society set forth in this book. This being the case, it seems to me logical and useful to include in this new edition an essay on recent developments in the Soviet Union, written jointly with my colleague Harry Magdoff and published in the March and April 1990 issues of *Monthly Review* of which he and I are co-editors. Part 2 is included in this volume. Entitled *"Perestroika* and the Future of Socialism," it aims to throw light on the question as to why the social system that enabled the Soviet Union to emerge victorious from World War II, reconstruct after the terrible losses of that conflict, and attain the status of a superpower was nevertheless unable to respond to the very different challenge of meeting the reasonable needs of the people under peacetime conditions.

The conclusion that emerges from this analysis is that the crisis of the Soviet Union and the collapse of its East European allies was not due to the failure of socialism. The struggle for socialism in the Soviet Union as recounted above, was lost long before with the consolidation of a class system, and it was this system which, despite its undoubted achievements, ultimately failed.

NOTES ON THE CONTRIBUTORS

Maria Helena Moreira Alves is associate professor of Latin American studies and political economy at the Universidade do Estado do Rio de Janeiro and is currently visiting professor at the University of Wisconsin, Madison. She is one of the founders of the Partido dos Trabalhadores and is the author of *State and Opposition in Military Brazil* (1985).

Samir Amin is currently director of the Africa Office, Third World Forum, Dakar, Senegal. He is the author of many books, including *Unequal Development* (Monthly Review Press, 1976), and *Eurocentrism* (Monthly Review Press, 1989).

Paul Buhle has long been active in student, antiwar, and labor support movements and founded the journal *Radical America* in 1967. He currently directs the Oral History of the American Left Project at New York University's Tamiment Library. His books include *C.L.R. James: The Artist as Revolutionary* (1980) and he is the coeditor of the *Encyclopedia of the American Left* (1990).

Michael Burawoy is professor of sociology at the University of California at Berkeley. He is currently researching democracy and the production process in Hungary and is the author of a number of books, including *Manufacturing Consent: Changes in the Labor Process under Capitalism* (1979) and (with Janos Lukacs) *The Radiant Past: Hungarian Workers in a Decade of Transition* (forthcoming).

293

Pat Devine teaches economics at the University of Manchester, England, and is coauthor of *An Introduction to Industrial Economics* (1985) and author of *Democracy and Economic Planning* (1988). He has had a lifelong commitment to communism, socialism, and political activism.

Eric Foner is the DeWitt Clinton Professor of History at Columbia University. He is the author of numerous books on American history, the most recent of which is *Reconstruction: America's Unfinished Revolution, 1863–1877* (1988).

Andre Gunder Frank is the author of many books and articles on third world development and antisystemic movements, including (with Immanuel Wallerstein, Giovanni Arrighi, and Samir Amin) *The Dynamics of Global Crisis* (Monthly Review Press, 1982) and *Transforming the Revolution: Social Movements and the World-System* (Monthly Review Press, 1990).

Pablo Gonzalez Casanova is professor at the Universidad Nacional Autonoma de Mexico and the author of many books, including *Democracy in Mexico* (1970), *El Estado y los Partidos Politicos en Mexico* (1981), and *America Latina, Hoy* (forthcoming).

Phil Hill is a freelance journalist living in Giessen, West Germany. He has written extensively on the socialist and ecology movements in Europe, Asia, and the United States, with particular emphasis on the West German Green Party. Since 1989 he has been especially concerned with investigating and reporting on the upheavals in East Germany.

Harry Magdoff is co-editor (with Paul M. Sweezy) of *Monthly Review* and the author of *The Age of Imperialism* (1969), *Imperialism: From the Colonial Age to the Present* (1978), and several books with Paul M. Sweezy, all published by Monthly Review Press.

Daniel Singer is the European correspondent of the *Nation* and writes frequently for *Monthly Review*. He is the author of *The Road to*

Gdansk (Monthly Review Press, 1982) and *Is Socialism Doomed? The Meaning of Mitterand* (1988).

Paul M. Sweezy is co-editor (with Harry Magdoff) of *Monthly Review* and author of many books, including *Theory of Capitalist Development, Monopoly Capital* (with Paul Baran), *Stagnation and the Financial Explosion* (1987) and *The Irreversible Crisis* (1988), both with Harry Magdoff, all published by Monthly Review Press.

William K. Tabb is professor of economics at Queens College and of sociology at the Graduate Center of the City University of New York. He is currently visiting professor of economics at Kansai University, Osaka, Japan. He is the author and editor of a number of books, including, most recently, *Instability and Change in the World Economy,* coedited with Arthur MacEwan (Monthly Review Press, 1989).

Carlos M. Vilas is professor of Latin American studies at the Universidad Nacional Autonoma de Mexico and author of *The Sandinista Revolution* (Monthly Review Press, 1986). From 1980 until 1989 he worked in Nicaragua, first at the Ministry of Planning and then at CIDCA, a research center concerned with the indigenous populations of Nicaragua's Atlantic Coast.